# The Ancient Mesopotamian City

# The Ancient Mesopotamian City

Marc Van De Mieroop

**OXFORD**
UNIVERSITY PRESS

# PREFACE TO THE PAPERBACK EDITION

After the completion of the original manuscript of this book in 1996, new research on several topics addressed here has appeared in print, which could not be integrated in the paperback edition. Especially important is the publication of the papers presented at a conference organized by the Deutsche Orient-Gesellschaft regarding the Middle Eastern city from antiquity to the modern period (G. Wilhelm (ed), *Die Orientalische Stadt: Kontinuität, Wandel, Bruch*, Berlin: Saarbrücker Druckerei und Verlag, 1997). Of great interest in that volume is the contribution by Mario Liverani, 'The ancient Near Eastern City and Modern Ideologies,' where the author demonstrates unequivocally that modern views on ancient Mesopotamian urbanism reflect the intellectual biases and ideological stances of individual scholars and their times. This book surely is no exception. In presenting my model of the ancient Mesopotamian city, I attempt to integrate it within Max Weber's ideal type of the "Ancient City." The stance consciously aims at undermining the Orientalist notions of West versus East and the Eurocentric teleology of history that sees Greece as the birthplace of "our" civilization. Perhaps I should have stressed that point more strongly, since other papers in the above mentioned volume, sadly, demonstrate that colonial discourse survives in ancient Near Eastern studies two decades after the humanities and social sciences in general have subjected it to devastating critiques. In my opinion, there is a pressing need to engage the scholarship on ancient Mesopotamia with post-colonial questions, and I hope that this book is a small step in that direction.

Hilary O'Shea, Senior Editor at Oxford University Press, kindly allowed me to make some minor changes in the original text. This has enabled me to remove several factual and grammatical errors, most of which were pointed out to me by Professor J. A. Brinkman. He has also generously provided me with a long list of insightful and detailed comments, resulting from a very careful reading of the hard cover edition of the book, and I am extremely grateful to him for his advice.

Marc Van De Mieroop

March 1, 1999

# CONTENTS

# LIST OF FIGURES

All drawings were made by Jo Ann Wood, New York.

## Babylonia        Assyria

| Historical period | Selected rulers | BC | Historical period | Selected rulers |
|---|---|---|---|---|
| Seleucid | Seleucus I (305–281) | 300 | Seleucid | |
| | | 400 | | |
| Achaemenid | | 500 | Achaemenid | |
| | Nabonidus (555–539) | | | |
| Neo-Babylonian | Nebuchadnezzar II (604–562) | 600 | | |
| | | | | Sennacherib (704–681) |
| | | 700 | | |
| | | | | Sargon II (721–705) |
| | | 800 | Neo-Assyrian | |
| | | 900 | | Assurnaṣirpal (883–859) |
| post-Kassite | | | | |
| | | 1000 | | |
| | | 1100 | | |
| | | 1200 | | Tukulti-Ninurta I (1243–1207) |
| | | 1300 | | |
| Kassite | Kurigalzu II (1332–1308) | | Middle Assyrian | |
| | | 1400 | | |
| | | 1500 | | |
| | | 1600 | | |
| | Ammiṣaduqa (1646–1626) | | | |
| Old Babylonian | | 1700 | Old Assyrian | Shamshi-Adad I (1813–1781) |
| | Hammurabi (1792–1750) | | | |
| | | 1800 | | |
| Isin/Larsa | | | | |
| | | 1900 | | |
| | | 2000 | | |
| Ur III | Shulgi (2094–2047) | | | |
| | | 2100 | | |
| | | 2200 | | |
| | | 2300 | | |
| Agade | Sargon (2334–2279) | | | |
| | | 2400 | | |
| | Uru'inimgina | | | |
| | | 2500 | | |
| | | 2600 | | |
| Early Dynastic | | | | |
| | | 2700 | | |
| | | 2800 | | |
| | | 2900 | | |
| | | 3000 | | |

Chronological chart of Mesopotamian History. All dates are according to J. A. Brinkman's appendix in A. L. Oppenheim, *Ancient Mesopotamia* (Chicago, 1977), 335–46.

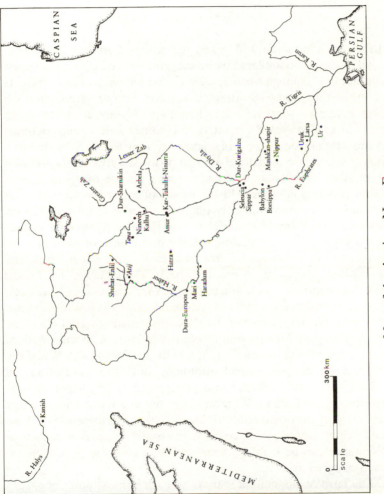

Map of the Ancient Near East

# INTRODUCTION

Although, after some 150 years, the study of ancient Mesopotamian history is no longer in its infancy, not much beyond the barest outlines of a political history seems to be known to most students of other disciplines. Studies in ancient history often overlook Mesopotamian material, or, when they do pay attention to it, reproduce a standard narrative including some main political events and personalities. This ignorance may not only be due to a lack of interest on the part of ancient historians and others, but also to a failure of scholars of ancient Mesopotamia to communicate with colleagues in other fields. The lack of communication is often a result of the predominantly philological approach by the latter, working with primary material in several relatively poorly understood languages, and entailing lengthy discussions of grammar and lexicography, which are incomprehensible to all but a few fellow specialists. Moreover, there has been a reluctance to engage broader historical topics, due to the concern that many of the basic textual interpretations are still equivocal. Indeed these worries are very real, but by excluding the Mesopotamian material from the study of ancient history, one discards a gold mine of information, often unparalleled in other regions of the ancient world. While the clarification of philological problems and the publication of primary data will continue and progress, it is important to start investigations of what this material can tell us about ancient society and to apply historical methodologies to the interpretation of these data. Many topics that have been extensively discussed in various disciplines can be fruitfully explored with the help of Mesopotamian material as well.

The term Mesopotamia is used here, as in most other books, in more than one way. It refers to the geographical area covering the entirety of modern Iraq and the northern part of modern Syria from its eastern border to the Euphrates river in the west. The confines of the area are not firmly fixed in anyone's mind, and vary according to the extent of political influence of the ancient Mesopotamian political powers. 'Mesopotamia' also denotes a civilization which developed in that region in prehistory, and survived under numerous ethnic groups until it was gradually replaced by Hellenistic and Persian traditions. Thus the use of the term Mesopotamia is also fluid from the point of view of chronology. It applies primarily to the region's history from its very beginning around 3100 BC to the integration of the Middle East in the Hellenistic world in the late fourth century BC, but can also include developments and characteristics both before and after this time span. The lack of strict boundaries, both geographical and chronological, is a reflection of the mixture of continuity and exposure to new political and cultural influences, which characterizes the entire history of the Middle East.

In this book I will attempt to provide a purely historical study of one of the crucial aspects of Mesopotamian civilization, the city. I hope to demonstrate that the city in Ancient Mesopotamia was a pivotal institution on which the entire civilization was based. In politics, the economy, social life, and culture, the city was of crucial importance, and none of these aspects of Mesopotamian life can be properly understood without a comprehension of their urban background. Historians commonly accept Mesopotamia's importance in the history of urbanism as the region of primary urbanization that influenced, at a minimum, the entire Mediterranean world and south Asia. But to talk of the region solely as the locus of the rise of the first urban culture does not pay due attention to the subsequent developments in Mesopotamia. Instead of jumping from the accomplishments of the late fourth millennium to the classical Greek situation in the first millennium BC, it is necessary to investigate the Mesopotamian city in the historical periods.

Is it meaningful to speak of the ancient Mesopotamian city? The answer to this question depends on whether or not one believes in the validity of establishing models that obscure the peculiarities of individual cases, and indeed the enormous time-span of Mesopotamian history may make such an abstraction a daunting idea. However, if the Mesopotamian historian wants to communicate with other historians, such a model needs to be developed, and the fear of oversimplification is outweighed by the need to present a concept that can be compared to other historical situations. A long list of particular cases whose characteristics can be discarded as idiosyncrasies does not stand up in comparison to the Greek, Roman, or any other urban type that is discussed in scholarship. If we do not develop a vision of the ancient Mesopotamian city, we could end up with the same attitude as Aristotle, who saw Babylon as a city so unusual that it did not merit comparison to real cities.

By using the term the Ancient Mesopotamian city I propose to consider urbanism in the entirety of Mesopotamia, hence both in Babylonia and Assyria, within the context of ancient urbanism in general. Many historians regard the 'ancient city' as a type, without any acknowledgement of the existence of cities other than those in the Graeco-Roman world. For such a Eurocentric ideology to be modified, if not overthrown, it is necessary for the Mesopotamian scholar to present a model of a non-western ancient city. Obviously, the use of types ignoring a great number of nuances and variants that existed in reality, especially in an opposition of East to West, has the danger of perpetuating Orientalist notions that these areas were fundamentally antithetical, and that their differences can be illustrated by a reduction of their characteristics into a simple list. This is certainly not my intention. In proposing to regard the ancient Mesopotamian city as a type, I wish to enable comparison with the existing notions of urbanism in the ancient Graeco-Roman world, which equally are abstractions, the validity of which is debatable, but which are commonly used in scholarship.

This book is not an exposé of what is known about the Mesopotamian city in layman's terms, but an investigation of various topics regarding urban life, that will hopefully be accessible to all interested readers. As much as possible I have avoided the use of terms in the native Mesopotamian languages, and all texts quoted are presented without a philological commentary. This is not a statement of my belief that the translations of these terms and texts are certain, but I leave it to others to justify them, as I do not think that a historical work is a suitable place for philological argument. Also in the spelling of proper names I have striven for as much simplicity and clarity as possible, usually using spellings found in well-known books on Mesopotamian history. I have refrained from writing numerous and extensive footnotes, and instead I have provided detailed bibliographical essays with recommendations for further reading at the end of each chapter. Obviously these guides are based on a personal selection, and they are certainly not exhaustive, but I have chosen those books and articles that were most useful to me in the writing of the chapter, as well as those that I thought would be most accessible to the general reader.

In the translations of ancient sources the following conventions are used: square brackets around broken text that is restored with certainty; angled brackets around text added by the translator for clarity's sake; round brackets for parentheses only. When the translation of one or more words is uncertain the text is rendered in italics. When part of the original text is not provided in the translation three points of ellipsis are indicated.

No typographic distinction is made to indicate Sumerian or Akkadian words in the text, but when needed the abbreviations Sum. and Akk. are provided in parentheses.

# 1

# City and Society in Ancient Mesopotamia

> From the walls I had an uninterrupted view over a vast plain
> stretching westward to the Euphrates, and losing itself in the
> hazy distance. The ruins of ancient towns and villages rose on
> all sides; and, as the sun went down, I counted above one
> hundred mounds, throwing their dark and long thinning shad-
> ows across the plain. These were the remains of Assyrian
> civilisation and prosperity.[1]

These words by Austen Henry Layard standing on Tell Afar in
northern Iraq announced the birth of modern Western exploration
in ancient Mesopotamia, and identify what is most striking about
this region. The innumerable mounds scattered throughout the
countryside of modern-day Iraq and northern Syria cover the remains of myriad ancient cities and towns, many of which survived
for hundreds, if not thousands of years. Mesopotamia was not only
the oldest urban civilization, but also the most urbanized society of
antiquity. From the mid-fourth millennium BC onwards, cities were
in existence in Babylonia (southern Mesopotamia), and despite
many vicissitudes they never disappeared entirely from the landscape. Urbanism may have emerged only later in Assyria (northern
Mesopotamia), but soon some Assyrian cities became gigantic in
extent. At their most flourishing, the most important Mesopotamian cities dwarfed their contemporaries in the rest of the ancient
world, to the amazement of Greeks, such as Aristotle, who could
not consider Babylon to be a city, but only as the equivalent of a
nation because of its enormous dimensions. The dense concentration of Mesopotamian cities was also unparalleled; large urban
centres lay within sight of one another.

The Mesopotamian known to us today was a citizen, a resident

[1] Austen Henry Layard, *Nineveh and its Remains*, 2nd edn. 1 (London, 1849),
315.

of one of these many ancient towns. The art and literature we admire was created by these citizens, the bureaucracies we study were urban bureaucracies, and the politicians and military leaders we know were living in cities. Mesopotamian civilization, as it is known to us, was an urban civilization. Nomads and villagers lived in the area as well, and their culture was different from that of the city-dwellers. But we have no direct contact with them, and we can only study them through the eyes of the urbanites who mentioned them in their writing, or who were influenced by them in some way. Villages have rarely been investigated by archaeologists, and probably writing was scarcely used by their inhabitants. Nomads have left us no archaeological remains or texts at all. Hence, we cannot study these non-urban Mesopotamians directly.

The study of urbanism in Mesopotamia would thus seem of primary importance to the historians of this civilization, yet few of them have devoted specific attention to it. An enormous amount of research, spearheaded by anthropologists who find there a rare and well-documented example of primary urbanization, has focused on the origins of cities in the area. But their studies usually leave off just when we enter the historical period, or soon afterwards. The invention of writing, and the advent of history, somehow seem to discourage further research by anthropologists, who leave the subsequent developments to be studied by historians. Historians, however, have been concerned with other problems, primarily those of political history. As was the case among historians of Classical Greece, cities were often identified by scholars of Mesopotamia with city-states, and the study of them has focused on their political affairs rather than their function as urban centres.

Obviously the study of the city in Mesopotamia has not been totally ignored. In the 1950s and 1960s several research projects were initiated, which were seemingly influenced by the resurgence of the comparative approach in urban studies in general. The prime example of the comparative approach by a Mesopotamian specialist is Robert McC. Adams's *The Evolution of Urban Society* (Chicago, 1966), in which he compared Mesopotamian and Mesoamerican developments with great success. Symposia organized at the University of Chicago and the Institute of Archaeology in London also stressed the comparison of Mesopotamian developments with those in other regions. Similarly the Société Jean Bodin in France commissioned a paper on the cities of Mesopotamia for its 1955 issue on 'La ville'.

Major projects devoted to Mesopotamia alone were rarer. Under Adams's and A. L. Oppenheim's guidance all available documents from the Babylonian city of Sippar in the nineteenth to the sixteenth centuries BC were analysed, but soon Oppenheim himself started to stress the unusual aspects of this city rather than its common characteristics with other towns. He did, however, examine many facets of Mesopotamian city life in general in his wonderful book, *Ancient Mesopotamia*. This discussion, unfortunately, was dispersed throughout the work, and far from comprehensive. Simultaneously archaeologists started an extensive programme of settlement surveys in various parts of Babylonia, leading to three seminal books by Adams. Although changing settlement patterns were the focus of these works, many other aspects of urbanism were addressed in them as well. However, the books do not provide an analysis of urban life in general.

Recently this topic has received renewed interest, probably due to the explosion of the field of urban history. In the last two decades several archaeological projects have attempted to reconstruct entire urban layouts, rather than maintaining the customary focus on individual monumental remains. Almost all these projects took place in Iraq, and have been cut short by the Gulf War. Philologists also have taken an interest in the city, and at least three conferences have been recently devoted to the topic. Yet, it is disappointing to see how in the ensuing publications few contributors dealt with Mesopotamia proper or with the stated subject matter. Meanwhile, a few studies on individual cities have appeared, all concentrating on early second-millennium BC Babylonia, as the presence of large private archives—less available elsewhere—is thought to be a crucial requirement for such research. In all, this amounts to a rather meagre record, considering the number of scholars specializing in the study of Ancient Mesopotamian civilization. This scarcity is reflected in the fact that two recent books dealing with urbanism in antiquity basically reproduce the standard political history of Mesopotamia with the word 'city' highlighted. One can even say that many classical historians, including some who specialize in urban studies, deny the existence of the city in the East in antiquity altogether.

The resulting image of the Mesopotamian city, even in the

specialist's mind, is thus very vague. Although palaces and temples were always urban foundations, it seems that their presence and activities are often considered to be inconsequential to the rest of the city, as if they existed in a world of their own. The non-monumental sectors of towns—if considered at all—are portrayed very much like the present-day villages we encounter on the *tell*s we excavate: poor, dirty, and totally unaware of the existence of majestic complexes nearby. Ethno-archaeologists have tried to institutionalize this portrayal by telling us that modern Middle Eastern villages provide an insight into Ancient Mesopotamian city life, as if these cities were just large villages.

Classical historians often continue to see the origin of the city as a Greek phenomenon, and either deny the existence of the Near Eastern city, or see it as inconsequential for later urbanism. In the latest edition of the standard English-language history of the ancient world we can find this statement:

At the start of our (i.e. the Hellenistic) period, in Asia and the Levant as in Greece and the Mediterranean generally, large urban agglomerations were rare and exceptional. Babylon, however, was certainly one until it was supplanted by Seleucia-on-the-Tigris. Susa, Uruk, and Sippar may have been others, and the existence of large cities elsewhere cannot be discounted. However, there is little doubt that outwith the narrow band of Greek or semi-Greek coastal city-state settlement the predominant form of nucleated settlement all over the region was the so-called village, either on its own or (as often) grouped together in various ways.[2]

The author of this passage seems to ignore entirely the archaeological and textual evidence concerning large-sized cities, not only in Mesopotamia, but also in other Near Eastern regions, such as Syria and Egypt. When they do acknowledge the existence of cities in these areas historians often see them as totally different from the Greek examples, because of the lack of 'democracy' and free enterprise. Thus a history of urbanism in the ancient world states: 'Mesopotamia still afforded magnificent urban complexes like Babylon or Nineveh, which deeply impressed Greek travellers. But these were too vast to serve as models for incipient cities in Greece and were creatures of monarchies, not self-governing communities.'[3] Besides perpetuating some old prejudices, such as the idea

[2] J. K. Davies, 'Cultural, social and economic features of the Hellenistic world', *The Cambridge Ancient History*, 2nd edn., 7: 1 (Cambridge 1984), 297–8.
[3] Mason Hammond, *The City in the Ancient World* (Cambridge, 1972), 152–3.

of Oriental Despotism, these opinions seem to be based on a lack of knowledge of the Mesopotamian situation, perhaps due to the scarcity of studies regarding the topic.

Of course, there are serious obstacles to our understanding of Mesopotamian urbanism. There is no such thing as *the* Mesopotamian city, as each one of the hundreds that existed had its own peculiarities, and to generalize from one of them would be misleading. And if we limit our research to one city only, we are faced with a dearth or complete lack of information on most of the issues we would like to address. The most extensive excavations have uncovered only a minute part of the sites under investigation. Moreover, when textual information is abundant, it almost always derives from one source, giving excessive emphasis to its activities: the palace, a temple, or a small number of private citizens. Even when a mixture of sources is available, the subject matter detailed is limited and not directly relevant to most of the questions we ask. Some of the documents on which urban historians of other cultures rely extensively, such as census lists and tax records, are absent from Mesopotamia. Most texts available to us were not written to inform later historians, or absent people, through description or explanation. Rather, the majority of the so-called economic texts put down in writing a transfer of property, be it silver, land, or a bowl of barley, from one person or office to another person or office, with a vague reference to the reason for the transfer, a payment, a loan, an inheritance, and so on. Such documents are very hard to understand without knowledge of their context. It is thus tempting to say that it is impossible to arrive at an overall picture of Mesopotamian urbanism, or for that matter any other aspect of its culture, and better to limit oneself to analysing the material that is readily available.

Such a defeatist attitude is not very satisfying, however. After all, other historians face similar problems of limited documentation, and no culture had a typical city to be used as a paradigm. Yet books on the Greek city, for instance, appear with great regularity. Although a single paragraph of Thucydides may provide insights into the Athenian government that we will never arrive at for Mesopotamia, some aspects of the economy, for instance, are much better documented in Mesopotamia than they are in Greece.

Can we then develop a model of the Mesopotamian city? I think so, if we cast a wide net, and if we abandon a strictly positivistic approach to our sources. Both conditions are to be met with great caution, and require elaboration. The Mesopotamian documentation may be abundant, but it derives from an enormous time-span and a large geographical area. Instead of the few centuries of Greek history, Mesopotamian history covers close to three millennia, a period equal to that which separates us from Homer, and that is when we exclude prehistoric and Hellenistic material from consideration. During these 2,800 years numerous political changes took place with newcomers dominating the events narrated in our history books: Sumerians, Akkadians, Amorites, Hurrians, Kassites, Persians, and so on. Didn't some of them fundamentally change urban life?

The issue of continuity and change in Mesopotamian history has rarely been explicitly addressed in scholarship. The existence of a discipline of Mesopotamian studies, and the abundance of books on Mesopotamia assumes the reality of a field of research with enough coherence to permit the delineation of a distinct identity. Yet that by itself is not sufficient justification to present a study of the city throughout Mesopotamian history. A simple reference to Braudel's *longue durée*[4] may be fashionable, but is also too facile. Matters need to be considered in more detail, despite the fact that scholars seem to recognize an internal unity in Mesopotamian civilization, based on the characteristic that newcomers attempted to integrate themselves within the existing structures rather than overthrowing them.

All too often in our vision of Mesopotamian history, political and military events are taken as the only important ones, and have consequently provided the chronological framework for that history. But politics and the activities of the military are only two dimensions of society, and although they do indeed show the most evidence for change throughout Mesopotamian history, the changes are exaggerated in modern scholarship. Textbooks describe in detail the succession of dynasties and their military exploits in and outside Mesopotamia. They present an *histoire événementielle* culled from the rich historiographic remains of this civilization. A long list of dynasties based both on native traditions and on modern scholarly classification has been developed. Dynasties that are prominent in the textual record have been assigned

---

[4] See Fernand Braudel, *On History* (Chicago, 1980), 25–54.

their own period: for instance, those of the Third Dynasty of Ur, the First Dynasty of Babylon, the Neo-Assyrian. Other, less documented royal houses have been grouped together and subsumed under designations such as Early Dynastic, Isin-Larsa, post-Kassite, etc. When the centre of political power shifted from Akkad to Ur, or from Ur to Isin, or when a Persian king replaced a Chaldean one, we have established insurmountable boundaries in our political histories. Consequently we do not investigate whether these changes in dynastic control were of crucial importance in political terms. The practice of categorizing the studies of economics, law, society, and even literature and religion within the resulting dynastic framework has inflated the importance of political events even more. Thus the 'Old Akkadian' society, for instance, is investigated in isolation from the preceding and succeeding situations, Middle Assyrian laws are studied in a vacuum, and so on. The resulting periodization is flawed and misleading. Instead of acknowledging patterns of continuity, it stresses instability and change. And this fragmentation becomes even more misleading when aspects of Mesopotamian civilization not directly dependent upon the fortunes of the royal house are studied.

A. Leo Oppenheim has argued forcefully that instead of the fragmented sequence of the traditional historical periods we should see an essential unity in Mesopotamian civilization during its millennial history. In order to do so, he described a cultural continuum involving social, intellectual, and technological traditions. Especially in a study of urban life, an aspect such as the economic infrastructure of a region, for instance, should be of more relevance than the ethnic or linguistic background of the ruling class. The basic economic structure of Mesopotamia remained the same throughout its history: it was a pre-industrial society based on an agricultural economy. The ecological conditions of the region were never fundamentally altered from the moment agriculture was developed until the discovery of oil as a valuable commodity. The fundamental dependence of cities upon their agricultural base remained the same during the whole of antiquity, regardless of variations in the agricultural potential of their surroundings. Manufacturing relied on agricultural resources as well, or on imports of materials from abroad. At no time in Mesopotamian history did the discovery of a new material or a new technique substantially alter this aspect of the economy. The cities were also essential to the tertiary sector of the economy, services. Their administrative and financial roles basically remained the same throughout Mesopotamian history. We need to look for such continuities, rather than focus upon the overt changes in political control.

The idea of a unity in Mesopotamian civilization should not lead to a static view of its history. Oppenheim outlined five phases in its evolution, which were unfortunately rather impressionistically named and vaguely delineated in time, and need not be imposed upon the study of a single institution. What is important about his periodization is that it stresses the existence of a continuum rather than a sequence of disjointed periods. An element of evolution in the model of urban life developed in this book needs then to be acknowledged. Due to the nature of the evidence it will not always be possible to detail all the stages of this evolution, but I hope to be able to demonstrate the unity of the subject matter.

In geographical extent Mesopotamia is perhaps not especially large—it is comparable to France in size—but it includes at least two clearly different ecological and cultural zones: Lower and Upper Mesopotamia. In different historical periods these areas were identified with the polities of Babylonia and Assyria, and I will use the latter designations for the sake of simplicity. Babylonia is a flat, dry region where permanent settlement is possible only near natural or artificial waterways; Assyria is more varied in relief and receives sufficient rainfall to enable dry-farming and settlement throughout the countryside. Culturally the two regions showed many differences; yet Assyria was greatly dependent on Babylonia, emulating and adopting many of its traditions. The concept of the city itself may have been introduced to Assyria from the South. The fates of the two regions became intrinsically tied after 1500 with the continuous movements of peoples and ideas back and forth. The ecological differences between the two regions did affect many aspects of urbanism within them, especially with respect to the economy. These differences will have to be kept in mind and investigated under particular topics such as agricultural resources or urban origins. But I hope to show that the Babylonian and Assyrian cities shared so many characteristics that they can be regarded as variations of a theme, and that material from both regions can be used in the study of the Mesopotamian city.

I think thus that it is acceptable to regard the entirety of Mesopotamia, both in temporal and geographical terms, as a single unit. Of course, if more information were available differences in time and space would become more obvious and a focus upon the Babylonian city in the nineteenth century BC or the like would be possible, but not necessarily more useful. Just as we can study the pre-industrial European city or the ancient city, we can study urbanism in Ancient Mesopotamia.

The problem of the limitations of our sources can be somewhat mitigated if we abandon the strictly positivistic approach that predominates the field of Mesopotamian studies, especially among philologists. All too often reconstructions are based on the presence or absence of documentation, giving excessive importance to the material we have and assuming that only what is reported in it took place. Let me repeat a famous example: for more than fifty years we talked of the Sumerian temple-city in the twenty-sixth and twenty-fifth centuries, a city-state where all means of production and economic activity were owned and controlled by the temple. This idea was based on the study of one archive from the Bau temple at Lagash, the only archive analysed from that period of time. It took many years and great persistence by a handful of scholars to convince others that private and palatial economic activity existed as well. Often the economic history of Mesopotamia looks like a chronological list of the various archives available, each one determining the economic structure of its time!

The lack of documentation may be due to many factors other than the absence of an activity. Most scholars acknowledge the accident of recovery, but still basically assume that everything was somehow recorded. Instead, we should question why what we have was recorded, and why other possible activities were not. For instance, we have no records of retail sales of food or manufactured goods. Is this because such sales did not take place, or can we explain their absence in the records otherwise? We have to acknowledge that many enterprises could have remained outside the written record, and even a simple acceptance of the fact that they could have taken place provides a more refined picture than if we just state what is at hand.

The procedure of inquiry in this book will not amount to a didactic narration of what is known about certain urban issues, or about certain cities at a particular moment in time. Instead, I will select issues of urban life that were important in my opinion, develop a model about them, and then illustrate the model with examples from the entirety of Mesopotamian history, acknowledging temporal and regional variations. The resulting portrait will thus be idiosyncratic: after all both the selection of topics and of documentation are my own, while someone else could choose to discuss entirely different problems with other material. I fear that this is unavoidable unless one provides a complete catalogue of the documentation for all aspects of urban life, if such were possible.

It is customary in a study of this nature to seek a definition of 'the city', and to establish a means of distinction between cities and towns, villages, and hamlets. The native Mesopotamian terminology is of no help here. An enormous number of settlements were referred to with the Sumerian and Akkadian terms we translate as 'city': *uru* (Sum.) and *ālum* (Akk.). The Akkadian term was used for anything from the metropolis of Babylon in the sixth century to a farmstead with seven inhabitants in the area of Harran in the seventh century. It was used for the entire city of Nineveh as well as for a section of it. The Akkadian language had a few other terms to allude to permanent settlements, such as *kaprum*, a farmstead, *dūrum*, a fortified settlement that could be the size of a large city like Dur-Sharrukin, and *māhazum*, which could be anything from a small enclosure to a large town. But in the great majority of cases the term *ālum* was used. The translation 'city' is thus misleading, since we classify settlements by size, and reserve the term city for larger ones, although an exact definition also eludes us. The lack of differentiation among settlements seems to reflect a perception that all of them were equivalent and sovereign communities. The Mesopotamian languages were not alone in their lack of distinguishing settlements according to size. The Ancient Egyptian language, for instance, also failed to do so, and this has led to the false conclusion that ancient Egypt was a civilization without cities. It is only in recent years that historians of ancient Egypt have started to acknowledge the urban character of the civilization, culling data from rare archaeological remains.[5]

Thus we have to turn to criteria other than the native terminology in order to arrive at a definition of a city. Many scholars have

---

[5] For the Egyptian terminology see Manfred Bietak, 'Urban Archaeology and the "Town Problem" in Ancient Egypt', in Kent Weeks (ed.), *Egyptology and the Social Sciences* (Cairo, 1979), 98–100.

attempted to provide a definition valid for all cultures and time periods, usually without success. Wheatley devoted thirty-nine pages to this topic in his monumental book on the Chinese city, rejecting such prominent theories as those by Weber, Pirenne, and Childe, to end with a statement that the question is metaphysical rather than scientific.[6] He did, however, stress the importance of the city as an organizing force in its geographical setting. This idea derives from the 'Central Place Theory' developed by geographers, which states that each settlement can be assigned a position in a hierarchy based on the number of lower-ranked communities it serves, and particular patterns of settlement in a region will appear if the hierarchy is mapped out. Yet there remains an aspect of uncertainty about what type of settlement can be called a city rather than a town or a village, as was clearly stated by Richard Blanton:

In a society with a hierarchy of central places, cities are communities in the highest range of the hierarchy, while towns are those communities occupying the middle and lower ranges of the hierarchy. Where the researcher draws the boundary between what are called cities and what are called towns is always arbitrary and will vary from society to society.[7]

This ambiguity cannot be resolved.

We can, however, maintain that the primary functional characteristic of a city is its role as a mediator between various permanent and seasonal settlements in its surroundings. Or, as Braudel has stated: 'The town only exists as a town in relation to a form of life lower than its own.'[8] That mediating role has several dimensions: economic, ideological, military, and political.[9] It is important that several, if not all, of these dimensions are present simultaneously. A religious institution—such as a temple in the countryside—can be an ideological centre, but does not constitute a city. In order to observe the mediating role of a city we need geographical studies that provide regional maps indicating all settlements and the means

---

[6] Paul Wheatley, *The Pivot of the Four Quarters* (Chicago, 1971), 371–409.

[7] Richard E. Blanton, 'Anthropological Studies of Cities', *Annual Review of Anthropology* 5 (1976), 253.

[8] Fernand Braudel, *The Structures of Everyday Life: Civilization and Capitalism, 15th–18th Century* 1 (New York, 1981), 481.

[9] I am using here the model of the four dimensions of social power—ideological, economic, military, and political—developed by Michael Mann, *The Sources of Social Power* 1 (Cambridge, 1986).

of communication between them. Fortunately, we have such maps for southern Babylonia through the efforts of Robert McC. Adams, but we lack them for the rest of Mesopotamia.

Can we use other criteria, identifiable in an isolated settlement, to recognize a city? V. Gordon Childe developed a list of ten elements distinguishing cities from villages,[10] but this list has been justly criticized as a mixed bag of unrelated characteristics. It is thus preferable to limit the criteria in number, and perhaps common sense should be our main guide. A book on European urbanization states reasonably:

[There are] commonly accepted quantifiable dimensions that distinguish cities from other forms of settlement: population size, density of settlement, share of non-agricultural occupations and diversity of non-agricultural occupations. All four of these criteria are continuums, so that one must draw a line at some point dividing cities from non-cities. This cannot help but be arbitrary. But a settlement must score sufficiently high in all four of these criteria to be a city, a requirement that does not make the task easier but does reflect the existence of a broadly shared intuitive understanding of what constitutes an urban place.[11]

The problem of distinguishing between urban and non-urban settlements is somewhat alleviated in the study of Mesopotamian urbanism in that archaeologists have concentrated their work on settlements that have urban characteristics, because these are still most visible in the countryside and promise the most sensational results. The textual material from these sites will thus also derive from an urban environment. In this study the term city will be rather broadly applied to many of the Mesopotamian settlements we know. I will use town as a synonym for city, as it seems impossible to differentiate between the two with the information available, and contrast these terms only with village. The latter I will interpret as a rural settlement of limited size, whose inhabitants are primarily involved in agricultural production or in a specialized aspect of industry, for their own needs and for the needs of the inhabitants of a neighbouring city. It seems futile to attempt a more refined distinction than that between city and village.

The reconstruction of urban life presented here perforce will be

---

[10] V. Gordon Childe, 'The Urban Revolution', *Town Planning Review* 21 (1950), 3–17.

[11] Jan de Vries, *European Urbanization 1500–1800* (Cambridge, 1984), 11.

greatly influenced by ideas on the structure of Mesopotamian society in general. Every scholar works with such a bias, yet few state their views clearly. A survey of the current theories on the social and economic structures of Mesopotamia would be useful, but cannot be provided here. A variety of opinions is inspired by the scholarship devoted to the societies and economies of ancient Greece and Rome, where the discussion has been more public. The fundamental issue in the debate, which is especially pertinent to the study of urbanism, is whether the ancient economies were 'primitive' or 'modern'. The polemic around this question has been going on for a century among ancient historians, but has seemingly escaped the attention of Mesopotamian ones.[12] It is paralleled by the so-called 'substantivist–formalist' controversy among economic anthropologists, which has been set off by the work of Karl Polanyi. The 'primitivist' or 'substantivist' points of view state that pre-capitalist or non-capitalist economies were and are so radically different from the modern Western economy that the concepts or models used in modern economics cannot be applied to them. The 'modernist' school thinks that the ancient Greek and Roman economies showed such an advanced stage of capitalist development that they differed only quantitatively from the modern economy, not qualitatively. 'Formalist' anthropologists believe that economic theories used for the analysis of the modern economy can be used in the study of 'primitive' economies.

The 'primitivist' point of view is clearly dominant among those scholars who have formulated a coherent theory on the Mesopotamian economy, especially the 'schools' around the Marxist scholars I. M. Diakonoff and M. Liverani, as well as I. J. Gelb, A. L. Oppenheim, and J. Renger. The majority of Western scholars seems to adhere to the modernist point of view, and actually extends it further back in time to ascribe capitalist practices to Mesopotamia in the early second, if not the third, millennium BC.

An entire set of 'modern' economic values and motivations can

---

[12] The only explicit references to the primitivism–modernism debate known to me are in the recent articles by Johannes Renger, 'Probleme und Perspektiven einer Wirtschaftsgeschichte Mesopotamiens', *Saeculum* 40 (1989), 166–78; and by Carlo Zaccagnini, 'In margine all'*emporion*: modelli di scambio nelle economie del Vicino Oriente antico', in Alain Bresson and Pierre Rouillard (eds.), *L'emporion* (Publications du centre Pierre Paris (URA 991); Paris, 1993), 127–43.

be demonstrated to have been present in ancient Mesopotamia: a desire for profit, the maximal use of economic resources, and a price-setting market economy including a labour market. There are many empirical data that point to the existence of these economic factors; loan documents, bills of sale, hiring contracts, etc. The crucial problem lies in the evaluation of their role within the economy. Do these documents reveal 'capitalist' activities that had a substantial or even dominant importance in the economic life? Or are they merely peripheral to an economy dominated by the public institutions of palace and temple, which controlled the majority of labour, remunerated with standardized rations, set prices, and extracted economic resources for unproductive purposes such as ostentatious display? In 1909 the German sociologist Max Weber stated that such an evaluation could not yet be made as most of the 200,000 cuneiform texts excavated at that time had not been translated and the interpretation of those studied was still highly uncertain.[13] Today, when the number of published documents is infinitely higher and our understanding of them, although still open to debate, has improved vastly, we are in the same position. Since we are unable to quantify information on any sector of the Mesopotamian economy, we cannot evaluate the relative importance of the data we have. For example, the agricultural production in Babylonia managed by the state under the Third Dynasty of Ur (twenty-first century) seems enormous. Huge tracts of land were worked by numerous state dependants, accounted for by bureaucrats. We know that next to these seemingly gigantic state holdings privately or communally owned fields existed, but nothing is known about their production. Based on this information we can only venture the opinion that in this period most of the agricultural produce in Babylonia derived from the state enterprise, but one cannot say by any means what percentage of the total production was in the state's hands. Perhaps we are fooled by the documentary abundance from state archives, and the private sector in reality may have been dominant. If we accept that the state was the major agricultural producer, how can we determine its motives? Did it organize production merely to guarantee the survival of the official bureaucracy and all the state dependants with a marginal addi-

---

[13] See Max Weber, *The Agrarian Sociology of Ancient Civilizations*, trans. R. I. Frank (London and New York, 1988), 103–4.

tional surplus to enable the acquisition of foreign materials for a display of wealth in the palace and the temples? Or did the state strive for a maximization of production with the available resources of labour and land in order to enable the acquisition of as many prestige goods as possible? In the end our answers are determined by a theoretical stance, often based on an intuitive judgement, and an increase of the factual data will not enable us to settle these questions conclusively.

Since the work of the economic historian cannot be an unprejudiced description of facts this theoretical stance needs to be identified. In the model presented here in somewhat dogmatic terms I have incorporated many elements developed and argued by other scholars. References to these, and other works will be found in the bibliography. Of fundamental importance to our consideration of the economies of antiquity in general is the fact that the economy cannot be separated from its social setting. Hence the structure of society, again very incompletely known to us, needs to be considered first. The basic social unit within Mesopotamia was the household, which could vary enormously in size. At its smallest, it was formed by a nuclear family: a patriarch and his sons and grandsons with their wives and children. Dependent labour was part of the household, which thus could expand enormously to a large palace or temple complex headed by a secular or religious leader with hundreds of dependent families. At least originally, the household strove to be an autonomous unit of production and consumption. Ideally all that was consumed by it was grown and prepared within the household itself. But in reality this self-sufficiency was rarely attained above a level of mere subsistence. Since Mesopotamia had no mineral resources, for instance, metal objects could only be manufactured with materials obtained from the outside. Even the palace could not obtain all its needs through its own production or conquest, at least until the Assyrian empire.

Already in the early historical period, the households can be categorized into three sectors, which survived throughout Mesopotamian history: institutional, communal, and private. Other scholars see a dichotomy between institutional and communal (e.g. Diakonoff and Liverani), or institutional and private households (e.g. Gelb and Renger), but I believe that the idea that there was only one type of social unit outside the public institutions does not explain what we observe in the historical record.

The institutional households dominate the textual and archaeological data available to us, and include the secular palace and
the religious temples. The relationship between the two shifted
throughout Mesopotamian history. While the temples were dominant politically and economically in the very early periods, they
were incorporated into the palace hierarchy from the mid-third
millennium on, and may have become the representatives of the
community in late Babylonian history. Since temples and palaces
worked hand in hand during most of Mesopotamian history, they
can be considered together under the institutional heading. Their
households were large, in early history incorporating a large
number of dependants who provided labour and relied upon the
institutions for their livelihood. The complex system of the redistribution of all basic requirements developed later into one with self-
supporting tenant-farmers who supplied part of their yields to the
institutional landowner. In the first millennium, the Mesopotamian empires acquired huge tracts of land through conquest,
which were distributed to high officials who ran their estates like
feudal lords.

The communal households are very poorly documented, and
according to some scholars they are a figment of the imagination.
The idea of classless clan-based groups with communal ownership
of land that cannot be alienated by individuals derives from the
Marxist concept of the primitive mode of production preceding a
class society. Yet with the establishment of classes and the state,
the communities did not disappear entirely, although their activities were pushed to the fringes of the urban civilization that is the
focus of our attention. Autarkic rural communities leading a life
at the subsistence level may have remained a constant feature
in Mesopotamia at least until the late second millennium. Their
members were free, yet poor. The infiltration of new ethnic groups,
such as the Kassites, at times seems to have reinforced the communal sector, but that sector always remained on the margins of the
society as known to us.

The existence of a free private sector in Mesopotamian society,
in addition to the institutional and communal ones, seems rarely
accepted. The majority of scholars considers all the individuals we
see engaged in economic activity as belonging to the institutional
master class. Yet, although such persons often collaborated with
the temples and the palaces, they need not have been in the employ

of these institutions, as we see them also involved in transactions on their own account. Many of them never appear with a title that places them within an institutional household, and when the archaeological context of their records is known, they are often found in residential areas. The origins of these individuals are unclear. They may have been community members who had left their clan, or members of the upper echelons of the institutional households who had become financially secure enough to acquire land and conduct business independently. Perhaps a great impetus towards the creation of this sector came from the institutions' unwillingness to manage their own resources and their subcontracting of services to private individuals.

Obviously a rigid distinction between the activities of these three sectors did not exist. A look at present-day experience shows that, despite the rhetoric, no economy is completely managed by the state or by private enterprise. As usual, a scholarly classification obscures the details we can observe in our data. Individuals worked with institutions, the palace interacted with village communities, and many arrangements unknown to us must have been worked out. All three sectors of society played a role throughout history with varying degrees of importance, but never to the complete exclusion of the others.

An important question revolves around what motivated the economic activities we observe in the records. Although we cannot deny that the Mesopotamians were aware of the concepts of profit and loss, and that they are often documented as active in commercial enterprises, we need not look upon them as driven by the capitalist ideologies that have dominated the Western world in the modern era. We have to keep in mind that those activities that seem to us as having a commercial nature will dominate the textual records we use in our research. But it is obvious that economic activity could result from motives other than the desire for material gain. The acquisition of wealth may have been used to raise one's social status, and once the desired status was attained the individual might stop working. Institutions that made interest-bearing loans may have done so in order to help out people in need, but they may also have been interested in increasing their capital. Was the Mesopotamian economy a 'prestige economy' or one interested in 'filthy lucre'? These are questions we cannot answer, and not just because of the so-called lack of self-conscious literature in

Mesopotamia. One just has to look at the acerbity of the debate concerning the ancient Greeks and their attitudes towards commercial life to see that even an assertion by Aristotle cannot be taken at its face value. From our distance, and at the mercy of a textual record that emphasizes economic activity, we cannot judge the motivations of these ancient peoples.

Many of the statements made in this book will seem to substantiate the modernist claims concerning the ancient economy. I will use terms such as profit, the market, manufacturing industry, investments, all of which have particular capitalist connotations in our minds. Yet I do not want to portray the Mesopotamians as driven by the same economic desires we seem to have, or as archetypical 'Levantine' traders. Somehow they attempted to make the best of their lives with the limited resources available to them, and they often were not able to raise their standard of living above mere survival. But at times some of them, like the Assyrian emperors of the seventh century, were able to attain luxurious life-styles at the expense of many others, due to a fortuitous coincidence of political and economic factors. Those few are best known to us because their remains dominate both the textual and archaeological records available to the modern scholar, but they are the exception, not the rule.

Finally it is important to point out the restrictions of the textual documentation used in the study of Mesopotamian social and economic history. The three sectors of society I outlined above are not equally represented: there is a strong bias towards the affairs of the institutions in the records. This bias results both from the actual extent of writing used within the three sectors, and from the recovery of material in modern excavations. Writing in Mesopotamia was invented for the recording of economic transactions, and throughout the history of the region this remained the primary function of the written word, even when literature and the like were written down as well. But literacy was limited, and record keeping was primarily undertaken by the public institutions and by individuals with large economic interests. The village communities, producing little or nothing in excess of what they consumed, would not have needed to record anything, as the few transactions taking place were simple, and could be easily remembered. Large economic enterprises required a bureaucracy, however. They were primarily the enterprises of the palaces and large temples. Transactions, such as the issuing of rations to numerous employees, needed to be recorded. Also private individuals and family firms played an important role in the Mesopotamian economy and their activities became very complex at times, so complex that they required a record. Hence, in antiquity the affairs of public institutions and important private entrepreneurs dominated the record. In modern times the accounts of the large temple and palace organizations have gained an increased prominence, because both scientific and illicit archaeological exploration has focused on the monumental remains of palaces and temples. Private residences have been less explored, and thus the records of the people living in them often remain unexcavated. The bias of the written documentation available to us emphasizes thus the affairs of the public institutions, but this situation does not warrant the conclusion that they dominated economic life in Mesopotamia at all times. In our reconstructions we should remain aware of the activities of the communal and private sectors of the society as well, even if they remain poorly documented or not documented at all.

A detailed description of the economic interactions between the three sectors of society cannot be written here, and perhaps not even in a separate study. Their presence throughout Mesopotamian history, and their co-operation in the economy will be used as a basis of this study. They were variables in a complex system of interaction of social, political, economic, and cultural spheres, all of which played a role in urban life. It is that life I hope to elucidate in this book.

BIBLIOGRAPHY

Studies on Mesopotamian urbanism are rare: A. Leo Oppenheim's works include: 'A New Look at the Structure of Mesopotamian Society', *Journal of the Economic and Social History of the Orient* 10 (1967), 1–26; 'Mesopotamia—Land of Many Cities', in Ira M. Lapidus (ed.), *Middle Eastern Cities* (Berkeley and Los Angeles, 1969), 2nd edn. 3–16; and *Ancient Mesopotamia: Portrait of a Dead Civilization* (Chicago and London, 1977). The symposium on urbanism at the University of Chicago was published as *City Invincible*, C. H. Kraeling and R. McC. Adams (eds.) (Chicago, 1960). The conference at the University of London was published as *Man,*

*Settlement and Urbanism*, Peter J. Ucko, Ruth Tringham, and G.W. Dimbleby (eds.) (London, 1972). Robert McC. Adams published three seminal books on settlement patterns in ancient Babylonia: *Land behind Baghdad: A History of Settlement on the Diyala Plains* (Chicago and London, 1965); (with Hans J. Nissen), *The Uruk Countryside: The Natural Setting of Urban Societies* (Chicago and London, 1972); and *Heartland of Cities* (Chicago and London, 1981). G. Cardascia wrote an article 'Les villes de Mésopotamie', for the *Recueils de la Société Jean Bodin* 7 (1955), 51–61; and Wolfram von Soden gave some general remarks in 'Tempelstadt und Metropolis im Alten Orient', in Heinz Stoob (ed.), *Die Stadt: Gestalt und Wandel bis zum industriellen Zeitalter* (Cologne and Vienna, 1979), 37–82.

Three recent conferences on the city in Mesopotamia have been published: *La Ville dans le proche-orient ancien: Actes du Colloque de Cartigny*, Françoise Brüschweiler (ed.) (Louvain, 1983); *The Town as Regional Economic Centre in the Ancient Near East* (Session B-16, Proceedings Tenth International Economic History Congress, Leuven, August 1990), Erik Aerts and Horst Klengel (eds.) (Louvain, 1990); and *Nuove fondazioni nel Vicino Oriente antico: realtà e ideologia*, S. Mazzoni (ed.) (Pisa, 1994).

Important insights on urbanism can also be found in M. Liverani, 'La città vicino orientale antica', in Pietro Rossi (ed.), *Modelli di città* (Turin, 1987), 57–85, and J. N. Postgate, *Early Mesopotamia: Society and Economy at the Dawn of History* (London and New York, 1992). Jean-Louis Huot, *Naissance des cités* (Paris, 1990), is a more popular account addressing many aspects of urbanism.

General surveys of ancient urbanism that include remarks on Mesopotamia are Mason Hammond, *The City in the Ancient World* (Cambridge, 1972), for which the review by J. Renger in *Journal of the American Oriental Society* 95 (1975), 115–16 is important; and Frank Kolb, *Die Stadt im Altertum* (Munich, 1984).

Studies of individual cities include Sippar: Rivkah Harris, *Ancient Sippar: A Demographic Study of an Old Babylonian City (1894–1595 BC)* (Istanbul, 1975); Nippur: Elizabeth C. Stone, *Nippur Neighborhoods* (Chicago, 1987); and Ur: I. M. Diakonoff, *People of Ur* (Moscow, 1990); Marc Van De Mieroop, *Society and Enterprise in Old Babylonian Ur* (Berlin, 1992).

Archaeological projects attempting to reconstruct urban layouts include those at Abu Salabikh: J. N. Postgate in John Curtis (ed.), *Fifty Years of Mesopotamian Discovery* (London, 1982), 48–61; Abu Duwari: Elizabeth C. Stone and Paul Zimansky, 'Mashkan-shapir and the Anatomy of an Old Babylonian City', *Biblical Archaeologist* 55 (1992), 212–18; and Larsa: Jean-Louis Huot *et al.*, 'La Structure urbaine de Larsa: Une approche provisoire', in Jean-Louis Huot (ed.), *Larsa: Travaux de 1985* (Paris, 1989), 19–52. For a rare archaeological investigation of a Lower Mesopotamian village, see Henry T. Wright, *The Administration of Rural Production in an Early Mesopotamian Town* (Ann Arbor, 1969).

A powerful statement about the unity of Mesopotamian civilization was made by A. Leo Oppenheim in *Letters from Mesopotamia* (Chicago and London, 1967), 1–53, but his message has been mostly ignored. The issue of continuity in Mesopotamian history has been addressed recently by Norman Yoffee, 'The Collapse of Ancient Mesopotamian States and Civilization', in Norman Yoffee and George L. Cowgill (eds.), *The Collapse of Ancient States and Civilizations* (Tuscon, 1988), 44–68, and J. N. Postgate, *Early Mesopotamia*, (1992), 292–302.

On the Akkadian term *ālum* see I. M. Diakonoff, 'From a collective dwelling to an imperial city', *Oikumene* 5 (1986), 55–62; and William W. Hallo, 'Antediluvian Cities', *Journal of Cuneiform Studies* 23 (1970), 57–67.

A good survey of the methodological difficulties for the study of Ancient Mesopotamian economic history, with references to ancient history in general, was provided by Johannes Renger, 'Probleme und Perspektiven einer Wirtschaftsgeschichte Mesopotamiens', *Saeculum* 40 (1989), 166–78. The most important Marxist theoretical statements include the many contributions by I. M. Diakonoff, the most recent and accessible of which is in *Early Antiquity* (Chicago and London, 1991), 1–66; and Mario Liverani, 'Il modo di produzione', in S. Moscati (ed.), *L'alba della civiltà* 2: *L'economia*, (Turin, 1976), 1–126.

Non-Marxist scholars have never clearly outlined their ideas on the structure of Mesopotamian society. Important contributions have been made by I. J. Gelb in articles such as, 'On the Alleged Temple and State Economies in Ancient Mesopotamia', *Studi in onore di Edoardo Volterra* 6 (Milan, 1969), 137–54; 'From Freedom to Slavery', in D. O. Edzard (ed.), *Gesellschaftsklassen im Alten Zweistromland* (Munich, 1972), 81–92; and 'Household and

Family in Early Mesopotamia', in E. Lipinski (ed.), *State and Temple Economy in the Ancient Near East* (Louvain, 1979), 1–97. Johannes Renger has devoted several studies to the subject, e.g. 'Patterns of non-institutional trade and non-commercial exchange in ancient Mesopotamia at the beginning of the second millennium BC', in Alfonso Archi (ed.), *Circulation of Goods in Non-Palatial Context in the Ancient Near East* (Rome, 1984), 31–123; 'Wirtschaft und Gesellschaft', in B. Hrouda (ed.), *Der Alte Orient* (Gütersloh, 1991), 187–215; and 'On Economic Structures in Ancient Mesopotamia', *Orientalia* 63 (1994), 157–208.

# 2

# The Origins and Character of the Mesopotamian City

It is now generally accepted that Mesopotamia is the one region in the Old World where we can say with certainty that an urban civilization arose spontaneously. The origins of cities there have been extensively discussed in the past four decades, not so much by Near Eastern historians, who have often limited their comments to statements of archaeologically discernible facts, but by anthropologists, sociologists, and some urban historians specializing in later periods. The topic is of importance in the study of Mesopotamian urbanism, as our ideas about their origins influence to a great extent how we view the nature of cities in subsequent history. In this chapter I do not intend to give a survey of the events connected with the rise of urbanism, nor an overview and critique of all theories seeking to explain it. I will discuss some of the most influential theories on urban development and point out what elements in them seem most useful for understanding the Mesopotamian situation. This will lead to a consideration of the character of the Mesopotamian city once it was fully developed.

First, I have to restate a few well-known facts. Mesopotamia is the region where cities originated first in world history. Hence, the rise of cities there was an independent and indigenous event. Second, the entire evolution took place in prehistory. No textual sources are available from the time cities first arose, and texts from later periods can only be used to illustrate patterns visible in the earlier archaeological record. Third, the entire process from the first permanent settlement in southern Mesopotamia to the first cities there took an enormously long time, from around 5500 BC to around 3500 BC. The emergence of the city may have occurred relatively suddenly, but cannot be understood in isolation from what preceded it, and must be seen as a culmination of that process.

Of the numerous discussions on the origins of the city, three approaches have found the most adherents, each stressing a particular function of the earliest cities: ceremonial, commercial, or redistributive. The concept that the earliest cities, in all areas of primary urban generation, functioned foremost as ceremonial centres has been most extensively argued by Paul Wheatley, reviving an idea already developed by Fustel de Coulanges in the mid-nineteenth century. Wheatley maintained that religion provided the primary focus of social life in the period immediately preceding urbanism. Wherever cities first appeared, they contained a ceremonial complex, in his opinion, and even if the latter performed secular functions as well, these were part of the religious context. The priests were the first group to escape the 'daily round of subsistence labor',[1] hence setting the process of social stratification into motion. Only after ceremonial centres were firmly established did they obtain a redistributive economic role, and secular élites only developed after cities had been in existence for several centuries.

Although the observation that all the earliest cities contained a ceremonial centre is accurate, for Mesopotamia at least, the conclusion that religion drew people together in urban conglomerates is not warranted. The reasoning behind it seems to be one of *cum hoc ergo propter hoc*. The idea that temples are primarily religious institutions is a modern concept and does not apply to the early Mesopotamian temples. They fulfilled primarily a managerial role in the local economy. As I will demonstrate later, no urban settlement is possible without an agricultural base to support a dense population. Agricultural resources needed to be extracted from the countryside by an authority, and religion provided that authority. But people did not converge upon ceremonial centres for their spiritual leadership, and throughout the world many such centres exist in isolation. Moreover, the temple's importance in early Mesopotamia is greatly overstated, due to the archaeologists' focus on monumental architecture, and a misreading of mid-third-millennium archival records. The ideological focus provided by early cities clearly existed, but it was of insufficient strength to be the sole driving force towards urbanism.

A second theory emphasizes the role of long-distance trade in the

---

[1] Paul Wheatley, *The Pivot of the Four Quarters* (Chicago, 1971), 303.

development of cities. Its most extreme advocate is the urban theorist, Jane Jacobs, who has earned an almost legendary status in the USA for her 'visionary' ideas and is extensively quoted in anthropological and sociological literature. However, she is almost entirely unknown (or ignored) among ancient Near Eastern specialists. In her book *The Economy of Cities* (1969), she attacked the 'dogma' that agriculture preceded cities, and replaced it with a theory that the existence of cities led to agriculture, and that cities first originated because of long-distance trade in raw materials. The empirical basis for this theory is the existence of such eighth- to sixth-millennium settlements in the Levant and Anatolia as Jericho and Çatal Hüyük, interpreted by some scholars to have been cities. But, whereas the latter scholars acknowledge that an agricultural base was needed for these settlements, Jacobs hypothesized the existence of pre-agricultural cities antedating these excavated sites. She described an imaginary city, New Obsidian, which was involved in the long-distance trade in obsidian without being located near its sources. Food for the inhabitants would have been obtained partly through barter with nearby hunter-gatherers, but mainly through imports from foreign hunting territories. Because meat would have spoiled during its transport, live animals were driven to New Obsidian, where soon a selection of the tamest animals was made for breeding. Seeds and nuts were brought into town as they preserved better than fruits and vegetables, and when mixed together in bins and partly sown in wild patches, they were accidentally cross-bred and became 'better' than their wild progenitors. Soon the city began to grow most of its food. 'Cities First—Rural Development Later.'

Jacobs's theory is based entirely on false premises. It relies heavily on an unconvincing parallel with the modern world, where the most advanced urban areas are supposed to have the most advanced agriculture. And, when dealing with prehistory, Jacobs ignores altogether what Bairoch has called 'the tyranny of distance'.[2] The transport of food products is very expensive, as the transporter consumes part of his or her load. A man carrying the entire load, can daily transport 35–40 kilograms over 30–35 kilometres. Every day he has to consume about one kilogram, so he

---

[2] Paul Bairoch, *De Jéricho à Mexico: Villes et économie dans l'histoire* (Paris, 1985), 33–4.

eats his entire load in about seventeen days when he has marched at the most 600 kilometres one way, taking into account that he has to eat on his way back. Of course, to be able to barter the food he cannot consume all of it. An example makes this problem obvious. If a man comes a distance of 100 kilometres to obtain obsidian at New Obsidian, he will start out with 40 kilograms of food. In three days he will have reached his destination with 37 kilograms, and he will be able to barter a maximum of 34 kilograms for obsidian. Those 34 kilograms will feed one inhabitant of the city for slightly more than one month. For the 5,000 inhabitants of Çatal Hüyük to be supported for one year, 60,000 trips of this type would be needed from a radius not surpassing 100 kilometres from the site. That area is only 157 square kilometres, and considering the extremely low population density in pre-agricultural times, there were not enough people in that region to provide all the food needed in New Obsidian. Moreover, all these calculations are based on the assumption that circumstances were optimal. It seems impossible to walk 33 kilometres a day in the region around Çatal Hüyük, while rest-stops on the road would have increased the consumption by the transporter. How long would it have taken to drive live undomesticated animals over this distance? The problems could not be alleviated by using draft animals, as Jacobs states that all this activity took place before the domestication of animals. Nor does river transport provide an alternative, as rivers are only navigable in one direction in the area of Çatal Hüyük. Jacobs's theory is thus entirely unacceptable.

Mellaart, whose work inspired Jacobs, was more careful as he acknowledged the existence of agriculture around sites such as Jericho, Çatal Hüyük, and others. He also stressed the role of religion in the creation of these settlements, referring to man as 'a religious animal' and to the fact that 'religious structures are among the earliest remains of the *homo sapiens*'.[3] But still the settlements of the eighth to sixth millennia he studied are not to be regarded as cities and certainly not as the beginnings of urban civilization. They were highly anomalous settlements, relying on unique coincidences of very fertile surroundings and location on trade routes, enabling and precipitating a dense habitation. No

---

[3] James Mellaart, 'The Origins and Development of Cities in the Near East', in Louis L. Orlin (ed.), *Janus: Essays in Ancient and Modern Studies* (Ann Anbor, 1975), 13.

social hierarchy is clear within these settlements, nor do their hinterlands show an urban infrastructure. Moreover, they were evolutionary 'dead-ends': after 5400 BC they disappeared and for over 1,000 years urban settlements are not to be found in the regions.

The last theory I will discuss here has gained the most popularity in the field of ancient Near Eastern studies after it was cogently argued by Robert McC. Adams in his seminal book *The Evolution of Urban Society* (1966). The book focuses on the societal changes which led to an urban civilization in two regions with primary urbanization: southern Mesopotamia and Mesoamerica. Adams recognized three major stages in this evolution. First, the development of agriculture led to increased stability of residence, increased yields, and incentives for population growth. As a result there was greater societal stability, and a surplus appeared in food production. Because of a specialization in food production, a mediatory role for the exchange of goods was needed, and the power of redistribution was concentrated in the hands of a small group within the society. Second, classes gradually replaced kin-based groups. Differences in access to the means of production led to a social stratification. Individuals identified themselves more with their equals in social status than with their kin. But kinship affiliation did not disappear altogether, as the relationship to a real or imaginary common ancestor was used as the basis for social stratification. Third, the upper classes in the social hierarchy took hold of the administration of the by now complex society. The first group to do so was a priesthood that may have justified its leadership through religion. The earliest Mesopotamian cults focused upon fertility, and ecological instability may have led people to rely on priests to intercede on their behalf with the gods. But the main function of the temple was one of economic redistribution. Increasingly large and complex temples organized the varied and multiple interactions between different groups within the society. The priests relied on technological innovations such as writing and bookkeeping for their trade. Craft centres grew up to provide for their needs with increasing specialization, and expensive raw materials were imported by them through long-distance trade. A physical separation from the rest of society ensued with the temple personnel residing in or around increasingly monumental temples in cities. Only centuries later were the powers held by the priests

usurped by a secular and military authority, whose influence
was nurtured by increased competition between the various urban
centres.

Adams considered the rise of the city as one aspect of the rise of
the state, i.e. a society that is hierarchically organized on political
and territorial lines rather than on the basis of kinship or other
ascriptive relationships. The political authority of the state happens
to be situated in the city where a dense and socially stratified
population resides. I would agree with this viewpoint, although I
do not want to broaden the discussion here to the rise of the state
in Mesopotamia. In Adams's opinion cities originated because
states developed. Society was structured with classes, differentiated
both through wealth or access to means of production, and through
occupation which could be agricultural, pastoral, industrial, commercial, cultic, or administrative. Cities were the loci where these
classes interacted or where the interactions between them were
regulated. In economic terms they were redistributive centres of
goods and services produced by these classes. Adams's theory has
earned widespread support among Mesopotamian scholars, who
have elaborated on it, and indeed its argument is highly persuasive.
In the present discussion I would like to stress why cities evolved in
southern Mesopotamia of all places, and to elaborate on the various aspects of their redistributive role.

It is very difficult for us to determine why cities appeared in
southern Mesopotamia, rather than in Anatolia or the Levant, for
instance. By the beginning of the fourth millennium the region
provided the three preconditions of city life, as determined by
Gideon Sjoberg: a favourable ecological base, an advanced technology (relative to the pre-urban form) in both agricultural and
non-agricultural spheres, and a complex social organization, especially with regard to the power structure.[4] But these circumstances
do not necessarily lead to an urban society. As Ester Boserup has
shown there is a need for a certain level of population density, as
the aggregate food surplus produced by the agriculturalists needs
to satisfy the requirements of the non-agricultural urban population.[5] The southern Mesopotamian countryside was certainly

---

[4] Gideon Sjoberg, *The Preindustrial City, Past and Present* (Glencoe, 1960), 27–
31.
[5] Ester Boserup, *Population and Technological Change: A Study of Long-Term
Trends* (Chicago, 1981), Part II.

fertile enough to sustain a dense population, but there was no shortage of agricultural land that would force people to live closely together. So why did they decide to remain in a small geographical zone, so that the prerequisite population density could be attained? I think we can answer this question by looking at the ecological diversity of the region. Several scholars, such as Adams and Liverani, have pointed out that the Near East contains a number of diverse ecological zones in close contact with one another: steppe, irrigated alluvium, and mountains with forests and pastures. This is also true on a more microscopic scale, especially for the very south of Mesopotamia. All too often it is imagined that this area was uninhabited until the arrival of irrigation farmers in the mid-sixth millennium. But many wild natural resources were available to non-farmers, and were exploited by them prior to the appearance of farming: pasture for herds of sheep and goats in the river valleys and the steppe, and extensive fishing and hunting grounds for fishermen and hunters in the marshes. When the technology to tap water from the numerous natural channels of the Euphrates river was introduced, large-scale farming became possible, but it did not replace herding, fishing, and hunting. All these activities took place in a small area in the very south of Mesopotamia, and it is thus not surprising that the earliest cities, Ur, Eridu, and Uruk, are to be found there as well. Exchange between the different food-producing groups became extensive and commonplace, and an organizing institution soon developed at the same time as the introduction of irrigation farming. Of course, exchange requires surplus production, something many scholars assume to have originated virtually spontaneously. Such an assumption is false and the origin of a surplus is the subject of much debate. No family will produce more than is needed for its subsistence unless it is forced to do so by a higher authority, or because the benefits of a surplus are obvious and indispensable. In theory, each of the specialized food-producing groups could be self-sufficient, and perhaps only the desire for a less restricted diet or for products that do not fulfil elementary needs pushed them to barter part of their produce. Still, the development is not inevitable and obvious.

The focus upon a small zone in the very south of Mesopotamia explains, in my opinion, why that was the area of primary urban development. Once the city had become a fact of life in the very south, the concept spread further north along the many channels of the Euphrates, which enabled easier exchange of bulky items along the river. By 2800 BC we find a system of city-states stretching from the Persian Gulf to the area just south of modern-day Baghdad. Inter-city trade of agricultural produce remained limited, however, and each city-state was self-sustaining in its food supplies and basic material needs until about 1800 BC when the military unification of Babylonia led to an integration of the agricultural economy as well.[6]

But this leads us too far in time, and we need to backtrack in order to explore further what the role of the earliest cities was. So far, I have referred only to their functions in the economy—moreover only in certain aspects of the economy—an approach that is too limited in its scope. The social stratification that characterizes urban life involves social power which relies on four sources, according to a theory developed by Michael Mann: economic, ideological, military, and political. With these sources of power, certain individuals or groups attain their goals in society. In the case of early cities, the urban élites were closer to these sources than were the other members of society. I would like to investigate here how this manifested itself. By treating these four areas separately, I do not intend to indicate that they had independent identities. They are interacting networks, whose separate consideration I hope will lead to a clearer understanding of their nature.

The economic power of urban élites has already been discussed in part. Their role was mainly managerial: the interaction between differently specialized producers of goods and services was controlled by a small segment of society. In the first cities that group had temple connections, and the anachronistic term priesthood is commonly used as its designation. An unknown number of these priests had the knowledge of writing, the ability to record transactions permanently on bulky clay tablets. The economic power was not limited to local affairs, but also extended to long-distance trade.

The importance of long-distance trade in early Mesopotamian civilization is not as easy to assess as is often assumed. A majority of scholars agree that southern Mesopotamia is a region lacking all raw materials but clay and reed, and that long-distance trade is needed to obtain access to basic materials such as timber, stone,

---

[6] See Marc Van De Mieroop, 'The Reign of Rim-Sin', *Revue d'assyriologie et d'archéologie orientale* 87 (1993), 47–69.

and metals, and luxury goods such as semi-precious stones. The need for such materials has been used as one, or even the most important, causal factor in the rise of cities in southern Mesopotamia, on the grounds that it would have necessitated the production of a surplus for exchange purposes. This explanation is not convincing, as it fails to show why other regions of the Mesopotamian alluvium, equally lacking in resources, did not develop cities at the same time as the South; besides, the poverty of southern Mesopotamia in raw materials has been greatly overstated. Wood and stone were available and useable, even though they were not of the best quality, and clay, bitumen, and reed could substitute for other materials. There was no necessity to acquire products from abroad, although it is clear that from the fifth millennium onwards trade contacts between southern Mesopotamia and the surrounding areas existed. Pottery produced in southern Mesopotamia dating to that millennium has been found along the Persian Gulf as far south as the United Arab Emirates, and in the second half of the fourth millennium an incredible expansion of the southern Mesopotamian Uruk culture throughout the Near East may have been driven by trade. But the economic importance of that trade remains to be assessed. A find in Saudi Arabia of a pot produced in Ur shows direct or indirect contacts between these two places, but not how common these contacts were.

Be this as it may, it seems likely that long-distance trade was originally controlled by the temples, and that the merchants had temple affiliations. This was probably caused by the fact that surplus production of textiles and other tradable goods was held by the temples. It is interesting that long-distance trade was the sector of the economy that was privatized earlier than any other state- or temple-controlled enterprise. Perhaps this can be explained as the result of the merchants' need for as much neutrality as possible, in order to avoid identification with a participant in a power struggle. Thus, we can conclude that the economic power of urban élites originally included long-distance trade, but that the importance of this trade has been exaggerated, and that it soon was delegated to private entrepreneurs.

The second source of power is ideological. At the time of urban origins, ideology was primarily religious. Although private shrines and ancestor cults survived throughout Mesopotamian history, urban temples grew increasingly large and the priesthood seems to have taken the role as mediator between the people and the gods. A late fourth-millennium carving on a stone vase found at Uruk (Fig. 2.1) shows a row of naked men carrying vessels and jars of produce to a goddess, identified by the symbols behind her as Inanna, the goddess of procreation. In front of her stands the city ruler, represented larger than his men and fully dressed in ceremonial robe, clearly acting as an intermediary. Rituals of fertility involving the ruler and the goddess were common until the eighteenth century at least. It is reasonable to assume that religious ideology was used by the priesthood to extract produce from the rural population, but its exact methods are not revealed to us.

Fig. 2.1   Uruk vase with reconstruction of the image of the city ruler in the top register

With the rise of kingship, a secular authority in need of an ideological basis developed alongside the religious one. This basis was provided through a combination of military and religious leadership. The latter had been provided by the priesthood, whose powers needed to be usurped before the military commander could claim religious leadership as well. The king fought battles against other city-states, but these battles allegedly were to protect the property of the city god. The conflict, lasting more than a century, over an agricultural area between the neighbouring city-states Umma and Lagash is portrayed as the defence of the rights of the god Ningirsu by successive kings of his city-state, Lagash. One king, Eanatum, even portrays himself as having been bred as Ningirsu's champion, and nurtured by the goddess Ninhursag:

Inanna stood by him, and named him 'Eana-Inanna-Ibgalkaka-atum'. She placed him on the good lap of Ninhursag. Ninhursag [laid him] on her good breast. Ningirsu rejoiced over Eanatum, semen placed in the womb by Ningirsu. Ningirsu measured him with his span: ⟨he was⟩ five cubits and one span tall! With joy Ningirsu [gave him the kingship of Lagash].[7]

Similarly, the 'Sacred Marriage Rite' came to involve the king who had intercourse with the goddess in order to assure the fertility of the land.

Traces of conflict between secular and religious leaders are noticeable in texts from the best documented city-state, Lagash. In the early twenty-fourth century the distinction between the two seems to have been eradicated when king Uru'inimgina proclaimed an edict ostensibly placing all lands in the hand of the city-gods, but in reality taking control of all temple domains himself. Later kings always held the position of high priest or even legitimized their rule by accepting divine status. The ideology of the secular power could thus not be separated from religion. Both temple and palace were located in the city, and the kings always stressed their urban background. So, here also the city acted as an ideological centre for the state.

Evidence for military engagement goes back to the pictorial representations of the late fourth millennium (Fig. 2.2), but it becomes abundant only in the mid-third millennium when royal inscriptions and monuments boast about military campaigns

---

[7] Stela of the Vultures, col. iv l. 18–col. v l. 17, Horst Steible, *Die altsumerische Bau- und Weihinschriften* I (Wiesbaden, 1982), 122–3.

F<small>IG</small>. 2.2   Late fourth-millennium sealing with combat scene

against neighbouring city-states or distant countries. All we know about the military involves such warfare, and the rise of the secular king has been convincingly related to the increased hostility between competing cities in southern Mesopotamia. Military power was always held by the palace located in the city, although the priest-ruler may have held that authority in the late fourth millennium as well. Feudal-style manor lords who delivered troops to the king when he needed them, and who raided on their own account, when free to do so, did not exist. Even when states relied on military levies from semi-nomadic tribes, as is documented in the texts from Mari, the administration and command of these troops remained an urban affair. The state's military power was thus centrally controlled in the city.

This military power relates, however, only to the 'international' affairs of the early city-states. Was military power also used by the urban élites in order to control the rural hinterland? Adams, for instance, has suggested that military coercion may have forced the exchange between villages and towns in the mid-fourth millennium.[8] In the early historical periods we do not find any direct evidence for such coercion, however. A standing army in the service of the king was perhaps only created in the twenty-fourth century by Sargon of Akkade, who claimed to have fed daily 5,400 soldiers, most likely a fictitious number. These men, and their successors in the employ of later dynasties, were involved in expeditions outside the heartland of their states. Yet the twenty-first-century kings of Ur appointed a military hierarchy, with blood ties to the royal house, next to the civil bureaucracy in the core provinces. These military men seem to have been installed to guarantee

---

[8]  Robert McC. Adams, *Heartland of Cities* (Chicago and London, 1981), 81.

to the king the loyalty of the civilian administrators who had local ties—not to help them extract resources from the local populations. Only in the peripheral areas of the state did the military fulfil the role of tax collectors for the kings in Ur.

Although active opposition to the king by his citizens is referred to in the omen literature,[9] the use of the army against residents of the countryside is never attested, as far as I know. No installations where such military troops could have been housed are visible in the archaeological record before the appearance of arsenals in Assyria of the first millennium. The collection of taxes seems to have been taken care of by bureaucrats without threat or violent resistance. Peasant revolts are not attested in Mesopotamian history. On the other hand, these bureaucrats may have relied on soldiers to enforce their demands. In early second-millennium texts, men with military titles are sometimes perceived as a threat, as can be seen from this passage of a letter from Ur:

Concerning the field, the allotment of Sin-abushu which you have taken unlawfully and have given to Ili-idinnam, Sin-abushu went and approached the king. The king gave him a soldier. Be quick! Before the soldier of the king arrives and they make you give compensation for the field, return the field to its owner. It is urgent![10]

The use of the military in internal affairs may thus have been more common than is suggested by the documentation.

The last source of power, political, is harder to define, especially since the military and ideological aspects have been stripped from it, a criticism that has been expressed against Mann's model. Mann separated political from military powers, describing as political 'those of centralized, institutionalized, territorial regulation',[11] as distinguished from decentralized, often independent, powers of military groups. If we regard politics as the actions and manœuvres of the state, both for its internal organization and for its diplomatic

---

[9] See J. Bottéro, 'Le Pouvoir royal et ses limitations d'après les textes divinatoires', in A. Finet (ed.), *La Voix de l'opposition en Mésopotamie* (Brussels, 1973), 119–65.

[10] H. H. Figulla and W. J. Martin, *Letters and Documents of the Old Babylonian Period* (Ur Excavations, Texts 5; London and Philadelphia, 1953), no. 45, lines 5–17.

[11] Michael Mann, *The Sources of Social Power* 1 (Cambridge, 1986), 11. The separation of military power from political power has been criticized, e.g. by Perry Anderson, *A Zone of Engagement* (London and New York, 1992), 77; and John A. Hall, *Powers and Liberties* (Oxford, 1985), 19 n. 13.

relations with other states, we can discuss them separately from economic, ideological, and military powers. From the outset cities clearly demanded a political organization different from that found in village communities. Royal political domination was established through a bureaucracy that expanded in size throughout the third millennium, culminating perhaps in the twenty-first century during the rule of the Third Dynasty of Ur. At that time, possibly the most prolific bureaucracy of the ancient world recorded minute aspects of administration, economy, and the courts, in a standardized format using an apparently dead language, Sumerian. Again, what is important for our consideration of the origins of the city is the fact that this aspect of power too was firmly founded in the city. The state was built around the city, as we aptly stress by our use of the term city-state when referring to early Mesopotamian political organization.

Thus, when we look at the late prehistoric and early historic city in Mesopotamia, we see that all four sources of power were centred in it: economically it acted as a redistributive centre, ideologically it contained the focal institutions of temple and palace, militarily it organized the army used by the kings, and politically it incorporated the organizing forces of the state. The city played thus a central role for its surroundings in many different ways; it grew up to provide that focus. The particular ecological conditions of southern Mesopotamia gave rise to this organization after an evolution lasting two millennia. In the mid-fourth century, the city was a fact of life in that area, never to disappear for the rest of ancient Mesopotamian history.

In my opinion, there are some amazing aspects of the early urbanization of the South, that need to be discussed before moving on to the North. Around 3200 a completely urban culture existed in southern Mesopotamia. Several technological innovations became visible simultaneously: writing, monumental arts and architecture, and mass-produced goods, especially pottery. The first written documentation shows the existence of developed systems of weights and measures, time-reckoning, and numeration. These accomplishments led V. Gordon Childe to his famous ten criteria to distinguish the earliest cities from older or contemporary villages:

1. size of settlements: the concentration of relatively large numbers of people in a restricted area;

2. specialization of agriculturalists and craftsmen;
3. payment of small amounts of taxes to a deity or divine king;
4. truly monumental architecture;
5. social stratification and a ruling class supported by a surplus;
6. writing;
7. emergence of exact and predictive sciences;
8. artistic expression;
9. foreign trade to import raw materials;
10. class rather than kinship affiliation.[12]

Although one can criticize the value of this list in identifying cities, it is true that all these elements were present in the earliest cities of southern Mesopotamia. Their simultaneous appearance is indicative of the 'revolutionary' changes that took place in society, changes whose importance cannot be overestimated.

What seems to me to be even more amazing is that these changes took place first and foremost in one specific place: the city of Uruk. Admittedly there is a real danger of overemphasizing Uruk's role, as it is the only extensively and intensively investigated site of this period. But many aspects of Uruk show its special status in southern Mesopotamia. Its size greatly surpasses that of contemporary cities: around 3200 it is estimated to have been about 100 hectares in size, while in the region to its north the largest city measured only 50 hectares, and in the south the only other city, Ur, covered only 10–15 hectares. A clear migration, not only to the city of Uruk itself but also to its surrounding countryside, at the expense of the region to the north, is visible. And Uruk continued to grow: around 2800 its walls encircled an area of 494 hectares and occupation outside the walls was likely. A comparison with later cities shows the magnitude of this size: Athens after the expansion by Themistocles only covered 250 hectares, Jerusalem in AD 43 only 100 hectares, and Rome as the capital of an enormous empire under Hadrian was only twice as large as Uruk had been 3,000 years earlier.[13]

Not only was the city itself enormous, but its temple complexes were also extremely monumental and elaborately decorated. The building history of the temples devoted to Anu, the sky god, and to

[12] V. Gordon Childe, 'The Urban Revolution', *Town Planning Review* 21 (1950), 3–17.
[13] Hans J. Nissen, *The Early History of the Ancient Near East, 9000–2000 BC* (Chicago and London, 1988), 72.

Inanna, the goddess of love and fertility, is extremely complicated and need not delay us here. It suffices to say that they were enormous in size and both contained various buildings. In the Inanna complex several examples of naturalistic sculpture of extremely fine artistic quality were found, as well as the first evidence of writing on clay tablets. Marvin Powell has suggested that writing was invented by a Sumerian-speaking citizen of Uruk,[14] a suggestion that is appealing if impossible to verify with the evidence available at present.

The importance of the city of Uruk was not limited to southern Mesopotamia. For about 500 years from the mid-fourth millennium on, the culture that we call the Uruk culture spread out over an enormous geographical area. Writing, mass-produced pottery, cylinder seals, and decorated monumental architecture were the hallmarks of that culture. At first it spread into western Iran where it influenced the culture at Susa, and then both cities established colonies: Susa as far east as Shahr-i-Sokhte in eastern Iran, Uruk in northern Syria at sites such as Habuba Kabira and Jebel Aruda, and as far west as the Egyptian Nile delta. The Uruk influence may have caused fundamental changes in Egyptian culture where individual marks of ownership were replaced by a real writing system and monumental funerary architecture appeared. The scope of the Uruk 'expansion' is thus overwhelming. Its stimuli are unclear; long-distance trade has been most often used as a justification, but its importance has been overstated and other factors must have played a role as well. Whatever the impetus of this expansion may have been, its driving force most likely was situated in the city of Uruk, the predominant centre of southern Mesopotamia. The leadership of Uruk, both locally and internationally, at a very early point in its urban development, is startling to say the least. It shows that much more complex factors were at work in urban development than the picture drawn here suggests.

The development of urbanism in northern Mesopotamia followed patterns quite different from those in the South, due to dissimilar ecological conditions. Rather than the great variety of natural settings in small geographical areas, the North consists of two physical regions. The western part, between the Tigris and

---

[14] Marvin A. Powell, 'Three problems in the history of cuneiform writing: origins, direction of script, literacy', *Visible Language* 15/iv (1981), 422.

Euphrates rivers, contains a vast rolling plain, the northern and eastern sectors of which receive sufficient rainfall for dry-farming. The southern sector of that area has to rely on irrigation for its agriculture, and permanent settlement is limited to the river valleys. The eastern part, from the left bank of the Tigris to the Zagros mountains, consists of a piedmont region with low hills, gradually rising to the east. The western flanks of the Zagros contain a number of intermontane valleys running parallel to the Tigris river. Although rainfall is often sufficient for dry-farming, its reliability is low, and often irrigation water supplements rain.

Whereas village settlement in this region dates back several millennia farther than in the South—as far back as the eighth millennium—internal processes did not lead to the development of cities. Cities first appeared in the late fourth millennium with the expansion of the Uruk culture described above. Extensive excavations of such cities are rare; only at Habuba Kabira is the entire extent of the city known. Although it occupied only eighteen hectares, its urban characteristics are clear: monumental architecture, dense domestic habitation, mass-produced goods, and proto-writing, all directly influenced by Uruk. Interestingly, the city was surrounded by a defensive wall, a characteristic that also distinguishes earlier northern villages from contemporary settlements in the South. The reasons for the need of a defensive structure are unknown. There is evidence of fires at several locations in Habuba Kabira at the time of its abandonment, which may have been the result of a violent conquest. The absence of textual sources prevents a clear reconstruction of what happened. In any case, with the disappearance of southern influence in the region, urban settlements declined, either being totally abandoned, or continuing as villages.

Five hundred years later, around 2500, a second period of urbanization occurred in northern Mesopotamia, which seems to have been part of a process of urban development encompassing an enormous geographical area from the Indus Valley to the Aegean, and throughout Syria and Palestine. Large fortified cities appeared, now equalling the urban centres of the South in size. Textual evidence from Mari and especially from Ebla shows a secular urban élite holding all sources of power. The culture of these cities was greatly influenced by southern Mesopotamia, and southern diffusion has usually been considered the driving force of this evolution. Although the urban development of the region may have declined around 2100, numerous cities survived in a framework of alternating political fragmentation and centralization under various powers. At the end of the Bronze Age in the fourteenth–thirteenth centuries all the main urban centres show signs of great decline, and only in the ninth–eighth centuries did cities reappear as a common feature throughout northern Mesopotamia. In the late seventh century BC, when the neo-Assyrian empire collapsed, the region suffered a total economic decline, and our knowledge of the level of urbanization becomes very vague.

Cities were thus not as easily maintained in the North as they were in the South. The agricultural potential of the region permitted the self-sufficiency of village communities, obviating the need for redistribution by cities. Only when southern powers installed centres to organize the extraction of northern goods for their own benefit, or when a centralizing political force arose in the North itself, were cities needed. Throughout the history of the region, cities were less common than in the South, and many of them owed their existence more to commercial, military, or political concerns than to agricultural ones.

In conclusion, this survey of the origins of cities in Mesopotamia has shown, I believe, that ecological conditions played an important role in their development. In the South the variety of zones with different agricultural potentials in close proximity to each other encouraged the growth of points of exchange. These nodal points gained a central role in other aspects of the economy as well as in religious, military, and political life. In the North, on the other hand, villages sufficed for the management of agricultural resources, and the city was at first introduced through southern influences. Throughout the history of the North the non-agricultural roles of the city predominated: trade, politics, militarism, and religion. They could only appear after the state had evolved, not before the state. The origins of urbanism in both areas had important repercussions for the characteristics of their cities, which I will explore in further detail in the following chapters.

BIBLIOGRAPHY

Of the many theories on urban origins I have only discussed a few. Paul Wheatley, *The Pivot of the Four Quarters* (Chicago, 1971) stresses religion. Jane Jacobs, *The Economy of Cities* (New York, 1969), views international trade as the sole catalyst. She relies heavily on James Mellaart's ideas, as expressed in, for instance, 'The Origins and Development of Cities in the Near East', in Louis L. Orlin (ed.), *Janus: Essays in Ancient and Modern Studies* (1975), 8–22. A similar emphasis on international trade for the rise of cities in southern Mesopotamia is found in H. E. W. Crawford, 'Stimuli towards Urbanization in Early South Mesopotamia', in Peter J. Ucko, Ruth Tringham, and G. W. Dimbleby (eds.), *Man, Settlement and Urbanism* (London, 1972), 761–2. Robert McC. Adams, *The Evolution of Urban Society* (Chicago, 1966), stresses the redistributive role of cities. His theory was further developed by Charles L. Redman, *The Rise of Civilization* (San Francisco, 1978). Adams's focus on cities as the prime movers towards civilization has been criticized by Richard T. Geruson and Dennis McGrath, *Cities and Urbanization* (New York, 1977). Mario Liverani, *L'origine delle città*, (Rome, 1986), sees population pressure and the decision to use surplus for communal works as the primary stimuli behind urban growth. Among the numerous other studies, Giorgio Buccellati, 'The "Urban Revolution" in a Socio-Political Perspective', *Mesopotamia* 12 (Turin, 1977), 19–39, provides an interesting approach to the problem, while the recent work by Jean-Louis Huot *et al.*, *Naissance des cités* (Paris, 1990), is easily accessible.

Michael Mann's theories are set forth in his *The Sources of Social Power* 1 (Cambridge, 1986). A very useful review is offered by Perry Anderson, *A Zone of Engagement* (London and New York, 1992), 76–86.

On the city of Uruk and the Uruk culture see among many others Hans J. Nissen, *The Early History of the Ancient Near East, 9000–2000 BC* (Chicago and London, 1988), ch. 4; and Guillermo Algaze, *The Uruk World System* (Chicago and London, 1993).

For the origins of cities in Assyria, see Abdul Jalil Jawad, *The Advent of the Era of Townships in Northern Mesopotamia* (Leiden, 1965); David Oates, 'The development of Assyrian towns and cities', in Peter J. Ucko, Ruth Tringham, and G. W. Dimbleby (eds.), *Man, Settlement and Urbanism* (London, 1972), 799–804; and Harvey Weiss (ed.), *The Origins of Cities in Dry-Farming Syria and Mesopotamia in the Third Millennium B.C.* (Guilford, Conn., 1986).

# 3

# City and Countryside:
# The Mesopotamian View

To an ancient Mesopotamian, city life was civilized life. The city was the seat of culture, and non-urban life was uncultured. The Mesopotamian visualized his or her city as being located at the centre of a world that could not exist without it, both in mundane and cosmic terms. The centrality of the city in the Mesopotamians' own concept of their culture was a constant theme throughout their literature. When a city and its god were in harmony, its inhabitants prospered and were happy. In the Sumerian composition, 'The Curse of Akkade', this prosperity was described as follows:

> In those days, she (Inanna) filled Akkade's stores for emmer wheat with gold,
> filled its stores for white emmer wheat with silver,
> copper, tin, and blocks of lapis lazuli were regularly delivered in its granaries,
> the outside of its grain silos she plastered over with mud.
> Its old women were given counsel,
> its old men were given eloquence,
> its maidens were given playgrounds,
> its young men were given the strength of weapons,
> its little ones were given happiness.
> Nursemaids holding the children of generals,
> played the *algasurrû*-lyre;
> Inside the city was the *tigi*-drum, outside were reed pipes and tambourines.
> Its harbour, where the ships moored, was full of joy.[1]

In the Akkadian literature the idea also was common. The city of Babylon, for instance, was praised in these terms:

---

[1] Curse of Akkade: ll. 25–37. Jerrold S. Cooper, *The Curse of Agade* (Baltimore, 1983), 50–2.

Babylon is such that one is filled with joy looking at it.
He who lives in Babylon, his life will be prolonged.
Babylon is like a Dilmun date whose fruit is uniquely sweet.[2]

The only surviving world map we have from Mesopotamia, dating to the first millennium, placed Babylon at the centre of the universe. Such an exalted opinion was not reserved for Babylon, indeed a cultural and political centre, but other, politically less important cities, were honoured similarly. About Arbela in Assyria the following was said:

Arbela, Arbela!
Heaven without rival, Arbela!
City of joyful music, Arbela!
City of festivals, Arbela!
City of happy households, Arbela![3]

Many people bore names that glorified their city, such as Mannu-kī-Babili 'Who is like Babylon', Larak-zēra-ibni 'Larak has created the seed', and Dilbat-abī 'Dilbat is my father', a chauvinism probably unparalleled in history.

The concept of the city as the basis of civilization was, perhaps, most strongly expressed when city life was contrasted to that of the uncivilized world. The latter was not thought to be the bucolic countryside, but the steppe, the desert, and the mountains; the habitats of the nomads. In a Sumerian literary composition of the early second millennium the life of the nomad was described in these negative terms:

He is dressed in sheep skins;
He lives in tents in wind and rain;
He doesn't offer sacrifices.
Armed [vagabond] in the steppe,
he digs up truffles and is restless.
He eats raw meat,
lives his life without a home,
and, when he dies, he is not buried according to proper rituals.[4]

---

[2] E. Ebeling, 'Ein Preislied auf Babylon', *Orientalische Literaturzeitung* 19 (1916), 132–3, ll. 10–15.

[3] Translation from Benjamin R. Foster, *Before the Muses: An Anthology of Akkadian Literature* 2 (Bethesda, 1993), 738, quoted by permission.

[4] Marriage of Martu, ll. 132–8; translation after Jean Bottéro and Samuel Noah Kramer, *Lorsque les dieux faisaient l'homme* (Paris, 1989), 434.

Such a description became a stereotype for the life of nomads and mountaineers throughout Mesopotamian history. In the first millennium Assyrian rulers used similar terms to refer to the inhabitants of the mountains in the east. Interestingly, they referred to them with archaic ethnic terms, such as Gutians, a people that had long disappeared from the face of the earth. Such designations promoted the image that time stood still among the nomads and that they lacked the ability to make progress.

The city represented order, the desert and the mountains embodied chaos. The progression from savagery to civilization in a human being was portrayed in the evolution of the legendary Enkidu, the creature that the gods made to challenge King Gilgamesh of Uruk. He arrived on earth as a wild creature, living as an animal in the steppe. His gradual development into a civilized human being was guided by the courtesan Shamhat, who introduced him to sexual intercourse, grooming, and the consumption of bread and beer. The completion of his education was symbolized by his introduction into the city of Uruk, his entrance into human civilization.

Erica Reiner has suggested that, parallel to the tradition of despising the life of nomads, an opposite trend existed in Mesopotamian literature that glorified the freedom of nomadism and loathed urban life as being effeminate. The suggestion is based on two almost identical passages in myths where curses were proclaimed, one by the queen of the netherworld, Ereshkigal, upon Aṣûshunamir, 'His Looks are Brilliant', who foiled her plans, the other by Enkidu upon Shamhat, who had introduced him to city life where he found an untimely death. The curses were devastating. This is what Ereshkigal said:

> Come, Aṣûshunamir, I will curse you with a great curse,
> Let me ordain you a fate never to be forgotten.
> May bread of public ploughing be your food,
> May the public sewer pipe be your drinking place.
> The shadow of a wall be your station,
> The threshold be your dwelling.
> May drunk and the sober slap your cheek![5]

[5] The Descent of Ishtar to the Netherworld, ll. 103–9, translation by Benjamin R. Foster, *From Distant Days* (Bethesda, 1995), 82, quoted by permission. Reiner's translation of this passage is, obviously, quite different: 'Come, Aṣûšu-namir, I will curse you with a great curse. May the bread from the city's *bakers* be your food, may

Rather than condemning Aṣûshunamir and Shamhat to an effeminate city life, as opposed to the freedom of the steppe, it seems to me that these curses have to be considered as being more malicious. The writers were aware of the existence of social outcasts, such as transvestites and prostitutes, who were tolerated in Mesopotamian society, but pushed to its fringes. Their presence in the cities was acknowledged, and they even fulfilled an important role in urban society, but their life was thought to be a miserable one at the margins of civilization. Theirs was a homeless life in the shadows of the city walls, eating food from the gutters and drinking water from the sewers, and these curses condemn their victims to such a life.[6]

Reiner also quotes a passage from the Erra epic where the god Erra is aroused by warmongering creatures, the 'Seven', with the following words:

Why have you been sitting in the city like a feeble old man,
Why sitting at home like a helpless child?
Shall we eat woman food, like non-combatants?
Have we turned timorous and trembling, as if we can't fight?
Going to the field for the young and the vigorous is like to a very feast,
⟨But⟩ the noble who stays in the city can never eat enough.
His people will hold him in low esteem, he will command no respect,
How could he threaten a campaigner?
However well developed is the strength of the city dweller,
How could he possibly best a campaigner?
However toothsome city bread, it holds nothing to the campfire loaf,
However sweet fine beer, it holds nothing to water from a skin,
The terraced palace holds nothing to the [wayside] sleeping spot![7]

The passage was included in a paean to military life, glorified because of its ability to frighten gods and men alike. The opposition here is not between urban life and nomadism, but between the city and the battlefield. A life on the battlefield could lead to glory, but it was also chaotic, and chaos was something to be avoided.

---

the jugs of the city be your drink, may the shade of the city wall be your residence, may the threshold be your sitting place, may the drunk and the thirsty slap your face.' See Erica Reiner, *Your Thwarts in Pieces. Your Mooring Rope Cut* (Ann Arbor, 1985), 44.

[6] See Jean Bottéro, *Mesopotamia: Writing, Reasoning, and the Gods* (Chicago and London, 1992), 193–7.

[7] Erra epic, Tablet I, ll. 47–59, translation by Benjamin R. Foster, *From Distant Days* (Bethesda, 1995), 135–6, quoted by permission.

Erra heeded the words of the 'Seven' and went on a terrifying rampage. Only when he returned to his city did he calm down, and order returned to earth; the audience of the Erra epic liked order. People copied excerpts of the text on amulets as protection against the terror described in it. To the Mesopotamian literate mind life on the fringes of civilization or on the battlefield was aberrant and repulsive. There was no admiration for the life of a 'noble savage'.

The negative attitude towards non-urban life is quite remarkable as the rulers of many dynasties had risen to power as tribal 'sheikhs'. Yet, once they had firmly established a foothold in a city, their nomadic past, at best, was recalled in an epithet, while attention to the cities, their temples, and their gods became a matter of pride. Hammurabi, who was still referred to as 'king of the Amorites' in a few of his inscriptions, ignored this connection entirely in the long list of epithets at the start of his famous law code. Instead he boasted of his accomplishments in embellishing or restoring cities and their cult places. A ruler's work in a city was considered to be of the greatest importance. The epic of Gilgamesh in its seventh-century version showed how the king's search for bodily immortality was futile, but predicted that he would be remembered for ever for the beauty of his city, Uruk:

> Climb the wall of Uruk, Ur-shanabi, and walk around.
> Inspect the foundation terrace, look over the brickwork,
>   if its bricks are not baked bricks,
> and if the Seven Counsellors themselves did not lay its foundations![8]

Why was the city so important to the Mesopotamian? The answer lies in its role both as a religious and as a political centre, two functions considered to be of utmost importance to society, and closely interrelated. Each Mesopotamian city was the home of a god or goddess, and each prominent god or goddess was the patron deity of a city. This concept probably arose in prehistory when all important settlements had their own pantheon headed by one deity, and it was so strong that it survived throughout the history of the region. In the third millennium, for instance, every city of the South was closely associated with a Sumerian deity: e.g. Nippur with Enlil, Ur with Nanna, and Girsu with Ningirsu. The

---

[8] Epic of Gilgamesh, Tablet XI, col. vi, ll. 303–5.

Mesopotamians thought that the gods had built the cities as their own dwellings. A hymn to Enlil describes the foundation of his city Nippur:

> Enlil, on the sacred place where you marked off your settlement,
> you built Nippur as your very own city.
> The Kiur, the mountain, your pure place, whose water is sweet,
> in the centre of the four corners ⟨of the universe⟩, in Duranki, you
>    founded.[9]

The connection between god and city was thought to have been so close that the decline of a city was usually blamed on its abandonment by the patron deity. Thus, when the Sumerian cities were overrun by invaders from the east in the last years of the third millennium, the literary compositions described their fall in terms of the gods' departure, not as a military disaster.

This concept did not disappear when the city-states were replaced by larger political entities of territorial states and empires. When Babylon became the political capital of the South and the cultural capital of the entirety of Mesopotamia, its patron deity, Marduk, rose in prominence in the pantheon. In the twelfth century a masterpiece of Babylonian literature, the so-called Creation Epic, was composed to explain his ascent as king of the gods. He defeated the gods' enemy, Tiamat, was granted royal status, and then the other gods built a dwelling as his reward, the city of Babylon.

> When Marduk heard this,
> his face lit up, like the light of the day.
> 'Build Babylon, whose construction you have desired.
> Let its brickwork be fashioned, name it The Shrine.'
> The Anunnaki wielded the hoe,
> in the first year they made its bricks.
> When the second year arrived,
> they raised high the top of the Esagila, equalling the Apsu,
> having built a ziggurat for the Apsu.
> For Anu, Enlil, and Ea they set up dwellings at its foot.
> In their presence Marduk was seated in splendour.[10]

---

[9] Hymn to Enlil, ll. 65–8, Adam Falkenstein, *Sumerische Götterlieder* 1 (Heidelberg, 1959), 14.

[10] The Epic of Creation, tablet VI, ll. 55–65.

ever Marduk abandoned the city, an event depicted in sev-
erary texts, disaster ensued:

People's corpses block the gates. Brother eats brother. Friend strikes
friend with a mace. Free citizens stretch out their hands to the poor ⟨to
beg⟩. The sceptre grows short. Evil lies across the land. *Usurpers* weaken
the country. Lions block the road. Dogs go mad and bite people. Whoever
they bite does not live, he dies.[11]

The absence of the patron deity from his or her city caused great
disruptions in the cult. The absence of the divinity was not always
metaphorical, but often the result of the theft of the cult statue by
raiding enemies. Divine statues were commonly carried off in wars
by the victors in order to weaken the power of the defeated cities.
The consequences were so dire that the loss of the statue merited
recording in the historiographic texts. When Marduk's statue was
not present in Babylon, the New Year's festival, crucial to the
entire cultic year, could not be celebrated. 'For [eight] years under
king Sennacherib, for twelve years under king Esarhaddon, thus for
twenty years ⟨altogether⟩, Bel (i.e. Marduk) s[tayed] in Assur and
the New Year's festival was not celebrated.'[12]

Despite the existence of a national pantheon headed by the god
Assur, whose name was used for the original capital and for the
country as well, the Assyrians also maintained a strong tradition of
associating gods with individual cities: Assur with Assur, Ishtar
with Nineveh and with Arbela, Ninurta with Kalhu, and Sin with
Harran. Deities of lesser rank probably were associated with
smaller urban centres. It is thus no exaggeration to say that,
throughout Mesopotamian history, cities were regarded as the
dwellings of individual deities, built by these divine beings, and
that the fortunes of these cities were thought to depend upon the
goodwill and the presence of those tutelary divinities.

The second crucial function of the city, closely related to its
religious role, was that of political centre. The Mesopotamians
always saw political power as being held within a city, not within a
nation or a region. Even if in reality a dynasty had firm control over
a territory with many urban centres, emphasis was placed on its

---

[11] Marduk Prophecy, col. ii, ll. 2–11. Rykle Borger, 'Gott Marduk und Gott-
König Šulgi als Propheten', *Bibliotheca Orientalis* 28 (1971), 8.
[12] Akītu Chronicle, translation after Jean-Jacques Glassner, *Chroniques
mésopotamiennes* (Paris, 1993), 190.

relationship to only one of them. The location of political power in a city was considered to be true not only in Mesopotamia itself, but also in the other areas of the Near East with which the Mesopotamians were in contact.

The origin of this concept lies in the time of the city-states, when each city truly constituted a separate political power. The Sumerian King List starts with the statement that 'when kingship was lowered from heaven, kingship was ⟨first⟩ in ⟨the city⟩ Eridu', and then the text goes on to list a number of cities with the names of their rulers. It expresses the ideology that kingship could only be present in one city at a time, a distortion of the actual historical situation where the existence of several contemporaneous city dynasties was the rule rather than the exception. It may thus seem that the Sumerian King List documents the existence of a concept of territorial dominion. The justification of the actual territorial control by one city may have been the reason for the King List's composition, but it is important that the text fails to define that territory, and instead focuses solely upon individual cities, all of which have the ability to act as the centre of political power. The succession of city dynasties was recorded in it from the mythological origin of kingship to the historically attested Isin dynasty (*c.*1800), and continued in other chronographic texts to register the dynasties of the cities of Larsa, Babylon, and Urukug, thus persisting in locating political power primarily in one city. Later, when Babylonia had irreversibly developed into a territorial state, the rulers continued to refer to themselves as 'king of the city of Babylon', rather than of the entire country.

The Assyrians applied the same ideology to the city-state of Assur, as is expressed in the Assyrian King List. The original purpose of that list may have been the legitimization of Shamshi-Adad's rule over the city of Assur (1813–1781). This foreign king was of nomadic descent, and his rule could only be explained by integrating his ancestors within a list of local city rulers. They were placed at the start of the list with the special notation that they were 'kings who lived in tents'. Hence, it was acknowledged that non-urban rule was possible, yet highly unusual and leading to an urban rule. Through later expansion of the list the local dynasty of Assur was portrayed as being continuous from the third millennium down to the reign of Shalmaneser V in the late eighth century. In reality, several kings did not consider the city to be their political

capital. Shamshi-Adad himself ruled from Shubat-Enlil in northern Syria, and Assur did not have a special political significance in
his state. From the ninth century on, Kalhu was Assyria's seat of
government, while Assur remained primarily a religious centre.
The city dynasty of Assur was thus a fiction, and the idea was
abandoned when Sargon moved to Dur-Sharrukin after he suc-
ceeded Shalmaneser V. But even then the attention of the Assyrian
kings remained focused upon one town, the seat of their political
power, despite the fact that they ruled an empire stretching from
Iran to Egypt.

The Mesopotamians did not only conceive of their own cities as
harbouring political and religious powers. They thought that the
same situation existed in the neighbouring lands that they encountered during their military campaigns. This is most obvious in the
Assyrian annals where conquests of foreign lands are depicted as
the capture of a series of towns, even in regions where cities must
have been rare, if not non-existent. A few examples from the
ancient descriptions of Assyrian campaigns will show this clearly.
When Sargon during his eighth campaign reached the mountain-
ous region of the Mannaeans, south of Lake Urmia, his opponent
Metattati was said to have abandoned all his cities. Sargon claimed,
'Their twelve strong and walled cities, together with eighty-four
cities in their neighbourhood, I captured. I destroyed their walls, I
set fire to the houses inside them, I destroyed them like a flood, I
turned them into mounds of ruins.'[13] Even in the marshes at the
head of the Persian Gulf Sennacherib asserted to have destroyed
numerous cities. In the account of his fourth campaign, against Bit-
Jakin, he stated: 'His (Merodach-Baladan's) brothers, the seed of
his father's house, whom he had left behind by the sea coast,
together with the rest of the people of his land, I forced to leave Bit-
Jakin, ⟨from⟩ the midst of the swamps and marshes, and counted
⟨them⟩ as booty. I turned around. His cities I destroyed and devastated, I turned them into ruins.'[14] Even if the last sentence was a
stock phrase, its constant appearance in the accounts of campaigns
in regions with very little urbanization shows that the city was seen
as the only possible seat of political power.

[13] François Thureau-Dangin, *Une relation de la huitième campagne de Sargon*
(Paris, 1912), 16 col. i, ll. 89–90.
[14] D. D. Luckenbill, *The Annals of Sennacherib* (Chicago, 1924), 35, col. iii, ll.
65–70.

And indeed, the total destruction of a city was used by the Mesopotamians as a military technique to instil terror in the defeated enemies, and to terminate their existence as an independent power. Although the annals talk about the levelling of cities as if it happened all the time, it is clear that this final solution was only used after repeated rebellions. But then it was done with a vengeance as is shown by the destruction of Babylon by Sennacherib:

With their corpses I filled the city squares. I carried off alive Shūzubu (Mushēzib-Marduk), king of Babylon, together with his family and [officials] into my land. The wealth of that city (Babylon)—silver, gold, precious stones, goods and valuables—I counted out into the hands of my people and they took it as their own. The hands of my people took hold of the gods' dwelling(s) there and smashed them. They took their property and goods . . . I destroyed the city and its houses, from foundation to parapet, I devastated and burned them. I razed the brick and earthenwork of the outer and inner walls, of the temples, and of the ziggurat, as much as there was, and I dumped these into the Arahtu canal. I dug canals through the midst of that city, I flooded it with water. I made its foundations disappear, and I destroyed it more completely than a devastating flood. So that in future days the site of that city and ⟨its⟩ temples would not be recognized, I totally dissolved it with water and made it like inundated land.[15]

The sight of the earth of Babylon carried down the Euphrates and deposited in the Persian Gulf is said to have terrified the inhabitants of Dilmun, modern-day Bahrain, to such an extent that they voluntarily submitted to Assur and presented Sennacherib with their treasures.[16] The total destruction of cities was used by the Babylonians as well. Probably their most ignominious act in today's opinion is the destruction of Jerusalem under Nebuchadnezar, repeatedly described in the Hebrew Bible. This event turned Judah into a sparsely populated state without any political or military significance.

Iconographic material also demonstrates the importance of the city as a political centre. From the ninth century on, a crown appears in Assyria, possibly only worn by queens, which had the

[15] Bavian Inscription. D. D. Luckenbill, *The Annals of Sennacherib* (Chicago, 1924), 83–4 ll. 46–8, 50–4.
[16] See Daniel D. Luckenbill, *Ancient Records of Assyria and Babylonia* II (Chicago, 1927), 185.

shape of a city wall (Fig. 3.1). This crown became very popular
later on. It was the standard royal crown of the Persians, and in the
West the Greeks after Alexander considered it an attribute of
goddesses such as Kybele, clearly with Near Eastern inspiration.
And it still influences the popular image of the royal crown today,
as any child's drawing of a king will show. Perhaps most indicative
of the idea that relinquishing a city was a symbol of giving up
political power are the depictions of people offering a model of
their city to the victorious Assyrian conqueror (Fig. 3.2). Again,
this image has a long history in Europe: in Byzantine and Renais-
sance art it became a symbol of submission to God, when rulers
offer him a model of their city.

Thus in the Mesopotamian concept of a city two ideas predominated: it was both a religious and a political centre. Temple and
palace were basic urban institutions, and they were the institutions
that defined a city. In the Mesopotamian mind, the city was contrasted to the steppe and the desert where permanent settlement
was impossible. Several rulers had nomadic ancestry, but this past
was not a matter of pride—rather the opposite.

Mesopotamia is famous for its numerous cities, many of which
grew out of villages over the centuries. Throughout the millennia of

0                    30 cm
scale

FIG. 3.1   Crown shaped as a city wall

FIG. 3.2    City-models being offered to the Assyrian king

Mesopotamian history, new cities were founded as well. Some of these were royal foundations, and we might expect that kings were proud of their work. Yet in the ancient Mesopotamian sources we notice an ambivalence towards the value of those endeavours and an apparent lack of pride among the founders of new cities. Mesopotamian kings are not known for their false modesty, thus the reasons for this restrained attitude deserve to be investigated. The inscriptional record on the foundation of new cities is surprisingly limited. Only a handful of Mesopotamian kings are known to have founded a city. Sargon of Akkade built the seat of his new dynasty in the twenty-fourth century. However, as its actual location remains uncertain, we have no local inscriptions describing the work. The Kassite king Kurigalzu I (early fourteenth century) built Dur-Kurigalzu, 'fortress of Kurigalzu', modern-day Aqar Quf, north of the traditional capital Babylon, but little is known about this city. The surviving inscriptions do not commemorate the construction of the entire city, only that of individual buildings within it. In the late thirteenth century Tukulti-Ninurta moved across the river from Assur to an enormous new settlement. The city, which he called Kar-Tukulti-Ninurta or 'Harbour of Tukulti-Ninurta', lost its special status upon his death. Assurnaṣirpal II's move to the newly established Kalhu, modern-day Nimrud, in the ninth century was more successful in that this city remained Assyria's capital for some 150 years. After that the centre of power was moved to Sargon's new capital Dur-Sharrukin, modern-day Khorsabad. This was perhaps the only city really intended to be founded on virgin soil in pre-Greek Mesopotamian history. However, it was left uncompleted by Sargon's successor, Sennacherib, who rebuilt the old city of Nineveh in its entirety in order that it might function as the state capital. We know of other settlements named after rulers, but there are no inscriptions commemorating their foundation. When we compare this record to that of Alexander of Macedon and his Hellenistic successors, who covered the Near Eastern countryside with large cities named after themselves, and used these as the backbone of their administration of the region, the contrast is obvious. Alexander alone is said to have founded seventy new cities.

The work involved in the construction of the new cities must have been enormous. Those we know archaeologically were gigantic in size and contained many monumental buildings. Very little evidence concerning the organization of the labour and the procurement of building materials is preserved. In their commemorative inscriptions, the kings usually pointed out that conquered people were set to work on the projects, and they also detailed how they obtained in distant lands the wood and stone needed. It is not accidental that all the builders of new capitals were highly successful in their military conquests and captured great amounts of booty and tribute. But local resources were also needed. Sargon II's correspondence gives some rare insights on that aspect during the building of Dur-Sharrukin. Countless bricks were produced by the local population of the region, seemingly with a quota set for each village.[17] The amounts of straw needed were apparently too great for the area to bear. The palace herald, Gabbu-ana-Assur, complained as follows: 'All the straw in my country is reserved for Dur-Sharrukin, and my recruitment officers are now running after me ⟨because⟩ there is no straw for the pack animals. Now, what are the king my lord's instructions?'[18] And where did Sargon find the funds

---

[17] See Giovanni B. Lafranchi and Simo Parpola, *The Correspondence of Sargon II*, Part II (Helsinki, 1990), no. 296.

[18] Ibid. no 119, translation quoted by permission.

to finance his project? A somewhat enigmatic letter suggests that he needed to borrow them from his citizens.

To the king, my lord: your servant Shulmanu-[   ]. Good health to the king, my lord! The king my lord told [me]: 'Nobody will pay back your loans until the work on Dur-Sharrukin is finished!' ⟨Now⟩ they have ref[unded] to the merchants ⟨loans on⟩ the portion of Dur-Sharrukin that has been constructed, but nobody [has reminded] ⟨the king⟩ about me; 570 pounds of silver with [my seal] and due this year have not been repaid as yet. When the king, my lord, sold gold and pre[cious stones] on *my account*, I told the king, my lord, that my father was much in debt to Har[   ], Huziru and [   ]. After my father⟨'s death⟩ I paid half of [his debts], but now their sons [are telling me]: 'Pay us the debts that [your] father owes to our fathers!' As soon as Dur-Sharrukin has been [*completely*] bu[ilt], the king my lord [will   ] to the house [   ] and pay the debts to [   ]. The king my lord may ask Shar[ru-emuranni]: half of [his work ass]ignment in Dur-Sharrukin [is finished].[19]

The need for funds to pay for the labour and supplies to be obtained locally must have been great, and it is not unlikely that the king had to turn to his wealthy citizens to obtain them. Unfortunately, we do not have much more information on these matters, but it seems safe to say that the building of new cities was a complex enterprise.

If this conclusion is correct, we would expect the kings who undertook the work to elaborate on their activities in their building inscriptions. Yet, when we study these texts, we find a lack of information on certain aspects of the undertaking. First, the kings must have had a motivation for the building of these vast cities, but when we look at their records no reason for the work is declared. Assurnasirpal's justification for the work on Kalhu is merely a statement that the city built by his predecessor Shalmaneser had become dilapidated. Divine requests are mentioned by Tukulti-Ninurta and Sargon, yet there is no elaboration of that in their inscriptions. Sargon seems to have been proud only of the idea that he was able to settle a place no one else had thought of before. His description depicts him as 'civilizing' an inhospitable place:

---

[19] Simo Parpola, *The Correspondence of Sargon II*, Part I (Helsinki, 1987), no. 159, translation quoted by permission. J. N. Postgate, 'The Economic Structure of the Assyrian Empire', in Mogens Trolle Larsen (ed.), *Power and Propaganda*, (Copenhagen, 1979), 221 n. 43 states that this letter indicates that Sargon imposed a moratorium on all debts during the work on Dur-Sharrukin. This seems unlikely as the creditors of the writer are demanding immediate repayment.

At that time, with the ⟨labour⟩ of the enemies I had captured, I built a city at the foot of Mount Musri above Nineveh, according to [the god's] command [and my wish. I named it Dur-Sharrukin]. A great park like on Mount Amanus, planted with all the aromatic plants of Hatti, fruits of every mountain, I laid out by its side. None of the 350 ancient princes who before me exercised dominion over Assyria and ruled the subjects of Enlil, had thought of this site, nor did they know how to settle it, nor did they think of digging its canal or setting out its orchards. [To settle that city], to build its shrines, the temples of the great gods, and the palaces, my royal seats, day and night I planned. I ordered that it be built. In a favourable month, on an auspicious day, in the month of Simânu, on an *eshsheshu* day, I made them carry baskets and mould bricks.[20]

It is only when Esarhaddon decided to restore the city of Babylon, demolished by his father Sennacherib, that an explicit reference is made to an order by the god Marduk. Esarhaddon described in detail how he was hesitant to undertake the work, and consulted the oracles to see whether the gods were at peace with Babylon. But this project involved the restoration of a previously damned city, destroyed and cursed by his father, and it was important for Esarhaddon to know the god's feelings about the rebuilding.

The lack of justification is all the more striking when compared to the lengthy explanations written when individual buildings were constructed or restored. In such cases a divine request was often cited as the incentive for the king's work. The most detailed description of such a request by a god is found in a literary composition of the late third millennium, a hymn in honour of the Eninnu temple at Girsu, built by Gudea. The king related two dreams in which deities came to him to ask for the construction of a temple for Ningirsu. He failed to understand the first dream, and needed his mother to explain its meaning to him:

The man, who is enormous like the heavens, enormous like the earth, whose head is like that of a god,
whose wing is like that of the thunderbird, whose lower parts are
    like a flood,
at whose right and left lions lay—

[20] Sargon, Display Inscription of Room XIV at Dur-Sharrukin, ll. 27–32. F. H. Weissbach, 'Zu den Inschriften der Säle im Palaste Sargon's II. von Assyrien', *Zeitschrift der Deutschen Morgenländischen Gesellschaft* 72 (1918), 180.

he certainly is my brother Ningirsu.
He ordered you to build his temple, the Eninnu.[21]

In the second dream the god Ningirsu told Gudea what the benefits of the new temple would be, and urged the king to start the project.

A very close parallel to this account is found sixteen centuries later in a text of king Nabonidus of Babylon, who described how the gods Marduk and Sin appeared to him in a dream and ordered the restoration of the temple of Sin in the northern Mesopotamian city of Harran. The Assyrian king Assurbanipal (ruled 668–627) also referred to a favourable dream that put him in a good mood, and caused him to order the restoration of the crown prince's palace. Such divine requests were thus common and were explicitly detailed when individual buildings were involved. But when the construction of entire cities rather than individual buildings took place, the divine request as its motivation was barely mentioned.

Another remarkable point in the descriptions of the foundation of new cities is the absence in the records of any omen readings used to determine whether the location was propitious. This fact is all the more surprising when we consider that divination played a very important role in Mesopotamia, both privately and officially. Kings asked their diviners to determine if the omens were favourable before they did anything of great importance, such as starting a military campaign. So why do we have no evidence of omen readings before the foundation of a new city? Indeed, there seems to have been a total lack of concern about the location of a town in general. The famous omen series *šumma ālum*, which starts with the statement 'if a city is located on a height, the inhabitants of that city will not prosper', is far from a handbook for the building of cities and houses. The series treats events in daily life that were thought to have an ominous significance. Only a few entries deal with the location and the layout of buildings, and we lack any references to the actual use of these when buildings were planned. The first entry, for instance, was clearly not taken very seriously, as most Mesopotamian towns were located on a height.[22]

---

[21] Gudea, Cylinder A, col. v, ll. 13–18. François Thureau-Dangin, *Les Cylindres de Goudéa* (Paris, 1925), pl. v.

[22] See Ann Guinan, 'The Perils of High Living: Divinatory Rhetoric in *Šumma Ālu*', in H. Behrens, D. Loding, and M. Roth (eds.) *DUMU-E₂-DUB-BA: Studies in*

Rituals to guarantee the good fortune of the city also are not attested. Only the time of the fashioning of the bricks was explicitly mentioned as having been important. Sargon indicated that this happened in the month Simânu, i.e. May–June. From the third millennium on this month was regarded the best moment for brick-making, with good reason, as at this moment of the year there was no agricultural work in southern Mesopotamia and the clay pits were moist, providing both a labour force and easily accessible clay. Moreover, there was no danger of subsequent rain which could have destroyed the bricks left in the open to dry.

There seems to have been more reliance on rituals when an individual building was constructed. Both textual and archaeological evidence for such rituals before and during construction or restoration exists. Several Babylonian rituals known from late manuscripts describe what needed to be done by a lamentation-priest 'when the wall of the temple falls into ruin'. They involved the offering of sacrificial animals and libations to various deities, and the singing of various lamentations on an auspicious day. The use of such rituals was probably inspired by the need to avoid the curses invoked by earlier builders, as every restoration entailed the partial destruction of the existing remains. However, when an entirely new building was erected rituals were also performed to ensure the purity of the place, and to protect the building from evil. Foundation trenches were purified with fire and filled with pure sand in which semi-precious stones, metals, and herbs were mixed. The first brick was specially prepared with honey, wine and beer mixed in the clay. Commemorative deposits were placed at various points in the foundations, as well as figurines in order to ward off evil. All these actions were undertaken following rigidly established ritual procedures.

A final element that is omitted in the available written documentation about the building of a new city involves its planning. The rectangular layout of the walls of a city such as Dur-Sharrukin could not have been realized without advanced planning. From existing ground plans of houses, some dating as early as the third millennium, we know that architects knew how to develop a blueprint. Yet, no one claims credit for the layout of new cities. Sargon

*Honor of Åke W. Sjöberg* (Philadelphia, 1989), 227–35, for an interpretation of the initial omen of this series as a warning against *hubris*.

boasted that he made plans to overcome the technical difficulties of the construction of Dur-Sharrukin, but his description does not show any awareness of the unusual character of the city's layout. Tukulti-Ninurta proudly proclaimed that the canal dug to provide Kar-Tukulti-Ninurta with water was straight, but, although he mentioned the walls of the new city,[23] he did not refer to the fact that they formed almost a perfect rectangle.

The silence in the building records of new cities concerning the motivations of the founders, the absence of rituals and omen readings before the work was started, and the apparent lack of pride about the layout of these cities, are all startling. Mesopotamian kings were eager to boast of their accomplishments, as they did when they constructed individual buildings, feats often described in great detail. The Mesopotamian situation is the complete opposite to what we see in ancient Rome. The choice of a site for a new Roman town was determined through extensive consultation of the oracles, the area of the town was ritually purified, and its layout was planned after oracular inquiries. Why this difference? After all, the Mesopotamians can hardly be regarded as less dependent than the Romans on omens and rituals for the running of their daily lives.

In my opinion, the reluctance of Mesopotamian kings to boast about their city building was grounded in the general attitude towards the merits of such an enterprise. Founding a new city was considered to be an act of *hubris*. A first-millennium tradition about Sargon of Akkade criticized the king for having built a new Babylon, whereby he incited the wrath of the god Marduk: 'He (Sargon) dug up earth from the clay pits of Babylon and built a replica of Babylon next to Akkade. Because of the wrong he committed, the great lord Marduk became angry and wiped out his people by a famine. From east to west there was a rebellion against him, and he was afflicted with insomnia.'[24] And we can understand this feeling, as any new city detracts from the importance of the existing ones. Tukulti-Ninurta highlighted in his inscriptions that Kar-Tukulti-Ninurta was a religious centre to complement the old

---

[23] See Karlheinz Deller, Abdulilah Fadhil, and Kazad M. Ahmad, 'Two new royal inscriptions dealing with construction work in Kar-Tukulti-Ninurta', *Baghdader Mitteilungen* 25 (1994), 467.

[24] Chronicle of Early Kings A, ll. 18–23, translation after Glassner, *Chroniques mésopotamiennes*, 219.

city of Assur, not a new city to replace it. New work was depicted as the expansion of something that already existed.

The only exception was the building of Dur-Sharrukin by Sargon of Assyria. The king was proud that he settled a previously uninhabited place. He depicted himself as expanding the cultivated area of Assyria:

> The wise king, full of kind thoughts, who focused his mind on the resettlement of the abandoned countryside, the cultivation of lands left fallow, and the planting of orchards, who conceived the idea of raising a crop on slopes so steep that nothing had grown there since time immemorial, whose heart caused him to cultivate desolate areas which earlier kings had not known how to plough, in order to hear the work song, to cause the springs of the surrounding area to flow, to open ditches, and to make the water of abundance rise like the sea, above and below. The king, with open mind, sharp of eye, in everything the equal of the Master (Adapa), who became great in wisdom and intelligence, and grew in understanding—to provide the wide land of Assyria with food to repletion and well-being, as befitting a king through the filling of their canals, to save ⟨the people⟩ from want and hunger, so that ⟨even⟩ the beggar will not . . . at the bringing of the wine, and so no interruption may occur in the offerings of the sick, so that the oil of abundance, which soothes men, does not become expensive in my land, and that sesame be bought at the ⟨same⟩ price as barley, to provide sumptuous offerings, fitting for the tables of god and king, the price of every article had its limit fixed, day and night I planned to build that city.[25]

The city was the cornerstone of his programme of civilizing the area. A new beginning was made, but perhaps this was acceptable as no important city was located nearby Dur-Sharrukin. Other kings did not stress innovation. Continuity was what mattered to them. Cities had histories going back for hundreds of years, and that history made them important. Huge rebuilding programmes, such as those that took place in Babylon in the first millennium, were not depicted as new beginnings, but as the restorations of cities to their former glory. Bigger may have been better in the Mesopotamian opinion, but the extension needed to be based on an old and respectable structure with a long history behind it. Existing cities could be expanded with new buildings without shame, and such actions were glorified in inscriptions, but the

[25] D. G. Lyon, *Keilschrifttexte Sargon's Königs von Assyrien* (Leipzig, 1883), 34, ll. 34–43.

foundation of a city itself was too important a task to be left to a mere human.

The Mesopotamians' idea of their cities was thus tied to a respect for the past. Cities were monuments of the age-old culture; they were not new and modern, but old and respectable. They were not human creations but divine ones. When the walls of Uruk were praised, the fact that their foundations were laid by the seven primordial sages was stressed. When Sargon of Assyria—the only king who readily admitted to having built a new city—described his work on Dur-Sharrukin, he likened himself to one of these sages, Adapa. It was as if he re-enacted a primordial accomplishment. Adapa had brought civilized life to the people of Babylonia at the beginning of time, and had introduced the building of cities. Berossos, the Hellenized Babylonian priest of Marduk writing around 300 BC, stated it in these words:

In Babylonia a great mass of foreign people was settled in the land of the Chaldeans, and they lived an uncivilized life, like that of beasts and animals. In the first year a frightening monster appeared out of the Red Sea in the region of the Babylonians, and its name was Oannes (= Adapa) . . . Of the same animal he says that it lived in the day among the people without eating anything and that it taught the people writing, science and technology of all types, the foundation of cities, the building of temples, jurisprudence, and geometry. He also showed them how to harvest grains and fruits. He gave mankind all that constitutes civilized life.[26]

In sum, the Mesopotamians took the idea that cities are at the root of civilization literally.

BIBLIOGRAPHY

The image of the city in Sumerian literature has been studied by Françoise Brüschweiler, 'La Ville dans les textes littéraires sumériens', in F. Brüschweiler (ed.), *La ville dans le proche-orient ancien: Actes du Colloque de Cartigny* (Leuven, 1983), 181–98. No equivalent study for the Akkadian material exists as yet.

For the negative image of nomads, see Peter Machinist, 'On

---

[26] Paul Schnabel, *Berossos und die babylonisch-hellenistische Literatur* (Berlin, 1923), 253–4.

Self-Consciousness in Mesopotamia', in S. N. Eisenstadt (ed.), *The Origins and Diversity of Axial Age Civilizations* (New York, 1986), 183–202; and Mario Liverani, *Prestige and Interest* (Padua, 1990).

Several representations of defeated enemies presenting a model city to the victorious Assyrian ruler can be found in Pauline Albenda, *The Palace of Sargon King of Assyria* (Paris, 1986). For the mural crown of Assyrian queens see Peter Calmeyer, 'Mauerkrone', *Reallexikon der Assyriologie* 7 (1987–90), 595–6.

The foundation of new cities was studied in an article by Jean-Louis Huot, 'Les Villes neuves de l'orient ancien', in J.-L. Huot (ed.), *La Ville neuve: Une idée de l'Antiquité?* (Paris, 1988), 7–35. He denied that cities were ever created 'ex nihilo' in Mesopotamia, either because the settlements were abandoned immediately after the death of their founder, or because the regular town plan noticed in the archaeological record was imposed upon an existing settlement. It appears, however, that these objections cannot prevent us from stating that certain Mesopotamian rulers intended to create newly planned cities and that such an undertaking was considered to be feasible. In a later publication, Jean-Louis Huot, *et al.*, *Naissance des cités* (Paris, 1990), 215–16, this scepticism seems to have diminished somewhat. More recently the practice of founding new cities was the subject of an entire conference published by S. Mazzoni (ed.), *Nuove fondazioni nel Vicino Oriente antico: realtà e ideologie* (Pisa, 1994).

Building accounts by Assyrian kings were analysed by Sylvie Lackenbacher, *Le Roi bâtisseur: Les récits de construction assyriens des origines à Teglathphalasar III* (Paris, 1982), which formed the basis for her more accessible book, *Le Palais sans rival: Le récit de construction en Assyrie* (Paris, 1990). For building deposits see Richard S. Ellis, *Foundation Deposits in Ancient Mesopotamia* (New Haven and London, 1968), and for ritual texts used for a new building see F. A. M. Wiggermann, *Mesopotamian Protective Spirits: The Ritual Texts* (Groningen, 1992), 119–40.

The rituals and omen readings performed at the building of a new Roman city are discussed by Joseph Rykwert, *The Idea of a Town: The Anthropology of Urban Form in Rome, Italy and the Ancient World* (Cambridge, Mass., and London, 1988).

# 4

## The Urban Landscape

A modern-day traveller through the countryside of Mesopotamia does not see the remains of majestic stone temples and funerary monuments, as is the case in Egypt, but encounters nothing other than earthen mounds, distinguished from their surroundings only by their height. These mounds, usually referred to with the Arabic term *tell*, are the remnants of great and small cities, the accumulation through millennia of the debris of mud-brick houses, palaces, and temples. To recognize the layout of the ancient cities of Mesopotamia from these remains is not an easy task. Although aerial photographs can provide us with a map of their main features, this map will always be a palimpsest with details from many different eras. The collection of datable objects on the surface of the *tell*, usually pottery shards, permits to some degree the determination of when certain zones were occupied, but still in a very imprecise way. Only excavation guarantees the clear recognition of buildings and their date of occupation. It is, however, an extremely expensive and time-consuming procedure, and not a single urban site in Mesopotamia has been completely excavated. In fact, most excavations have uncovered only a very small percentage of the total area of the site under investigation.

Ancient Mesopotamian sources on urban layout are very restricted in number, but they do provide useful information. A very small number of ancient summary maps of a few Babylonian cities exists. Best preserved is a plan of the city of Nippur, probably produced around 1300 BC (Fig. 4.1). It focuses on the city wall, its gates, the course of the Euphrates river, subsidiary canals, and the temples; its accuracy has been confirmed by excavations at the site. Moreover, some texts, somewhat optimistically called 'The Description of Babylon', or 'The Description of Assur' by modern scholars, contain lists of the names of gates, streets, temples, and quarters of these cities. If much of the monumental architecture is

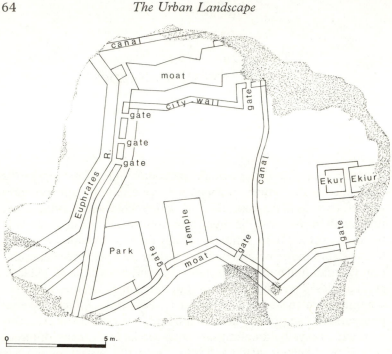

FIG. 4.1  Ancient map of Nippur

archaeologically known as well, the combination of the two sets of data permits the drawing of city plans with many buildings exactly identified by name. A careful examination of topographic indications in ritual and economic texts, again combined with archaeological data, may produce comparable results. Thus, we have something resembling a modern tourist map for such cities as Assur, Babylon, Borsippa, Nippur, and Uruk, useful for the principal monuments of these cities, but less so for the details of the plans.

The information on the layout of individual cities is thus always partial and fragmentary. Yet we are in a unique position to study urban layout by the mere fact that so many cities existed in ancient Mesopotamia. Many parts of the region are literally covered with *tell*s of all sizes. Mesopotamia was, after all, the most densely urbanized region in the ancient world, and the accumulation of data from various sites allows us to develop quite an accurate picture of the Mesopotamian town. It is a common misconception that the Mesopotamian city was limited to its walled centre. A city had several built-up parts, a walled inner city, suburbs, a harbour district, as well as fields and orchards adjoining these areas. These were all integral elements of the city and an evaluation of Mesopotamian urbanism cannot ignore the role each of them played. Archaeological research has concentrated on the walled inner city, which is consequently best known to us. A variety of plans, determined by geography and by the time of foundation, are attested, and the various layouts seem to reflect different attitudes towards the function of the city. But the other sectors of town, surrounding the inner city, need to be considered as well. Due to the lack of documentation we cannot distinguish temporal or geographical variations in their layout.

When someone in antiquity approached a Mesopotamian city, along a road or by boat on a waterway, he or she would have been aware of the city's presence long before reaching it. More cultivated fields would appear, together with the villages of farm labourers tending them. The city's monumental buildings would have been visible from afar, especially the ziggurat towering over the rest of the town. The first urban element encountered would have been the harbour district, where inter-city trade took place. In southern Mesopotamia and along the rivers in the North this was a real harbour on a river or canal, while elsewhere it was a mercantile centre located on the overland routes passing by the city. The Akkadian language refers to both centres of trade with the same term, *kārum*. Texts from various sites indicate that the harbour district was distinct from the inner city and situated outside the city walls, and thus cannot be equated with the intramural harbours shown on some archaeological maps. Many toponyms of Babylonia and Assyria contain the element 'harbour of', but usually the settlements are not located archaeologically.

Consequently, the only extensive remains of a *kārum* were found outside Mesopotamia, at a settlement that was founded by merchants from Assur, and is thus likely to reflect Mesopotamian traditions. The site in question was called *kārum Kanish*, 'harbour Kanish' in antiquity, and was located at the foot of the central Anatolian city Nesha, some 150 metres north-east of the citadel (Fig. 4.2). The settlement survived for only about 150 years starting around 1950 BC, with a hiatus in occupation of thirty to sixty

FIG. 4.2  Plan of Kultepe-Kanish. Shaded portions indicate areas excavated by early archaeologists. Contours indicate intervals in metres above
the level of the plain

years, and reflects thus a relatively short period of time. Kanish was
primarily inhabited by merchants coming from Assyria, whose
correspondence and contracts were found in their houses. These
texts make clear that the Assyrians settled there in a community
structured along Mesopotamian lines, and acting as a branch of the
government of Assur. Some Anatolian merchants lived in the
Assyrian colony, but their role is unclear as their records remain
unpublished. The excavations have revealed a dense cluster of
small houses along winding and narrow streets. These streets were
paved with stones, something that would not have been found in

Mesopotamia proper, where pottery shards might have been laid on the surface of streets. Also stone-lined drains were in use at Kanish, a feature that most likely would have been absent in Mesopotamia. The major streets were seemingly wide enough to permit the use of a cart. The *kārum* contained not only dwellings, but also workshops, primarily located in the areas settled by Anatolians. Yet no religious or secular monumental buildings have been excavated so far. The harbour district had its own defensive wall, emphasizing its detachment from the inner walled city.

At Kanish the harbour district was located relatively close to the walled city itself, perhaps because it functioned as the centre of the Assyrian trading system throughout Anatolia, and needed close interactions with the king of Nesha who provided protection and the permission to trade. But elsewhere the *kārum* was further removed from the city. This physical separation resulted from the fact that the harbour acted as a neutral zone where citizens from various communities could interact without direct and obvious supervision of the urban political powers. One can visualize these districts filled with activity and life, with people loading and unloading boats and pack animals, and buying and selling. Traders from such distant regions as India and Egypt at times mingled with the natives. The lack of information on this sector of town is unfortunate, and an archaeological investigation of a *kārum* in Mesopotamia proper would seem a promising project.

Coming closer to the town, a visitor would start to walk through gardens and orchards, owned by the urban residents who grew fresh produce there to complement their diet of barley, fish, and meat, brought in from further afield. In Babylonia the orchards were mainly used to cultivate date palms, still the most common tree in the area today. Other fruit trees and some vegetables were grown in between the palm trees or in special plots. As these crops required a lot of water, the orchards and gardens were usually located on the banks of the numerous canals near the cities. In Assyria the date palm was less commonplace, and orchards of different trees were laid out near the cities. Several kings boasted that they imported exotic trees from the regions in which they campaigned, and the presence of gardens near capital cities is recorded with pride in their building inscriptions. The most extensive record of such an accomplishment is provided by king

Assurnaṣirpal II (ruled 883–859), who collected saplings of some forty-one types of trees on his campaigns and planted them near his capital city, Kalhu:

> I dug a canal from the Upper Zab, cut it through a mountain top, and called it Patti-hegalli. I irrigated the lowlands of the Tigris and planted orchards with all kinds of fruit trees in them. I pressed wine and offered first-fruit offerings to Assur, my lord, and to the temples of my land.
> . . . (Here he lists the names of forty-one trees and bushes, many of which cannot be identified.) The canal cascades from above into the gardens. The alleys smell sweet, brooks like the stars of heaven flow in the pleasure garden.[1]

Many of these trees were, of course, not commonly found in Assyria, and the orchards around other cities were less exotic. The orchards and gardens continued into the suburbs and even inside the city walls. The trees furnished not only food, but also shadow and protection against the heat of the sun. In the summer their greenery must have provided a pleasant retreat from a parched countryside.

Soon the visitor would enter the city's suburbs. As is the case today, the distinction between satellite villages and suburbs would not always have been clear, as habitation around the city walls was far from continuous and permanent. In contrast to the inner cities, which were almost continuously occupied for millennia, suburbs were only intermittently inhabited, when the city's population outgrew its walls, and when they would not be exposed to constant attacks and looting by armies and raiding bandits. Archaeologists unfortunately have not devoted much time to the areas outside city walls, as they do not contain monumental buildings considered to produce the most spectacular finds. The periodic settlement of the suburbs has both a positive and a negative consequence for modern researchers. Advantageous is the fact that, when a suburb is found and mapped out, we are not presented with a plan that incorporates data from many different time periods, but with one of a single period of occupation. Of course, that period may have lasted for more than a century, and changes in the layout of the settlement must have taken place, but these changes were relatively

---

[1] A. Kirk Grayson, *Assyrian Rulers of the Early First Millennium BC. I (1114–859 BC)* (The Royal Inscriptions of Mesopotamia. Assyrian Periods 2; Toronto, Buffalo, and London, 1991), 290, ll. 36–40, 48–50.

minor. On the negative side is the fact that the areas of the suburbs are often indistinguishable from the surrounding countryside due to the lack of accumulation of remains; they are thus often ploughed over by farmers or, if outside the agricultural zone, a small amount of sand deposit can hide all traces of them.

As a result, very little information is available on suburbs, and their existence has been recorded only at a few sites. In just one case these remains have been mapped extensively, at a site called Tell Taya, its ancient name unknown, located in the Assyrian plain near Tell Afar in north-western Iraq. The most conspicuous element of the site is a high round citadel, 50 metres in diameter, situated on the left bank of the Wadi Taya. Around this citadel was a small walled city of only 5 hectares. Tell Taya is unique so far because its extensive ruined suburbs can still be seen on the plain: stone foundations were used for the houses, and these are still visible on the surface due to wind erosion of other debris. Only one-third of the suburbs have been surveyed in detail, but their total extent has been determined. Around the walled city were 65 hectares of dense occupation, themselves surrounded by 90 hectares of scattered development (Fig. 4.3). Considering the small walled city and the extensive suburbs, Tell Taya may have been a very unusual settlement. Yet the features of its suburbs must reflect those of other cities to some extent, and can thus be used as a guide to visualize those.

Although Tell Taya's citadel was occupied intermittently from 2400 to the first centuries AD, the suburbs were only in use during its first period of occupation in the twenty-fourth century. The remains provide ample documentation on their layout. The suburbs were located primarily to the north and the east of the walled city. They were intersected by two small rivers, the Wadi Taya and the East Wadi, which in antiquity must have contained more water than they do today. The walled inner city could be approached by two major roads, one to the west of the Wadi Taya, the other to the east of it. Yet these road systems were, it seems, concerned with communication to the districts outside the city, rather than with providing access to the town centre. They did not converge on the citadel, but only led the traveller to its general area. Within the framework of larger roads was a system of small and narrow side streets, without any obvious pattern. A number of them led to the Wadi Taya and it is clear that they were intended to give access to

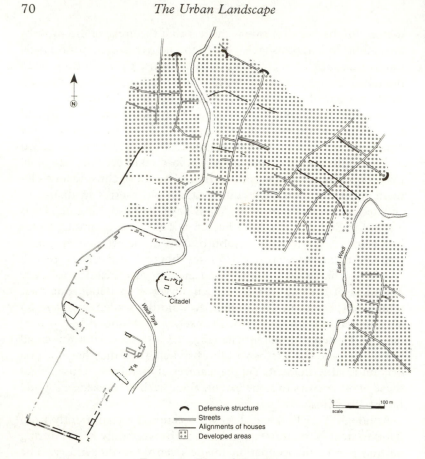

FIG. 4.3   Plan of Tell Taya

its water. There are some open spaces in the plan, but it is impossible to determine whether these existed in antiquity or are the result of stone quarrying by more recent occupants of the region. In general, the occupation between the streets is very dense. Not only houses are visible, but also a number of buildings that are too large to have served for domestic purposes, and may have had an official function. Industrial workshops existed also, and can perhaps be recognized by the large amounts of pottery debris found near them.

It is clear that the suburbs of Taya grew over time, although all within the twenty-fourth century. Three concentric bands of aligned houses are visible in the plan, each representing the limit of the dense occupation at one time. In its final phase the entrance to the major streets was guarded by semi-circular walls, in one case with an adjoining tower. Thus, although the suburbs were not surrounded by a defensive wall, the outer row of houses was laid out so that it formed a clear limit, and the entrances to major streets were protected. The erosion that uncovered the foundations of the houses unfortunately also removed most of their contents. Here and there remnants of kilns, slag, and pottery wasters can be seen, but it is impossible to determine the functions of the various neighbourhoods of the suburbs in any detail. They contained primarily residential and industrial areas, while the religious and official buildings were seemingly restricted to the citadel and the walled city.

Another Assyrian site where some evidence of suburbs was supposedly uncovered is Nuzi in north-eastern Iraq. The mid-second-millennium levels show, outside the small main mound, only 4 hectares in size, the remains of large houses belonging to prominent families according to the tablets found in them. The excavator believed these houses to be located in the suburbs, but it is more likely that they were part of the lower town occupation of the city of Nuzi.[2]

Early Babylonian cities also had suburbs, but their remains have only been uncovered by accident. The most intensive research on them was done at Ur, where the excavator, Leonard Woolley, noticed that his workmen picked up many objects on their way to the excavations. He dug for a few days in the area to the north of the walled city, but the excavation was considered to be too expensive for the meagre architectural results, and was soon abandoned for a system where workmen were paid for objects picked up and brought in. These collected finds indicate that part of the site was used for the production of pottery, clay figurines, stone amulets, and cylinder seals. Other craft activities probably took place there as well, or in other suburbs located at various sites outside the inner city. The location of craft areas outside city walls was, of course, a sensible practice: access to raw materials and water was easier, bad

---

[2] See G. Wilhelm *apud* Mirko Novak, 'Eine Typologie der Wohnhäuser von Nuzi', *Baghdader Mitteilungen* 25 (1994), 342 n. 8.

odours were less likely to irritate citizens, and space was less restricted.

Freedom of space was a major reason why people settled outside the city walls, which would have been laid out many centuries earlier, when the population had been much smaller. This option was only available when the countryside was not exposed to warfare or raids. In case of an occasional raid the suburban population could withdraw within the city walls, but such an arrangement could not last for prolonged periods of time. Consequently, some cities seem to have established subsidiary walled settlements instead of a corona of suburbs. This led to the existence of agglomerations of two or more cities in close proximity to one another. A peculiar example of such an arrangement was found on the northern border of Babylonia, an area exposed to attacks from Assyria and the Syrian desert, where in the early second millennium twin Sippars were located a mere 5 kilometres apart. Thus, the suburb was not the only way to deal with a population outgrowing the city walls. But suburbs were a common feature throughout Mesopotamia, and future archaeological research should devote more attention to them.

After traversing the suburbs the Mesopotamian visitor would finally reach the inner city, the centre of the urban settlement. This sector has almost always been the sole focus of attention, both of the archaeologist and of the illicit digger, as it is most visible on the surface and promises to produce the most sensational finds. It is thus best known to us, and because of our detailed knowledge we are able to distinguish different plans of the inner cities, determined by geographical circumstances and by the history of their foundation. Yet all inner cities of Mesopotamia had certain common characteristics; before discussing the different layouts we are able to discern, I will describe their standard features.

An inner city was always, at least partly, located on a higher elevation than the other sectors of the city. This elevation was due to artificial terracing in the few cases of new foundations, but usually it was a result of the natural growth of the city. The inner city customarily remained occupied for several millennia in antiquity, and even more recent settlements, typically only villages, tend to be located on the remains of these ancient towns. There were several advantages to keeping a settlement in the same location.

The accumulated collapse of the buildings of earlier occupants provided a height that clearly delineated the settlement and had a defensive value. Xenophon reports that the villagers of the area around the former city of Kalhu took refuge on top of the ziggurat's ruins when his troops passed by. Once a city wall was built, it required less energy to keep it in good order than to build a new one around a new settlement. Moreover, once the ground level of the city had risen above that of the countryside, it became impossible to irrigate its surface, and rather than settling on badly needed agricultural land, it made more sense to remain on top of the old site. Finally, religious sentiments dictated that temples must remain in the same location. Thus many settlements were occupied continuously for several millennia starting in prehistory, and the collapse of earlier buildings provided a natural height demarcating them from their surroundings.

The inner cities were also clearly distinguished by their defensive walls. Perhaps the presence of walls was the main characteristic of a city in the eyes of an ancient Mesopotamian: all representations of cities prominently display walls, many kings boast of their building or repairing city walls, and even literary works sing their praise. A city without a wall might thus not have been conceivable. Of the relatively few Mesopotamian depictions of cities, Assyrian palace reliefs provide the best record. The typical image of a city consisted of one or more rings of fortification walls with numerous towers at regular intervals, which seem to indicate a walled citadel and one or more town walls (Fig. 4.4). The same idea, with only a single wall, is shown in the city-models offered to Assyrian kings as a gesture of submission, and, interestingly, also in representations of Assyrian army camps (Fig. 4.5). The ubiquitous emphasis on the walls in iconographic material reveals the Mesopotamian concept that they were a crucial characteristic of the city.

That concept is also reflected in the numerous royal building inscriptions commemorating the construction or repair of city walls. For instance, Tukulti-Ninurta I described his work on the wall of Assur in these terms:

At that time the ancient wall of my city, Assur, which had been built by previous kings, had become dilapidated and old. I removed its broken down parts, renewed and restored that wall. Around that wall I dug a large

F<small>IG</small>. 4.4   Assyrian representation of walled city

<figure>Fig. 4.5 Assyrian representation of army camp</figure>

moat—a large moat which no previous king had ever built. Its bottom I cut into the bedrock with copper picks. Twenty *mušaru* down I reached the water level. I placed my foundation inscriptions in that wall.[3]

Even the literature of Mesopotamia celebrates city walls. Most famous is the praise of the walls of Uruk at the beginning and the end of the Epic of Gilgamesh in its first-millennium version.[4] And indeed, the excavated remains of this city's walls are impressive. In antiquity they were 9.5 kilometres long and had nearly a thousand semi-circular bastions. Much later Herodotus started his description of Babylon with an account praising the size of its walls:

It is surrounded by a broad deep moat full of water, and within the moat there is a wall fifty cubits wide and two hundred high . . . On the top of the

---

[3] A. Kirk Grayson, *Assyrian Rulers of the Third and Second Millennia BC. I (to 1115 BC)* (The Royal Inscriptions of Mesopotamia. Assyrian Periods 1; Toronto, Buffalo, and London, 1987), 267, ll. 3–10. The exact value of the *mušaru* measure is unknown.

[4] See Ch. 3, p. 46.

wall they constructed, along each edge, a row of one-roomed buildings facing inwards with enough space between for a four-horse chariot to pass. There are a hundred gates in the circuit of the wall, all of bronze with bronze uprights and lintels.[5]

From this quote it is clear that a city's defences were not limited to walls, but also included monumental gates and a moat. For the latter, advantage was often taken of the presence of a river adjoining the city, while other sides were protected by excavated channels. An Assyrian account describes the moat dug around Dur-Jakin, an archaeologically unidentified Babylonian city conquered by Sargon. The moat was almost 100 metres wide, 9 metres deep, and located some 60 metres in front of the city wall. Bridges were built across it, which were cut under attack, while the army was positioned in between the moat and the walls. Clearly this description does not refer to a hastily constructed defence: the digging of the moat had been a massive undertaking. It has been calculated that to excavate a moat of these dimensions for a medium-sized city of 50 hectares, ten thousand men would have had to work three and a half months.[6]

Massive gates gave access to the inner cities. Some gates, like the famous Ishtar gate at Babylon, were extensively decorated. The location of the northern and southern palaces between that gate and the point where the Euphrates river entered the inner city shows the need to guard these access points to the city. Although many town plans show numerous gates, it is not certain that all of them were in use. For instance, at Dur-Sharrukin several of them were blocked off. Access was restricted as much as possible for security reasons, and city gates were closed at night to protect the inhabitants, as is revealed in an Akkadian literary *topos*, describing a city sleeping under a starry sky:

> The countryside is quiet, the land is totally still,
> the cattle lie down, the people are asleep,
> the doors are fastened, the city gates closed.[7]

[5] Herodotus, *Histories*, 1. 178–9. Translation by Aubrey de Sélincourt (New York, 1983), 113.

[6] Marvin A. Powell, 'Merodach-Baladan at Dur-Jakin: A Note on the Defense of Babylonian Cities', *Journal of Cuneiform Studies* 34 (1982), 59–61.

[7] A. Leo Oppenheim, 'A New Prayer to the "Gods of the Night"', *Analecta Biblica* 12 (1959), 283, ll. 36–8.

All inner cities were characterized by the presence of monumental buildings. Palaces were always located there, as were the main city temples. Some shrines may have been located in the suburbs, but all important temples were within the walled inner city. In Babylonian cities the temple of the patron deity was usually the oldest monumental building, hence situated in or near the centre of town, and on a height in order to be visible from the surroundings. This elevation was not necessarily due to artificial terracing, but often resulted from the tradition of locating temples exactly on the same spot, a habit that originated early in prehistory. At the site of Eridu, for instance, a succession of sixteen shrines was excavated in exactly the same location, spanning a period from the sixth to the late third millennium. The ruins of each earlier shrine were contained within the foundations of its successor. The sequence started with a small one-room shrine, and the temple expanded continuously, culminating in a ziggurat of the twenty-first century. The exact location of the earlier temple remains was a matter of concern to later builders. In the sixth century, king Nabonidus related how the temple of Shamash at Sippar had fallen into ruin, although it had been restored just forty-five years earlier. Specialists examined the situation, and concluded that the last restoration had been flawed because the original foundations had not been followed.[8] In order to determine exactly where the earlier temple had been, kings of this period were careful to excavate the underlying infrastructure, as failure to adhere to the original plan was thought to lead to a weak construction.

The accumulation of the debris of earlier monumental buildings naturally led to a greater rise of the temple's ground level than for the rest of the town. But it became also a special aim of the builders. In the late third millennium the ziggurat was developed by creating a succession of massive platforms on top of which a small shrine was located. This ziggurat was situated either adjacent to the main temple, or at a distance, but then connected to the temple by a succession of courtyards. It towered over the rest of the city, and must have presented an impressive sight, considering that the authors of the Biblical book of Genesis saw in Babylon's ziggurat a prime example of man's *hubris*.

---

[8] See Stephen Langdon, *Die neubabylonischen Königsinschriften* (Vorderasiatische Bibliothek 4; Leipzig, 1912), Nabonid Nr. 6.

The palace was the second monumental building in town, distinguished from the temple by its fortified character. In Assyrian cities several palaces were located on artificially constructed citadels, clearly visible from the surrounding countryside. The buildings were often enormous in size, and considerable energy was expended on their construction and decoration. They were a powerful symbol of royal might.

Most inner cities also had non-monumental areas, except perhaps for the early cities of Assyria, which I will discuss later. The cities were after all the main residential centres of Mesopotamia, and often largely occupied by domestic quarters. They were divided into monumental and residential sectors by a system of streets and canals, the latter primarily found in Babylonia. It is clear, however, that these urban divisions were quite flexible, and that domestic dwellings could infringe upon the monumental sectors, if space was needed. Certain scholars have doubted that inner city canals existed, as they wonder how water could have run through them, considering that the level of the *tell* is usually several metres above that of the countryside. The Nippur map confirms their reality, however, and we have to imagine that the banks of these canals sloped steeply upward in antiquity. Silt deposit probably caused the canals to dry up over time, and then they were most likely converted into streets.

The streets of Mesopotamian cities were rarely monumental. Notable exceptions existed, such as the Processional Way in Babylon, leading from the New Year's temple outside the walls to the Marduk temple complex in the centre of the city. It formed a kilometre-long straight avenue from the Ishtar gate to the Marduk temple, and was named 'May the arrogant not flourish'. Sennacherib described in detail how he enlarged the streets of Nineveh when he turned it into his capital city:

At that time I enlarged the site of Nineveh, my royal city. I widened its streets enough for a royal procession, and made them shine like daylight . . . In order that in the future there would not be a narrowing of the royal road, I had steles made which stand opposite one another. Sixty-two great cubits I measured as the width of the royal road, up to the Gate of the Orchard. If ever any of the inhabitants of that city tears down his old house and builds a new one, and the foundation of his house encroaches upon the royal road, he shall be hung on a stake in front of his ⟨own⟩ house.[9]

Roads only rarely transected the entirety of the town as a thoroughfare from one gate to another. In cities that resulted from organic growth no straight streets can be observed. In planned cities we find some straight streets behind the gates, but these usually led to the cult centre in the middle of the town, or even only to the nearest monumental building, as far as we can see. They did not provide a grid, or even a means to get quickly from one end of town to another. As was observed in the suburbs of Tell Taya, the primary function of the streets leading into the inner cities seems to have been to provide access from the outside. But once inside one was caught up in a maze of narrow, winding streets, totally lacking a plan. Such a street pattern was probably determined by the natural conditions in Mesopotamia. Narrow winding streets provided protection against the sun and against dust blown in by desert winds. Moreover, due to the lack of wheeled transportation, wide streets were unnecessary. Yet the entire city became subdivided into sectors delineated by these irregular streets. The circulation pattern within these sectors often consisted of small squares from which a number of streets radiated (Fig. 4.6). In this way conglomerations were created of neighbourhoods with internal circulation but with restricted access from the outside. Many of the streets were dead ends, and could perhaps be closed off with gates, creating an isolated community inside them.

Street names were not rare. Many of the streets in Babylon of the sixth century had exalted names, such as 'Pray and he will hear you'. Legal documents throughout Mesopotamian history locate a piece of property by street, often named after a god or after the ethnicity of the inhabitants. A humorous tale of the first millennium describes the confusion of a visitor to Nippur who wants to find a doctor's house and is given these directions: 'When you come to Nippur my [city], you should enter by the Grand Gate and leave a street, a boulevard, a square, [Til]lazida Street and the ways

[9] D. D. Luckenbill, *The Annals of Sennacherib* (Chicago, 1924), 152–3, xvii ll. 13–16, 19–27. The exact length of a great cubit is unknown, but it is about 50 cm. The road would thus have been about 31 m wide. The Gate of the Orchard is not one of the known city gates of Nineveh.

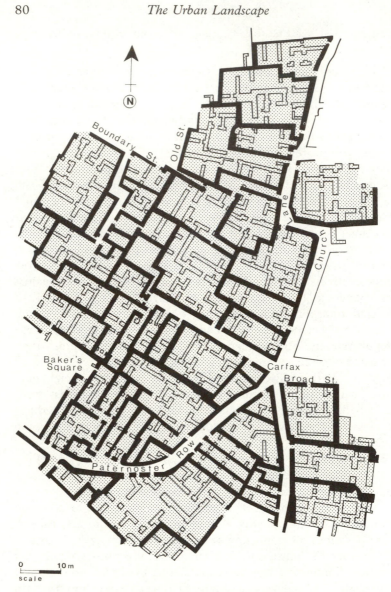

FIG. 4.6   Plan of AH site at Ur

of Nusku and Ninimma to your left.'[10] Thus, there must have been some order in the clutter of streets we perceive in the archaeological plans.

Along the streets houses were packed closely together in agglomerations resembling Roman domestic *insulae*. This building pattern was, and is, very common in the Mediterranean and Middle Eastern world, and obviously has the advantage that it protects the inhabitants against the heat by reducing the number of walls exposed to the sun. Protection against the heat dictated many other aspects of the layout of Mesopotamian houses. Although there existed innumerable variations in the house plans, two basic variants existed in Mesopotamia. One consisted of a set of rooms merged together in an agglutinative pattern. The other was formed by a courtyard, surrounded by rooms that were accessed only from that courtyard. The courtyard house was ideally suited to protect its inhabitants from excessive heat in the daytime and cold at night. At night the courtyard and the rooms filled up with cool air, which during the daytime became heated by the sun. The rising hot air provided cooling currents in the rooms. In the afternoon, when the house was at its hottest, increasing shadow produced similar currents to offset the heat. It is thus no surprise that the courtyard house remains the preferred style of dwelling in the Middle East to this day.

Outside windows were rare in the Mesopotamian house, and the streets were lined by blank façades. Both the inside and outside walls of unbaked bricks were very thick, and occupied almost half of the house's surface. Due to the lack of long roof beams, the rooms were small, and many domestic activities may have taken place in the courtyard. Second storeys probably did not exist in the south of Babylonia, but further north they may have been common. It is likely that people slept on the roofs, if not under the open sky, under reed structures or the like that would never survive in the archaeological record.

The plans of houses changed constantly as individual rooms were often bought and sold, or houses were divided among brothers at the father's death. As space limitations were great in inner cities, open spaces between the houses would have been soon

---

[10] Translation by Benjamin R. Foster, *From Distant Days* (Bethesda, 1995), 363, quoted by permission.

occupied by additional rooms. There were obviously differences according to the wealth of the inhabitants of neighbourhoods. Richer citizens probably had the ability to build larger houses, with some empty spaces between them, while the poor lived packed together in restricted spaces. Unfortunately, archaeologists so far have devoted insufficient attention to the domestic areas of towns for us to distinguish clearly between the characters of different neighbourhoods.

Mixed together with the domestic areas were industrial sectors where craft production took place. Usually the archaeological record only allows us to recognize remains of kilns for the production of pottery and for metal smelting, but texts also attest to the existence of quarters of jewellers, fullers, tanners, and so on. There is no firm evidence, however, that each craft was concentrated in a specific neighbourhood. The location of industrial zones was dictated by common sense. In Larsa, for instance, kilns were located in the south-eastern sector of town, while the prevailing winds came from the north-east. Clearly attention was paid to these winds, and the bad odours of the industries were blown away from the residential areas, rather than over them. For the same reasons many craft centres were located in the suburbs, as I mentioned before. Again we are insufficiently informed about these areas of towns, a situation which is only recently being rectified through the changing attitudes of archaeologists.

Finally, an inner city also contained open areas. This is clear from the Nippur map (Fig. 4.1) where the location of a park is shown in the south-west corner of town. The Epic of Gilgamesh indicates the existence of such areas in town: 'The city is one square mile, the orchards are one square mile, the claypits, the open ground of the Ishtar temple, are one square mile as well. Three square miles and the open ground comprise Uruk.'[11] The extent of these areas depended on the number of city residents, and the statement that two-thirds of the city was reserved for open spaces and gardens is probably wishful thinking rather than fact. In the open areas cattle and sheep were probably herded, while they were used also for the growing of vegetables, date palms, and fruit trees. They could provide a cool area in the excessive heat of the Mesopotamian summer. So far, no surface survey of a site has

---

[11] Epic of Gilgamesh, Tablet XI col. vi, ll. 306–7.

allowed us to locate these zones with certainty. It is important, however, to keep their existence in mind when population estimates are made based on the size of settlements.

A word needs to be said about the location of burials in ancient Mesopotamian cities. Two types of interment existed seemingly throughout the history of Mesopotamia: burial underneath the floors of houses, streets, and squares, and burial in special cemeteries. Due to the focus of the archaeologists' attention on built-up areas in towns, the first type seems to have predominated, but it seems unlikely that all inhabitants could have been buried in that manner. The tradition of burying a dead family member underneath one's house was inspired by the cult of the dead. Deceased ancestors were greatly respected, and at times meals were held within the house which involved offerings to those family members. Pipes in the floor enabled the pouring of food and drink into the tombs. Interestingly, burial-chambers were often reopened, and the bones present were swept aside, in order to lay out a new corpse. It is unclear to us how it was decided who was to be buried underneath the family home, and who was taken to a cemetery. The location of cemeteries in or outside inner cities is rarely known. We have some notable exceptions at Ur, for instance, where in the centre of town a large cemetery was in use for several centuries in the middle of the third millennium. Again more archaeological research on this aspect of urban occupation would be useful.

Despite the fact that all Mesopotamian inner cities had the above-mentioned characteristics in common, we can distinguish four major variants in their layouts. The differences derive from the geographical surroundings of the cities, and from their building histories. The geographical conditions were quite distinct between Upper and Lower Mesopotamia, and both regions had two types of urban settlements. The majority of cities developed naturally over time from villages to urban centres, and showed no advanced planning in their layout. They were the result of organic growth over the centuries. Throughout the history of Mesopotamia, however, cities were founded according to preconceived artificial plans as well. These planned cities need not have been built on virgin soil, but were also created on top of existing towns or villages. What is important, however, is that at a particular moment a decision was taken to build a city according to some regular and preconceived plan. The four variants in the layout of Mesopotamian inner cities can thus be summed up as Upper and Lower Mesopotamian cities resulting from organic growth, and as planned cities in both regions. In the following I will discuss each variant with special emphasis on those aspects that distinguish them from one another.

Lower Mesopotamian cities that had grown organically were characterized by a dense occupation of the inner towns with buildings of varied nature. Religious complexes, palaces, administrative buildings, residential, and industrial areas were all part of the inner cities. The cities were intersected with canals and major streets, but no effort was made to make these straight, and consequently the divisions of the town they created were irregular. Although it may be possible to assign predominant functions to quarters, such as religious or administrative, the separation between them was not strict. Temple complexes, for instance, were only surrounded with monumental walls in the first millennium: previously, houses often abutted the temples themselves. Even if the inhabitants of such houses were often temple personnel, they were not exclusively so.

The main religious complex of a town dominated its plan and its skyline, as it was large and built on a height. The second important monumental building was the palace, but seemingly not all Lower Mesopotamian cities contained one, including some cities that were politically prominent. Palaces were often located at the edge of the inner cities that had been founded in prehistory or the early historical period. When the cities developed after secular élites had become firmly established in the region, by the mid-third millennium, the palace and temple complexes were located in each other's vicinity in or near the centre of town. The city walls were often constructed after a settlement had already attained a substantial size, and by necessity they followed the contours of the settlement, usually more or less oval shaped. The natural height of the *tell* formed by earlier building deposits facilitated the erection of a defensive wall on its edges. No prior planning of the wall's outlines is thus noticeable. There were a great many cities that developed organically in Lower Mesopotamia, and local circumstances influenced their particular layouts.

Upper Mesopotamian cities usually developed differently from those in the South. Instead of a gradual growth from village to city over the centuries, many villages suddenly expanded in the mid-third millennium when the region was urbanized, possibly under Lower Mesopotamian influence. The cities developed two clearly distinct sections, an upper and a lower town. The local Akkadian dialect used two terms to refer to these divisions: *kerḫum* for the acropolis and *adaššum* for the lower town. Access to the former was restricted as is illustrated by this quote from a letter found at Mari:

> The day after tomorrow Simahlânê will arrive with his troops in Mari . . . 150 Babylonians and 50 Numhaians, 200 men in total, will accompany him . . . To the men that accompany him I will assign lodgings in the *adaššum*. Not a single soldier will be given a tablet for access to the *kerḫum*. But I will make Simahlânê enter the *kerḫum*, and according to circumstances I will give his attendants [*comfortable*] lodgings, so that he will not get upset.[12]

The upper town was located on top of the debris of the earlier village, several metres above the level of the plain, not in the centre of the lower town, but at one of the edges. The monumental buildings were situated on it, clearly visible from the surroundings. It is clear from the excavations at Shubat-Enlil and Qattara that in the early second millennium those buildings were all of a religious character, while the palace and administrative buildings were located in the lower town. If the location of the so-called palace of Naram-Sin in the lower town at Tell Brak is not unusual, this may also have been the case in the mid-third millennium.

The upper town was separated from the lower one only by its height and by the monumental walls of its buildings. This is different from the situation in the South where canals or streets separated the religious sector from the rest of town. In the only site where this has been examined, Shubat-Enlil, the lower town contained some domestic architecture besides monumental palace buildings. But there seems to have been an evolution in that practice. A carefully planned residential area with a straight paved street leading to the acropolis was found in the mid-third-millennium town. In the second millennium that residential area was not occupied, and just a few domestic remains have been found on the edges of the town, near the city walls. It seems, therefore, that there was almost no domestic occupation of the

---

[12] Georges Dossin, '*Adaššum* et *kirḫum* dans les textes de Mari', *Revue d'assyriologie et d'archéologie orientale* 66 (1972), 117, ll. 11–13, 18–20, 24–33.

walled city in the early second millennium, when Shubat-Enlil was the capital city of the state created by King Shamshi-Adad (ruled 1813–1781). People must have lived in the suburbs and villages surrounding the city, which was reserved for religious and administrative purposes. Such a situation was never encountered in Lower Mesopotamia. Plenty of open spaces were thus available within the Upper Mesopotamian lower city, which could be used for agricultural activity, and provided a safe haven for the inhabitants of the suburbs and their flocks in times of crisis.

The differences between those cities of the South and the North that resulted from organic growth are thus the following: southern cities contained a dense occupation of varied nature within their walls, while northern ones reserved the walled cities for official purposes and the residential areas were mainly located in the suburbs. The citadels of Upper Mesopotamia have no counterpart in the South where a less clearly delineated sector of town contained the city's temples. The remains of southern cities contain several mounds separated by gullies, where canals and streets used to be. In the North the remains are limited to one high mound, the acropolis or upper town, while the lower city shows little relief.

Although cities that had evolved over the centuries were by far the most common in the entirety of Mesopotamia, throughout the history of the region new settlements were founded with advanced planning, or at times older ones were entirely rebuilt with a radically new and planned layout. Usually these settlements were either new capital cities or trading and military foundations in Mesopotamia's periphery. Although the tradition of founding new capital cities is attested in Babylonia as early as the twenty-fourth century, when King Sargon built Akkade, only one example of it is known archaeologically—Dur-Kurigalzu, built in the second half of the second millennium, just south of modern Baghdad. It is an unusual site in that it stretches for some 5 kilometres along a branch of the Euphrates, joining together three earlier settlements, and no evidence of planning can be seen. Information on planned cities only becomes available in the seventh and sixth centuries, when Babylonia gained political and military supremacy over Western Asia, and its kings undertook massive building projects in many of the ancient Babylonian cities, completely redesigning several of them. These refurbished cities were planned on the same pattern, as is exemplified by Babylon (Fig. 4.7) and Borsippa (Fig. 4.8).

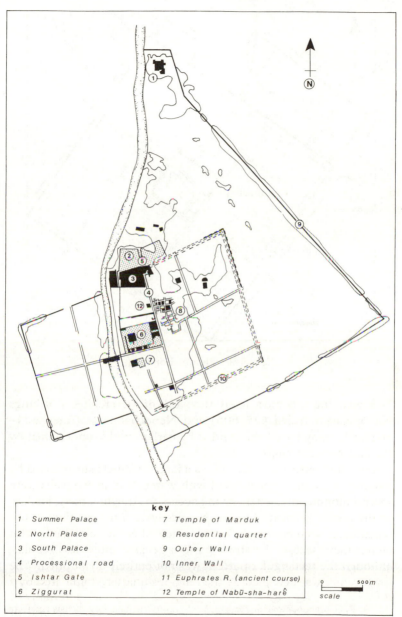

| key | |
|---|---|
| 1  Summer Palace | 7  Temple of Marduk |
| 2  North Palace | 8  Residential quarter |
| 3  South Palace | 9  Outer Wall |
| 4  Processional road | 10  Inner Wall |
| 5  Ishtar Gate | 11  Euphrates R. (ancient course) |
| 6  Ziggurat | 12  Temple of Nabū-sha-harê |

Fɪɢ. 4.7   Plan of Babylon. Solid areas are fully excavated, shaded areas
have been partly excavated

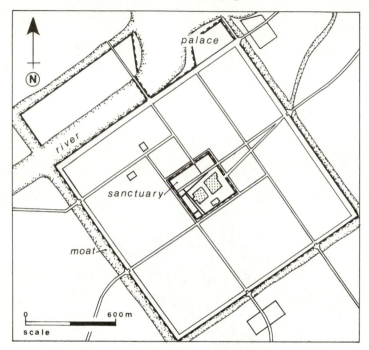

FIG. 4.8  Plan of Borsippa

The planning was most likely the work of the architects of kings Nabopolassar (ruled 625–605) and Nebuchadnezar (ruled 604–562), who may have been guided by earlier works, undertaken by the late Assyrian kings.[13]

The inner cities were laid out as a large rectangle surrounded by massive walls and a moat filled with water. Within the walls were several monumental gates, giving access to straight streets, leading to the centre of town. The inner cities were thus partitioned into rectangular sectors, which were named after the city gates. But within these sectors the street pattern became much less regular, although the rectangular pattern was not entirely abandoned. The town centre was occupied by the religious quarter, dominated by a

---

[13] A. R. George, *Babylonian Topographical Texts* (Orientalia Lovaniensia Analecta 40; Louvain, 1992), 15, suggests that the rebuilding of Babylon on a rectangular plan dated to the 13th-12th cents., but the evidence for this is limited to a later literary text.

ziggurat. This quarter was not located on a height, but separated from its surroundings by a massive wall. The centrality of the temple complex was emphasized by the fact that the roads from the city gates led to it. Moreover, the ziggurats were particularly elaborate and must have been visible from a great distance. Indeed, the temple was intended to be the city's focal point.

The palace, on the other hand, was located on the edge of the cities, at the point where the rivers entered them. This was a weak point in the defences, and the military installations adjoining the palace were probably located there for a good reason. Herodotus (1. 191) recounts, however, that Cyrus of Persia was still able to penetrate Babylon through the bed of the Euphrates after he had diverted the water upstream. The palace was not entirely enclosed by the city wall, but, as was the case in Assyria, it extended into the countryside, probably indicating that its function surpassed the city limits.

Babylon and Borsippa were bisected by rivers. In Babylon the Euphrates cut the inner city into two almost equal parts. The monumental buildings were concentrated in the eastern part, while the western part may have been reserved for residences. In Borsippa a branch of the Euphrates turned into a lake just north of the city. A run-off channel from that lake separated the northern fifth of the city from the rest. In both places water from these rivers was diverted to fill the moat around the walls.

Babylon had the unusual feature that a second wall was built to form an enormous triangle around the eastern part of the city, along the Euphrates. It may have been intended to integrate within the city the so-called summer palace, situated 2 kilometres to the north of the inner town wall. This outer wall was 7.5 kilometres long, and together with the Euphrates on its western edge, created a triangle measuring 12.5 kilometres in circumference. The eastern inner city was situated at its corner as a highly defended fortress containing temples, palaces, and élite residences.

Advance planning was not only used for Babylonian cities of the late period, but also for earlier settlements built by southern Mesopotamians on the fringes of the region, for trading and military purposes. Excavated examples of such planned towns are Habuba Kabira in northern Syria, founded in the mid-fourth millennium, Shaduppum, now in a suburb of Baghdad, and Haradum in western Iraq near the Syrian border, both early second millennium foundations. The last site shows all the characteristics of these settlements (Fig. 4.9). It was founded by Babylonians on top of an older settlement in the eighteenth century and survived for little more than one hundred years. Its plan was almost a perfect square, covering only 1.3 hectares. The town was intersected by a number of straight thoroughfares, leading to a religious complex in the centre of town. To the north of the temple was located a large residence that belonged to the so-called mayor. The thickness of the walls, and the defensive character of the city gate suggest that the settlement had a military character. But the location of the site close to the river and the texts found in it indicate that it had an

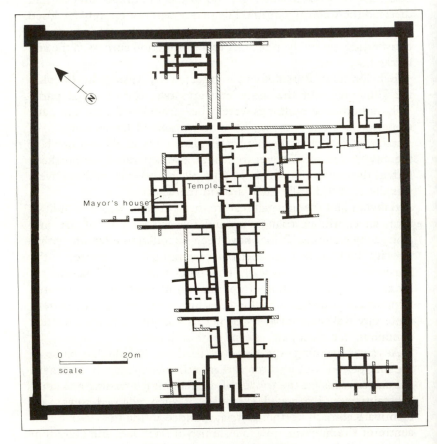

FIG. 4.9   Plan of Haradum

important role to play in the trade between Babylonia and the areas to its north and west. City planning was thus in existence from the very beginning of Babylonian history, and new foundations were ideally laid out as rectangles, allowing for special circumstances that were easily accommodated. The main roads of these cities led to the religious centre in their centre, which stresses again the fact that the temple was considered to be the Babylonian city's most important monumental building.

Planned cities are best known in Assyria where several new capital cities were constructed in the late second to the mid-first millennia: Kar-Tukulti-Ninurta (thirteenth century), Kalhu (ninth century), Dur-Sharrukin (eighth century; Fig. 4.10), and Nineveh (seventh century). Kalhu and Nineveh were built over much smaller earlier cities, and at that time their layout was entirely refashioned. Both survived under several kings, all of whom worked on them and slightly refurbished them. The other two sites reflect the original plan of their builders accurately, and are thus ideal illustrations of a planned Assyrian city.

The architects designed these cities as a large rectangle, surrounded by a massive wall. In Kar-Tukulti-Ninurta and Dur-Sharrukin this rectangle is almost perfect, in Kalhu and Nineveh much less so, probably because earlier features had to be included (Kalhu), or because of the topography of the surroundings (Nineveh). On every side of the rectangle, the wall was pierced by several monumental gates, some of which were seemingly not used. The gates were never located exactly opposite one another, although this could have been very easily accomplished. Major streets were laid out behind some of them, yet they did not transect the entire city, and just led to the nearest monumental building, as far as we can see. In a sense we have here a total reversal of the Hippodamian scheme of ancient Greece and Rome, where the grid pattern of thoroughfares was strictly maintained even when the circumference of the city was highly irregular. In Assyria the city walls were regular and linear, while internally the street pattern was irregular.

Each city, except perhaps Kar-Tukulti-Ninurta, had two citadels substantially raised above ground level and surrounded by their own walls. They were always located on the city wall, not in the centre of town. Often they extended slightly beyond the limits of the city wall, as if to show their association with the surrounding

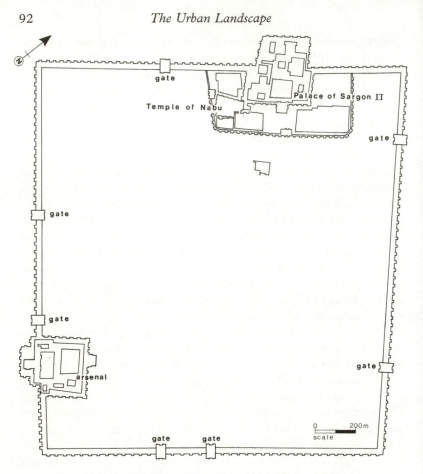

FIG. 4.10    Plan of Dur-Sharrukin (Khorsabad)

countryside as well. The largest citadel was used for one or more palaces and for temples; the second one contained military installations. All these buildings were of massive proportions, and extensively decorated. Their construction was glorified in numerous inscriptions as the king's major accomplishment.

Because of the imposing character of the monumental buildings on the citadels, archaeologists have had little or no time to investigate the lower towns. Only a small section of Nineveh has been surveyed, and the research has shown the existence of élite residences just north of the Kuyundjik citadel, with an industrial quarter somewhat further north. Large areas of these immense Assyrian cities were probably not occupied, but used for pleasure gardens, areas to provide refuge to villagers in times of danger, and for pasture, if we can believe the biblical book of Jonah's mention of many cattle inside Nineveh. It is clear that extensive gardens were considered to have added to the city's pleasures, and several kings boast of having laid them out. According to the building inscriptions all kings who established a new capital started out by digging canals to provide their cities with additional water and to irrigate the fields near and possibly inside them. Sennacherib, for instance, built an extensive aqueduct system, bringing water in from distant mountains. The economic importance of these canals is debated. They may have been needed to support the dense populations of these artificial foundations; yet Sennacherib's own statement that he used a large part of the water to create an artificial swamp suggests that an image of grandeur may have been striven for by these works.

The planned cities of Babylonia and Assyria thus show similarities in that their general layouts were highly regular, and preferably rectangular. They differed, however, in the location of their cult centres. In Babylonia, these were in the centre of the city, separated from the palace, while in Assyria they were located with the palace on a citadel on the city wall. The cities of Assyria seem to have had much more open space than those of Babylonia, perhaps because they were more artificial creations than their southern counterparts, which were usually refurbished ancient and prominent cities.

The four different layouts reflect varied attitudes towards the cities. The differences are greater between Lower and Upper Mesopotamia than between unplanned and planned cities. In Lower Mesopotamia numerous cities were located near the rivers and canals that provided the water indispensable for agriculture. Often several of these waterways entered the city walls. Settlement outside the agricultural zone was impossible, so space was restricted. In Upper Mesopotamia the well-watered plains allowed settlement almost everywhere, and the need for artificial canals was less immediate. The cities were not clustered along the major rivers; instead they could rely for their water supply on smaller streams. Consequently the attitudes towards cities as residential centres were different between the two regions. Throughout Lower

Mesopotamian history inner cities were densely occupied by domestic dwellings, and they were the logical form of settlement in a limited area. In Upper Mesopotamia houses in inner cities were less numerous, and at times perhaps barely present, because settlement in villages throughout the countryside was possible.

In the South, the primacy of the temple as the main public building in town never disappeared, while in the North the palace became the dominant structure, especially in the planned cities of the first millennium. Military installations were also much more prominent in Assyria than they were in Babylonia. The first millennium cities of Assyria had massive arsenals, while in Babylonia no military buildings separate from the palace are known. These differences suggest the greater importance of military and secular matters in Assyria than in Babylonia, where the cultic importance of the city remained a constant through its history.

The differences between unplanned and planned cities in both regions were really not so great. Planned cities show a concern with an outward regularity, but inside the cities this order soon disappeared. The emphasis on the linearity of the wall may have resulted from the city wall's pre-eminence in the Mesopotamian concept of a city. When a wall was built around an existing settlement it was easier to follow its established contours, which were usually oval. Throughout the planning of inner cities in Mesopotamia we see an ability to adapt to existing circumstances. No dogged adherence to architectural principles is visible, but flexibility in the design is a major characteristic.

Finally, a word about the sizes of these Mesopotamian cities is in order. When talking about urban dimensions we can only take into account the inner cities, clearly delineated by walls, as measurements of suburbs are absent at the moment. There is an enormous variation in the areas of excavated cities. A settlement such as Abu Salabikh in the early third millennium only covered 20 hectares, while at the same time Uruk's wall surrounded an area of 494 hectares, about 400 of which were settled.[14] The latter city was very

---

[14] The numbers given in different publications for the sizes of cities vary enormously. I use here mainly those provided by Wolfram Nagel and Eva Strommenger, 'Altorientalische Städte–von der Dorfkultur zur Hochkultur seit Habubah bis Babylon', *Kölner Jahrbuch für Vor- und Frühgeschichte* 16 (1978–79), 61–75, with some additions and corrections.

unusual in its size and remained the largest walled city in Mesopotamia for two millennia. More common were Babylonian cities such as Ur, with 61 hectares, and Mashkan-shapir, with about 72 hectares in size, or in the North Shubat-Enlil, which covered 75 hectares in the early second millennium.

The new foundations of the late second and early first millennia greatly surpassed these dimensions: Kar-Tukulti-Ninurta covered at least 240 hectares, Kalhu 360, Dur-Sharrukin 300, and Nineveh 750 hectares. The largest city in antiquity until imperial Rome was Babylon, where the outer wall encircled an area of 890 hectares. Its size startled the Greeks: Aristotle describes Babylon in his *Politics* (3. 1. 12) as a 'city that has the circuit of a nation rather than of a city, for it is said that when Babylon was captured a considerable part of the city was not aware of it three days later'.[15] Of course, not all the area within the city walls was occupied, and the kings who commissioned the building of these new capital cities clearly wanted their size to reflect grandeur.

The issue of settlement size relates closely to that of population size, but estimating the latter is virtually impossible.[16] The textual record is disappointing: there are no census lists, and references such as Assurnaṣirpal II's claim that he fed 69,574 men and women after the founding of Kalhu are probably not very reliable indicators of the size of the population. We are thus forced to look at the archaeological record for estimating populations. Three techniques are currently popular among prehistorians, based on the total size of settlement, the sustaining area available to a settlement, and the domestic architecture. All three techniques have an enormous margin of error, which cannot be reduced by their combined use.

It is not easy to determine the area of settlement in a city at any moment in time, because no city has been completely excavated. Occupation within the city walls was usually only partial, and we cannot establish the extent of the open areas. Habitation outside city walls certainly existed at times, but figures about the spread of suburbs are totally lacking. The number of inhabitants per hectare

---

[15] Translation H. Rackham, *Aristotle: Politics* (Cambridge, Mass., 1977).

[16] The information provided by Tertius Chandler in *Four Thousand Years of Urban Growth*, 2nd edn. (Lewiston and Queensten, 1987), is based on an entirely uncritical use of data from widely varying sources, and is therefore unreliable.

of settlement is essentially impossible to establish. Comparison with contemporary, or early twentieth-century AD Middle Eastern cities provides a guideline, but the variation there is enormous, and the applicability of the figures is doubtful. Most scholars have adopted a figure of 100–400 persons per hectare, but this is inappropriate as the range is too wide and as 'the use of later statistics begins from an assumption we should be setting out to prove'.[17] Moreover, the supposition that population density remains the same whatever the size of the settlement is most likely false. A study of numerous modern Middle Eastern villages indicates that density actually decreases when the settlements grow larger,[18] which might have been true in antiquity as well. If so, there is no linear correlation between area and population of a settlement, making estimates of the latter even less secure.

It is equally difficult to calculate the sustaining area of a site, i.e. the amount of agricultural land available for the feeding of its population. Even when one city dominates an isolated and well-delineated area, we cannot determine how much land was developed for agriculture in antiquity. It is usually stated that one person can be fed by the income of 1.5 hectares of irrigated agricultural land or 3 hectares of rain-fed land. This figure may help us to set the upper limit of the number of people in a certain territory, although it is always possible that food was imported over long distances. A useful lower limit can never be established on this basis.

Population estimates based on the size of houses are also unreliable. The method involves two uncertain figures: the number of dwellings in a settlement and the number of inhabitants per house. Since we cannot determine the area of occupation of a city at any particular moment in time with certainty, we cannot calculate how many houses were located in it. Even if we knew from excavation how many residences existed in one area, we cannot assume that the density of buildings was the same all over town. Moreover, the number of inhabitants per house cannot be established. The size of a house in a densely inhabited city does not vary with the size of the family residing in it, as expansion of the dwelling to accommodate

---

[17] J. N. Postgate, *Early Mesopotamia: Society and Economy at the Dawn of History* (London and New York, 1992), 79–80.

[18] O. Aurenche, 'Essai de démographie archéologique. L'exemple des villages du proche orient ancien', *Paléorient* 7/1 (1981), 93–105.

for family growth is restricted by the presence of neighbours and the lack of open spaces adjacent to the house.

In order to demonstrate existing uncertainties about population sizes, it may be useful to quote some examples of the numbers published for a specific city: Nineveh after its rebuilding by Sennacherib in the early seventh century. The enormously large city of some 750 hectares drew attention even in antiquity. The biblical book of Jonah states that it had 120,000 inhabitants, which has been regarded as at best based on a contemporary guess, or as most likely too high. The most recent estimates consider the number too low, suggesting 300,000 as a round population figure, or too high with 75,000 inhabitants as more reasonable. These last opinions both presume that the entire walled city was inhabited, but that the population density was either 400 or 100 persons per hectare.[19] Obviously the divergence of the published numbers is so great that none can be used for acceptable demographic analyses.

Paul Bairoch, a specialist in demographic studies for Western Europe in the historical periods, calculated a factor of error of one to twelve when discussing ancient Near Eastern population sizes. According to him, urban density is determined by three factors, each with a great margin of inaccuracy: (1) area of occupation within the city walls; (2) number of storeys per house; (3) number of inhabitants per room.[20] None of these elements can be properly ascertained at the moment. We are thus confronted with a high degree of uncertainty when discussing population size. Even the assumption that variation in settlement size is reflective of variation in population size is not proven. Some very general statements can be made with a high degree of conjecture. We can presume that Babylon in the sixth century had an extremely large population, or that Dur-Sharrukin in the late eighth century was probably not fully settled. But more detail is at present unavailable, and demographic studies remain a remote goal.

---

[19] The estimates mentioned here can be found in David Oates, *Studies in the Ancient History of Northern Iraq* (London, 1968), 49 (perhaps 120,000); Mario Liverani, *Antico Oriente. Storia, società, economia* (Rome, 1988), 815 (less than 120,000); S. Parpola in Jack M. Sasson, *Jonah* (New York, 1990), 312 (300,000); and David Stronach in S. Mazzoni (ed.), *Nuove fondazioni nel vicino oriente antico* (Pisa, 1994), 103. (75,000).

[20] Paul Bairoch, *De Jéricho à Mexico: Villes et économie dans l'histoire* (Paris, 1985), 44–5.

98     *The Urban Landscape*

BIBLIOGRAPHY

A few discussions of the layout of inner cities have appeared. H. Frankfort, 'Town Planning in Ancient Mesopotamia', *Town Planning Review* 21/1 (1950), 98–115, provides a description of some of the best known towns at that time. Paul Lampl, *Cities and Planning in the Ancient Near East* (New York, 1968) contains a very superficial text, but has numerous illustrations. The study recently published by Elizabeth C. Stone, 'The Development of Cities in Ancient Mesopotamia', in Jack M. Sasson (ed.), *Civilizations of the Ancient Near East* (New York, 1995), 235–48 is the first attempt to classify the cities of the various regions and periods. See also her 'The Spacial Organization of Mesopotamian Cities', *Aula Orientalis* 9 (1991), 235–42. Some interesting remarks about Mesopotamian urban forms can be found in A. E. J. Morris, *History of Urban Form before the Industrial Revolutions*, 3rd edn. (New York, 1994); and Alexander Badawy, *Architecture in Ancient Egypt and the Near East* (Cambridge, Mass., 1966). For planned cities see several of the articles in S. Mazzoni (ed.), *Nuove fondazioni nel vicino oriente antico* (Pisa, 1994).

For ancient topographic texts see A. R. George, *Babylonian Topographical Texts* (Orientalia Lovaniensia Analecta 40; Louvain, 1992). An example of a reconstruction of urban topography based on building inscriptions, data of economic texts, and archaeological finds is Adam Falkenstein, *Topographie von Uruk 1: Uruk zur Seleukidenzeit* (Ausgrabungen der Deutschen Forschungsgemeinschaft in Uruk-Warka 3; Leipzig, 1941). For ancient maps see W. Röllig, 'Landkarten', *Reallexikon der Assyriologie* 6 (Berlin and New York, 1980–3), 464–7.

For the location of orchards around cities see Denise Cocquerillat, *Palmeraies et cultures de l'Eanna d'Uruk (559–520)* (Ausgrabungen der Deutschen Forschungsgemeinschaft in Uruk-Warka 8; Berlin, 1968). For city streets see Jürgen Schmidt, 'Strassen in altmesopotamischen Wohngebieten', *Baghdader Mitteilungen* 3 (1964), 125–47. For houses, see E. Heinrich, 'Haus. B. Archäologisch', *Reallexikon der Assyriologie* 4 (Berlin and New York, 1972–5), 176–220; and for burials, see E. Strommenger, 'Grab', *Reallexikon der Assyriologie* 3 (Berlin and New York, 1957–71), 581–93.

The literature on individual cities is enormous. The following is a very small selection of easily accessible works on the sites mentioned in this chapter. Sites excavated by the British School in Iraq, including Abu Salabikh, Tell Taya, Nimrud (= Kalhu), and Rimah (= Qattara), are summarily described in John Curtis (ed.), *Fifty Years of Mesopotamian Discovery* (London, 1982). For the other sites mentioned see Kanish: Tahsin Özgüç, 'An Assyrian Trading Outpost', *Scientific American* 208/2 (February 1963), 97–106; Tahsin Özgüç, *Kültepe—Kaniš* II (Ankara, 1986); Nuzi: Richard F. S. Starr, *Nuzi* (Cambridge, Mass., 1939); Ur: Marc Van De Mieroop, *Society and Enterprise in Old Babylonian Ur* (Berliner Beiträge zum Vorderen Orient 12; Berlin, 1992); Larsa: Jean-Louis Huot *et al.*, 'La Structure urbaine de Larsa: Une approche provisoire', in J.-L. Huot (ed.), *Larsa. Travaux de 1985* (Paris, 1989), 19–52; Shubat-Enlil: Dominique Parayre and Harvey Weiss, 'Cinq campagnes de fouilles à Tell Leilan dans la Haute Jezireh (1979–1987): bilan et perspectives', *Journal des Savants* (1991), 3–26; Kar-Tukulti-Ninurta: Tilman Eickhoff, *Kār Tukulti Ninurta: Eine mittelassyrische Kult- und Residenzstadt* (Abhandlungen der Deutschen Orient-Gesellschaft 21; Berlin 1985), Reinhard Dittman in Khaled Nashef, 'Archaeology in Iraq', *American Journal of Archaeology* 96 (1992), 309–12; Dur-Sharrukin: Gordon Loud and Charles Altman, *Khorsabad II: The Citadel and the Town* (Oriental Institute Publications XL; Chicago, 1939); Nineveh: David Stronach and Stephen Lumsden, 'UC Berkeley's Excavations at Nineveh', *Biblical Archaeologist* 55 (1992), 227–33; Dur-Kurigalzu: A. A. Al-Khayyat, 'Aqar Quf, capitale des Cassites', *Dossiers Histoire et Archéologie* 103 (March 1986), 59–61; Babylon: D. J. Wiseman, *Nebuchadnezzar and Babylon* (Oxford, 1985); A. R. George, 'Babylon revisited: archaeology and philology', *Antiquity* 67 (1993), 734–46; Borsippa: Eckhard Unger, 'Barsippa', *Reallexikon der Assyriologie* 1 (Berlin and Leipzig, 1932); 402–29; Haradum: Christine Kepinski and Olivier Lecomte, 'Haradum/ Harada: Une forteresse sur l'Euphrate', *Archéologia* 205 (Sept. 1985), 46–55, Christine Kepinski-Lecomte, *Haradum I: Une nouvelle ville sur le Moyen-Euphrate* (Paris, 1992).

For the issue of population estimates in ancient Mesopotamia, see Robert McC. Adams, *Heartland of Cities* (Chicago and London, 1981); and Carol Kramer, 'Estimating Prehistoric Populations: An Ethnoarchaeological Approach', in M. T. Barrelet (ed.), *L'Archéologie de l'Iraq du début de l'époque néolithique à 333 avant notre ère* (Paris, 1980), 315–34. J. N. Postgate, 'How Many Sumerians per Hectare?—Probing the Anatomy of an Early City', *Cambridge Archaeological Journal* 4 (1994), 47–65, ends his investigation of the question as it applies to the city of Abu Salabikh in the mid-third millennium with the telling conclusion: 'between 248 and 1,205 Sumerians per hectare . . . , provided we have not made any false assumptions.' On demographic issues in world history see Paul Bairoch, *De Jèricho à Mexico: Villes et économie dans l'histoire* (Paris, 1985).

# 5

## Social Organization

The social structure of the Mesopotamian city cannot be easily studied even in its most basic outlines. The absence of census lists, or even a relatively complete set of family names from any city, prevents us from recognizing even the familial ties of the inhabitants beyond their closest relatives. For most of Mesopotamian history, and with few exceptions, individuals were identified by their name, and, when further specification was needed, this was done by profession or by the name of the father: for instance, Nūr-Shamash, the shepherd, or the son of Ahi-shāgish. Rarely, an ethnic designation, such as the Amorite, Turukkean, or the like, was included. It was only in first millennium Babylonia that a more complete genealogy was consistently used. Before that date we are thus usually unable to establish family ties between individuals further removed than siblings.

We can determine with certainty that the most basic social unit in the city was the nuclear family: a married couple with a number of unmarried daughters and sons, and perhaps a widowed parent. Such a family could own domestic slaves residing in the same household. Widows and waifs not taken care of by a family were pitied, and their protection was a sign of royal beneficence. On the other side of the scale, the largest social unit was the entire city community, 'the city', which sometimes appears in the documents acting as one entity, especially in its interactions with authorities such as the king. People sometimes expressed their attachment to the home town by giving their children names such as 'Uruk preserves'.[1] Membership to the city community was probably based on residence, but we have no idea whether or not other requirements existed. Moreover, we do not know where the

[1] See Johann Jakob Stamm, *Die akkadische Namengebung* (Darmstadt, 1968), 84–5.

geographical boundaries of the city were located. It is likely that 'the city' did not refer only to the walled inner city, and that it incorporated the suburbs. But did the villages in the surrounding countryside qualify as well? The existence of boundaries between city territories was acknowledged, but their location is unknown to us. Thus we can say that 'the city' existed as a social unit, but we cannot define what it incorporated.

The major problem in the reconstruction of the social organization lies in the identification of groupings larger than the nuclear family, yet smaller than the entire city. If the Mesopotamian felt an allegiance to a social unit larger than his or her near family, what was that unit and what was its importance in daily life? We can hypothesize that individuals established social ties based on various shared affiliations, to a family, an ethnos, a place of residence, or a profession. Some of these different types of associations might have coincided or partly overlapped. For instance, the existence of craftsmen quarters shows that people residing in the same neighbourhood sometimes shared the same profession. All of these elements played a role in a citizen's social life, but the exact nature and importance of them is quite vague to us, as the following review will show. Moreover, the nature of these relationships probably changed over time, complicating the picture further. The documentation available to us derives primarily from southern Mesopotamia, or at least its material has been better analysed. For northern Mesopotamia, scholars have focused attention on the case of Arrapha in the second half of the second millennium, where we seem to find a system of extended family communities. This may reveal Hurrian practices rather than Assyrian ones, and may not be reflective of northern Mesopotamian society in general. The social structure of Assyrian cities has not drawn much attention otherwise.

It has to be kept in mind that the urban population was not static, but that there was a constant flux of people in and out of town due to various circumstances: war and uncertainty in the countryside probably led people to seek refuge within the city walls, while peaceful conditions may have encouraged rural settlement. Moreover, nomadic tribes constantly migrated through the Mesopotamian lowlands and some of their members settled in cities. Village and tribal communities were organized along different lines than urban ones, and it is usually assumed that family ties were very strong among them. Economically they lived at subsistence level, with little specialization of labour and no dependence on major temple and palace organizations, except in those villages with particular industries producing for an urban institution. When members of such communities moved into town, they partly abandoned their existing social contacts, and had to integrate themselves within urban social structures. The speed and degree to which they did so must have depended on many factors. If an entire village moved into the city due to a war, for instance, it was probably able to maintain its social ties for a long period of time. But when individual families came to town, they broke their existing ties and were forced to assimilate to city life much sooner. What were the social structures available to them?

In their consideration of social groupings scholars have focused their attention upon familial ties beyond the nuclear family. There seems to be a general assumption that remains of the tribe, clan, and extended family, social entities thought to have been prominent in the non-urban settings, survived to a certain extent within the cities. An evolution over time from these larger kinship groups to a fragmentation into individual nuclear families seems to be commonly accepted. Yet when we search for data on these kinship groups, we see that they are scanty at best, and that information for them increases over the millennia rather than the other way around.

The most debated problem with regard to social life is whether or not the extended family played a role in urban life in Mesopotamia. By the term 'extended family' is meant the grouping of relatives who maintain close economic and social contacts although they might not reside in the same residence. Its existence in Mesopotamia was established through the analysis of Babylonian land sale documents of the mid-third millennium. It is now commonly accepted among scholars that extended families played an important role at that time, but much less so in the second millennium, except in a few areas such as Arrapha in the north where 'archaic' social structures seem to have survived. The term archaic in this context reflects an evolutionary model of civilizations that goes back to the late nineteenth century AD, when Lewis Henry Morgan suggested a sequence of human development in three stages: savagery, barbarism, and civilization. Barbarism was characterized by a tribal organization with a subsistence agricultural economy, civilization was urban.[2] Morgan's book had a great impact on Friedrich Engels, whose *Origin of the Family, Private Property and the State*[3] has been very influential. The term family was meant to refer to the patriarchal nuclear family, or the single family in Engels's terminology, which is supposed to have developed simultaneously with private property and the state, intended to protect that property. Marxists and non-Marxists alike seem to think that the extended family, clan, or tribe, are social units to be found in an earlier, more primitive, stage of human development, and not in an urban civilization. But both do admit that we can find more remains of these larger kinship groups in cities during periods of transition, such as some time in third millennium Babylonia, and possibly other times and places in social environments considered to be 'archaic'. We can thus phrase a question along these lines: assuming that the countryside was characterized by a more 'primitive' social structure than the city, did people who moved from the countryside into the city shed their extended family ties immediately, or did their social structures survive? If they did survive, how long did they continue to play a role?

The slim evidence for extended families at our disposal derives mostly, if not entirely, from a rural environment. It seems that in the third millennium, land ownership in Babylonia was not individual, and that the sale of a field required the approval of the siblings of the nominal owner. The documentation for such sales is extremely limited in number, but it includes some very important records. A large-scale acquisition of fields by King Manishtushu (ruled 2269–2255), for instance, shows how the buyer had to compensate not only the nominal owner, but also a number of his relatives.[4] These were, however, members of village communities. The important question is whether the members of such communities maintained their extended family ties when they moved into the city. The scholar who first documented the existence of the extended family in the third millennium, I. M. Diakonoff, pointed out that such ties were often abandoned in an urban setting. First,

---

[2] Lewis Henry Morgan, *Ancient Society* (1877; repr. Tucson, 1985).

[3] 4th edn. 1891; repr. New York, 1972.

[4] For a discussion of kinship terms in this and similar documents, see I. J. Gelb, 'Household and Family in Early Mesopotamia', in E. Lipiński (ed.), *State and Temple Economy in the Ancient Near East* 1 (Orientalia Lovaniensia Analecta 5; Louvain, 1979), 1–97.

temple and palace administrations worked with individuals, and, second, private entrepreneurs, such as usurers, could not function with communal responsibilities.[5] Yet Diakonoff and other scholars have sought to identify large kinship groups in the cities. The evidence for these is very slim, however, and equivocal. In the late third millennium, for instance, Gudea, ruler of Lagash, stated that residents of certain sectors of town were called up for service to build the temple of Ningirsu. These sectors were identified with elaborate names, and after the levy the men were placed under divine standards.

> In 'Rampant wild bull without an opponent,
> holding the white cedar for its king',
> the *im-ru-a* of Ningirsu,
> he conscripted men
> and placed the standard of Lugalkurdub at their head.
>
> In 'Place of water, bank rising from the water,
> the high river, bounteous water, that brings abundance',
> the *im-ru-a* of Nanshe,
> he conscripted men
> and placed the sacred stern, the standard of Nanshe at their head.
>
> In 'Trap laid out for the animals of the steppe',
> and 'Prime donkeys of the famous team, the beloved team of Utu',
> the *im-ru-a* of Inanna, he conscripted men
> and placed the disk, the standard of Inanna at their head.[6]

The Sumerian term Gudea used, *im-ru-a*, has been identified with 'family' on lexical grounds, and the text has been understood as referring to clans within the city.[7] The term is extremely rare, however, and can also be interpreted as a purely geographical designation without any reference to family ties.[8] It is clear from the analysis of documents found in adjoining houses that family members did not live as neighbours, with few exceptions.[9] Upon the

[5] I. M. Diakonoff, 'Extended Families in Old Babylonian Ur', *Zeitschrift für Assyriologie* 75 (1985), 52.

[6] Cylinder A, col. xiv, ll. 14–27, François Thureau-Dangin, *Les Cylindres de Goudéa*, (Paris, 1925), pl. xiv.

[7] For instance, J. N. Postgate, *Early Mesopotamia* (London and New York, 1992), 82–3.

[8] See Åke W. Sjöberg, 'Zu einigen Verwandtschaftsbezeichnungen im Sumerischen', *Heidelberger Studien zum Alten Orient* (Wiesbaden, 1967), 202–9.

[9] See Marc Van De Mieroop, *Society and Enterprise in Old Babylonian Ur* (Berlin, 1992), ch. 5.

death of their father, brothers commonly divided the paternal home, and sometimes resided together with their individual families, but had no objections to selling off their part of the house and moving elsewhere.[10] The analysis of texts from residential areas shows that neighbours were not usually related by blood, and otherwise in the texts people act primarily as individuals, not as members of extended family communities. We do see how fields in the early second millennium were sometimes leased out by siblings acting together, but that should not be considered as a sign that land ownership was not individual. The division of fields through inheritance could threaten to reduce plots to such a small size that their exploitation would become economically unfeasible, hence it made more sense to keep plots together even if two brothers had to divide the income. The evidence for extended families in third and early second millennia urban environments in Babylonia is thus very limited, and such families clearly did not dominate economic life. We cannot determine whether or not they existed as social networks, or how rare or common they were. It seems, however, false to assume from later Islamic parallels that village communities or tribal groups that moved into towns maintained their strong family ties and resided in the same neighbourhoods. All ancient Mesopotamian textual evidence at our disposal contradicts such a conclusion.

The contemporary situation in Assyria is unknown, nor have attempts been made to determine the role of the family there. We see in the Old Assyrian trade documents that fathers and sons worked together, but that was most likely a matter of safety and trust rather than a reflection of the strength of the extended family as an economic unit. In the fifteenth and fourteenth centuries the textual evidence from Arrapha in the north-east of Mesopotamia attests to the importance of extended families in land ownership there. Seemingly no one could buy or sell land outside the family. To circumvent this restriction, buyers had themselves adopted into the seller's family, as a son or a brother. It seems, however, that this was a situation in a rural environment, not in an urban one, and we do not know what happened in cities at that time. Moreover, the Arrapha texts may reflect a Hurrian tradition rather than an

---

[10] See Elizabeth C. Stone, 'Texts, Architecture, and Ethnographic Analogy: Patterns of Residence in Old Babylonian Nippur', *Iraq* 43 (1981), 19–33.

Assyrian one. In the eighth and seventh centuries, information from the Assyrian countryside shows that the nuclear family was the dominant economic unit.[11] As centres of the enormous government bureaucracy, the large cities of the Assyrian heartland, which were often of artificial foundation, probably were inhabited by very diverse populations for whom the ties with the palace were of more importance than their kinship ties. But too little is known of the urban populations to say anything with certainty.

Surprisingly, the Babylonian material from the first millennium has never been analysed with respect to the question of extended families, while texts from that period are the most explicit in spelling out an individual's ancestry. A system came into use where almost every person mentioned in a text was identified as follows: personal name 1, son of personal name 2, descendant of personal name 3; for instance Iddin-Marduk, son of Iqīsha, descendant of Nūr-Sin. The third name is not of the grandfather, but of an ancestor, and scholars have commonly equated it with our family name. At times, the ancestral name was replaced by a professional designation, such as smith, weaver, or cowherd, which may not apply to the individual in the document but to his ancestor. It became standard practice to refer to ancestral or 'family' names in the seventh century, and their use lasted down to the most recent Akkadian administrative documents in the first century BC.

The origin of these family names seems to date to the mid- to late second millennium, however. Vague traces of their existence are preserved in the documents of that time, and the ancestral names used, such as Sin-leqê-unnini, were common in that period as well. Political pressure upon the Babylonian urban populations by invading Assyrian armies and by Aramaic and Chaldean tribesmen infiltrating the area, may have caused the recognition of such extended family groups.[12] Can we assume, however, that these 'families' remained merely associations of blood relatives with a common descent, or even that they ever did refer to actual extended families? Several indications argue against the latter conclusion. First, the number of family names was quite limited. A thorough analysis of references to professionals in sixth-century

---

[11] See F. M. Fales, 'Popolazione servile e programmazione padronale in tarda età neo-assira', *Oriens Antiquus* 14 (1975), 325–60.

[12] See J. A. Brinkman, *Prelude to Empire* (Philadelphia, 1984), 11.

documents of the city Uruk shows that seventy-seven family names were used by them.[13] This seems a rather small number for a city that was still substantial in size.[14] Furthermore, some of these names were simultaneously in use in other cities, such as Babylon. Second, all ancestral names were purely Babylonian, while in the centuries of the first half of the first millennium several Aramaic and Chaldean groups had arrived in southern Babylonia, and surely had also integrated themselves within the cities.

If descent was not the determining factor for membership in one of these families, what was? It has been observed that many people with the same ancestral name also held the same profession, a fact that has been explained as the result of fathers passing their craft on to their sons. But could it not be that professionals were organized as extended families, something that would also explain the use of professional designations as family names? Of the seventy-seven family names of professionals attested in texts from sixth-century Uruk, fifty-six were used for one type of professional only. Moreover, all men with the family names *rēʾi-ginê* 'shepherd of regular offerings' and *rab-banî* 'orchard inspector' exercised these functions. Admittedly, members of the Ekur-zākir family, for instance, appear as goldsmiths, shepherds, and scribes, but could this not have been the result of a diversification of the activities of an extended family after it had been firmly established? If my interpretation is correct, we would see here a merging of extended family ties and professional ties. Membership in a particular 'family' would indicate the licence to exercise a certain profession. The evidence for such a merger of social ties is clearly very slim, but the less preferable alternative is to assume that a limited number of extended families, with all their members related by blood, resided in Uruk.

The slim evidence on kinship groupings larger than the nuclear family can thus be interpreted quite differently from what we find in most publications. Instead of an assumed development from tribal ties to individual ties, a model inspired by late nineteenth-

---

[13] This number is based on the list provided by Hans M. Kümmel, *Familie, Beruf und Amt im spätbabylonischen Uruk* (Berlin, 1979).

[14] The exact size of Uruk at this time is unknown, see E. Cancik, in *Uruk. Kampagne 35–37* (Mainz am Rhein, 1991), 209–10. The map, Beilage 30, suggests an area of occupation of some 125 hectares. If a low population density of 100 persons per hectare is accepted, Uruk would have had 12,500 inhabitants.

century evolutionary theory, with ephemeral remnants of the more primitive social structure in the early Babylonian cities and in 'backward'[15] areas later on, we can hypothesize a very different set of social structures over time. I am reluctant to use the term evolution, since the evidence at hand is so limited and does not permit a diachronic view. From the earliest historical periods onwards the extended family, clan, or tribe, did not play a recognizable role in the Mesopotamian city. The nuclear family was the prevailing kinship unit, residing separately and acting as a basic economic unit. Obviously, close ties with blood relatives could exist: brothers or cousins could live under the same roof, each with their wives and children, or could be involved in joint economic enterprises. But this was the exception rather than the rule. Most evidence for the extended family as an economic unit comes from a rural environment.

In first millennium Babylonia fictional kinship groups dominated urban society. Residents of cities consistently used a limited number of 'family' names, referring to a long-deceased ancestor or a profession which might not be their own. These did not indicate actual agnatic groups, with all bearers of the same family name descendent from the same ancestor. The number of names was too small, and their purely Babylonian character would exclude the integration of different ethnic groups. Hence they were fictional, and not based on blood relations. The formation of artificial kinship groups is not unusual at all. It has been demonstrated, for instance, that the so-called tribal remnants in the classical Greek cities, *gentes*, *phratries*, and *phylai*, which were so important to Morgan's and Engels's models, were entirely artificial groupings that had no ancient tribal roots.[16] The common characteristic of these 'families' originally may have been their professions, with fellow professionals choosing a common ancestor. After a while this system may have become less rigorous in that certain sons kept their fathers' ancestral names, but not their fathers' professions. The origin of this system is entirely unknown to us. It may somehow have been related to the arrival of the Aramaean and Chaldean tribes in Babylonia in the late second millennium, but other explanations are possible as well; we need not adhere to the evolutionary

---

[15] Diakonoff, 'Extended Families in Old Babylonian Ur', 49.
[16] Denis Roussel, *Tribu et cité* (Annales littéraires de l'Université de Besançon 193; Paris, 1976).

model that suggests a unilinear development from tribal to urban. Such 'families' are not necessarily remnants of a society where kinship ties dominated in social life, but may actually have been purely urban creations without any reference to real blood ties.

Social bonds other than kinship have to be considered in the study of the Mesopotamian city as well. These could be based on profession, place of residence, and ethnicity, and played varied roles in the life of a Mesopotamian city-dweller. Again the evidence for these ties is scarce, but we can postulate that they existed. I have intimated the presence of professional associations in Mesopotamian cities by suggesting that professional ties explained the use of ancestral names in first-millennium Babylonia. A feeling of affinity with a fellow professional was surely not an innovation of the first millennium. A major factor in the development of urban society was the fact that people started to abandon their family ties for professional relations, a shift of focus from kin to class in Adams's apt terms.[17] We know that craftsmen were highly specialized and that some of them formed close associations and acted as one unit. To call these associations guilds is an overstatement, yet we cannot deny that they had certain powers and that they accorded certain privileges to their members.

Not only craftsmen identified with their fellows, but also bureaucrats, priests, and soldiers. These were united by their affiliation to one of the public institutions, the palace or a temple. As these institutions were of extreme importance in the cities their value as an organizing force in social interactions must have been great. Both in Assyria and in Babylonia the palace organizations were enormous, employing numerous administrators, courtiers, soldiers, and a great number of manual labourers. For all these people the palace may have been their primary social unit. Although there are indications that the bureaucrats of the Third Dynasty of Ur, for instance, had many family ties and that nepotism was widespread among them, it is not true that the palace bureaucracy was controlled by a small number of families. The bureaucrats owed their primary allegiance to the king who had appointed them from whatever family or region of his dominion he chose. Thus their institutional affiliation was what united them, not their family ties.

---

[17] Robert McC. Adams, *The Evolution of Urban Society* (Chicago, 1966), ch. 3.

Temples may have provided a social network to more citizens than did the palace, because the affiliation of individuals with temples was often part-time. In third-millennium Babylonia, temple offices were held by what could be called anachronistically professional priests, members of the cultic and administrative personnel of the temple whose livelihood depended on their temple employment. In that sense temple organizations were very similar to those of the palace. But, in the early second millennium temple offices became a commodity that could be inherited, traded, and divided, because they guaranteed the holder a financial reward. Instead of real temple offices, they became what we would call prebends, portions of the general temple income that were granted to individuals. Thus we see that the office of temple sweeper, for instance, could be held for as little as a quarter of a day per year, which meant that the owner received a very small fraction of the income assigned to that function. A system was established in which individuals could buy themselves a place within the temple organization, for which they probably did not have to provide any labour but which guaranteed them an income. This system remained in use throughout Babylonian history; some of the latest preserved administrative documents written in Akkadian record the distribution of temple income among such prebend holders. Because these prebends often involved a minute percentage of a temple office, numerous individuals could hold them simultaneously.

We see thus that in the mid-first millennium, the temple became the primary social organizing force of the Babylonian city, and that in places such as Uruk the organization of the main sanctuary and its hierarchy parallels that of the entire city. The professional organizations of a Mesopotamian city can be likened to corporations in that they appear in texts, speaking with one voice in their contacts with higher authorities and with one another. A professional association of goldsmiths, for instance, could represent its members in its contacts with the temple, while the temple community would act as a unit in its contacts with the king. Such corporations may have played a crucial role in a citizen's social life, providing a network of support not only in professional but also in personal affairs. Since the latter are not described to us in the documents, we cannot say much about them.

A citizen can also feel a certain social affinity to the people who

live in the same neighbourhood. There are several indications that
a city was subdivided into wards, but the social cohesion of these
subdivisions is less clear. The layout of the Mesopotamian city
shows the irregular subdivision of the inner city by roads and canals
into smaller sectors. Within these sectors the street pattern is
extremely irregular and the houses are closely knit together. Many
streets seem to have been dead ends, and could have been closed
off from the outside. In third-millennium Abu Salabikh it seems
even that some of these sectors were surrounded by walls.[18] These
subdivisions may have been called *babtum* in the Akkadian texts, a
term we translate as city ward. The *babtum* was a geographical unit
which had its own governmental structure and responsibilities. It
was sometimes named after a person, but that does not need to be
interpreted as a sign that it was originally the residential concentration of an extended family.[19] The social cohesion of these wards is
unclear. Some scholars have attempted to equate them with the
neighbourhoods of Islamic cities which show a great deal of familial, professional, or institutional cohesion,[20] but when we analyse
the legal records found in neighbouring houses we do not see such
ties at all.[21] Obviously people who worked for a particular temple,
for instance, often would reside near their place of employment,[22]
but that does not mean that neighbourhoods were set aside for
them or created by them. Similarly, the first-millennium evidence
of craftsmen quarters does not indicate that others were excluded
from these areas.[23]

Throughout history, the Mesopotamian city contained a great
variety of ethnic groups. From the beginning of urban civilization southern cities housed Sumerians, Akkadians, and whatever
other ethnic groups lived in the area. To this mixture were later
added Amorites, Elamites, Kassites, Hurrians, Chaldeans, and
Arameans, as well as a substantial number of peoples vaguely
known to us, such as Turukkeans, Guteans, and others. The most
prominent of these groups are distinguished by us through their

---

[18] Postgate, *Early Mesopotamia*, 91 and Fig. 5.4.
[19] Ibid. 82.
[20] e.g. Elizabeth C. Stone, *Nippur Neighborhoods* (Chicago, 1987), 4.
[21] Marc Van De Mieroop, 'Old Babylonian Ur: Portrait of an Ancient Mesopotamian City', *Journal of the Ancient Near Eastern Society* 21 (1992), 119–30.
[22] See e.g. Dominique Charpin, *Le Clergé d'Ur au siècle d'Hammurabi* (Paris,
1986).
[23] See Ch. 8.

different languages, yet we have no idea what, if anything, set them apart otherwise, and how long they continued to talk their native tongues. In the first millennium, when Assyria and Babylonia in succession ruled widespread empires, numerous people voluntarily came into their cities, to take advantage of economic opportunities there, or involuntarily as deportees. They included Egyptians, Judaeans, Israelites, Phoenicians, Arabs, Syrians, Phrygians, Medes, Persians, and many others. Originally they must have been very distinct, as they not only spoke different languages, but also looked different and brought their native customs and cultures with them. How long did they maintain their ethnic identity? Did they attempt to remain distinctive, or did they want to integrate within Babylonian and Assyrian society? Obviously the answers vary from case to case, as many different circumstances played a role.

As an example, we could compare what happened to two closely related peoples who seemingly suffered opposite fates: the Israelites and the Judaeans. The first were brought to various localities in Assyria after the loss of their independence in 721, and from that moment on they disappeared from history. The second, deported to Babylonia after 598 and 587, survived as a community for sixty years when they were liberated by the Persian king Cyrus who allowed them to return home in 538. But how dissimilar were these cases in reality? Possibly the Israelites had in vain waited for their release from Assyria, and had been unable to maintain their identity because they were cut off from their homeland for 120 years longer than the Judaeans. And how unassimilated were the Judaeans in reality? After sixty years many of them seem to have been pretty well settled in Babylonia and, according to Josephus at least, few wanted to return home: 'When Cyrus had made this announcement to the Israelites, the leaders of the two tribes of Judah and Benjamin and the Levites and priests set out for Jerusalem, but many remained in Babylon, being unwilling to leave their possessions.'[24]

According to Dandamaev,[25] the assimilation of foreigners in Babylonian society was a smooth and quick process, because of

---

[24] Flavius Josephus, *Jewish Antiquities* 11. 1. 3, trans. Ralph Marcus, Loeb Classical Library (Cambridge, Mass., 1966), 317.
[25] Mohammed A. Dandamaev, *Iranians in Achaemenid Babylonia* (Costa Mesa and New York, 1992), 173–5.

religious tolerance and the absence of racism. The use of Aramaic rather than Akkadian as the *lingua franca* facilitated integration as well. Many of the native tongues of the new immigrants from the west were akin to Aramaic, and the language had a great flexibility permitting its use by novices. The question remains, however: how fast did this assimilation take place? At first new arrivals were distinguished from the indigenous people by their foreign names and sometimes a special designation such as 'the Egyptian', or 'the Amorite'. Soon, however, they gave their children Babylonian names, and the ethnic designations became somewhat like a surname, to disappear in due course. The time-span involved is unclear to us, yet often seems to have been brief. Already in 653, for instance, we find a man, said to be of Egyptian descent, with a good Babylonian name, Bēl-shum-iddina.[26] His ancestors must have arrived in Babylonia less than thirty years earlier, as it was only in the early seventh century that Egypt became partly incorporated in the Assyrian empire. Why would an Egyptian, coming from a country with a long and proud cultural history, have become Babylonian so fast? Perhaps Dandamaev's idea of a non-racist society is too idyllic, and it may have been important for foreigners to assimilate as soon as possible in order to make a career.

The case of assimilation that has drawn the most scholarly attention in earlier Babylonian history is that of the Amorites. The designation of a person as being Amorite appears already around 2500,[27] but only from the twenty-first century onward are there in the textual record a substantial number of people with such a designation or with a name that can be interpreted as being Amorite. From that moment, they seem to have been integrated in all sectors of society, as agriculturalists and urbanites, even as Babylonians continued to use the term Amorite to refer to nomadic foreigners. In the early second millennium Amorites gained political ascendance in many cities, often maintaining their original names. Thus in the mid-seventeenth century the edict of Ammiṣaduqa could make a distinction between Akkadians and Amorites. Besides the adherence of the Amorites to their language, at least in their names, we do not see any other way in which they

---

[26] See I. Eph'al, 'The Western Minorities in Babylonia', *Orientalia* 47 (1978), 77.
[27] Jean-Robert Kupper, *Les Nomades en Mésopotamie* (Paris, 1957), 150.

clearly distinguished themselves from the other people in Babylonia. Nor do we see them adhering to a social structure of their own. The oft-quoted Old Babylonian list of Amorites[28] does not indicate the existence of city wards reserved for Amorites, only that a separate record was kept of Amorites living in the city.

The various ethnic groups that entered Babylonia seem to have been assimilated over the years and to have lost their separate identities, at least until the arrival of the Greeks in the fourth century BC. Obviously they had some type of social network during this process of assimilation that made them feel distinct from others in the community. But we have no means of studying these networks. It has so far proved impossible to relate archaeological remains to a specific ethnic group, and when people abandoned their language in naming their children we lose the ability to identify them as ethnically different. In any case, it is always dangerous to equate the language of someone's name with his or her ethnicity, as the members of the multi-lingual societies of Mesopotamia did not seem to have been averse to using a different language to name their children.

In conclusion, the social structure of the Mesopotamian city is poorly known, but the available evidence permits us to make some general suggestions. When a nuclear family moved to a city from a village, or from a nomadic or semi-nomadic group, or immigrated from another country, it seems to have abandoned its existing ties very quickly. The extended families of village communities or tribes do not seem to have survived, while a separate ethnic identity was maintained for only a few generations. Instead, professional ties became important. One associated with fellow members of the temple hierarchy or of the palace administration, or one joined professional associations which in first millennium Babylonia may have claimed a common fictional ancestor. Class became thus more important than kin. Obviously other ties played a role in people's lives as well. Family members were certainly considered to be important, and one would imagine that people with the same ethnic background sought each other's company. But such ties are not emphasized in the documentation, and may have been of secondary importance.

[28] I. J. Gelb, 'An Old Babylonian List of Amorites', *Journal of the American Oriental Society* 88 (1968), 39–46.

BIBLIOGRAPHY

A set of papers was devoted to the issue of extended families in the journal *Oikumene* 5 (1986). The contrasting opinions by Powell and Leemans expressed there show the uncertainty of any conclusion. I. M. Diakonoff identified the existence of extended families in third-millennium rural environments, e.g. in 'The Rise of the Despotic State in Ancient Mesopotamia', *Ancient Mesopotamia: Socio-Economic History* (Moscow, 1969), 177–9; and 'The Rural Community in the Ancient Near East', *Journal of the Economic and Social History of the Orient* 18 (1975), 121–33. See also Veysel Donbaz and Norman Yoffee, 'On Living Together in Kish', in *Old Babylonian Texts from Kish* (Malibu, 1986), 66–9, and the survey of the problem by J. N. Postgate, *Early Mesopotamia* (London and New York, 1992), 88–108.

Arthur Ungnad, 'Babylonische Familiennamen', *Miscellanea Orientalia dedicata Antonio Deimel* (Analecta Orientalia 12; Rome, 1935), 319–26, was the first to point out the importance of ancestral names and to date their origin to the mid to late second millennium. See also W. G. Lambert, 'Ancestors, Authors, and Canonicity', *Journal of Cuneiform Studies* 11 (1957), 1–14, 112. Hans M. Kümmel, *Familie, Beruf und Amt im spätbabylonischen Uruk* (Berlin, 1979), surveys all of the evidence from sixth-century Uruk. See also the remarks by David Weisberg, *Guild Structure and Political Allegiance in Early Achaemenid Mesopotamia* (New Haven and London, 1967), chapter 6.

For the identification of neighbourhoods in an early second-millennium city, see Elizabeth C. Stone, *Nippur Neighborhoods* (Chicago, 1987).

The subject of foreigners in Babylonia has been investigated primarily on the basis of the onomasticon. See, for instance, Ran Zadok, *On West Semites in Babylonia during the Chaldean and Achaemenian Periods* (Jerusalem, 1977); and 'On Some Foreign Population Groups in First-Millennium Babylonia', *Tel Aviv* 6 (1979), 164–81; and see several publications by Mohammed A. Dandamaev, most recently *Iranians in Achaemenid Babylonia* (Costa Mesa and New York, 1992); and 'Egyptians in Babylonia in the 6th–5th Centuries B.C.', in D. Charpin and F. Joannès (eds.), *La Circulation des biens* (Paris, 1992), 321–5. I. Eph'al, 'The Western Minorities in Babylonia in the 6th–5th Centuries B.C.: Maintenance and Cohesion', *Orientalia* 47 (1978), 74–90, maintains that resistance to assimilation, such as that by the Judeans, was great among many foreigners, but he only takes into account the fact that Babylonian toponyms can refer to ethnic groups without investigating how long these toponyms survived. For the problem of recognizing ethnicity in the early Mesopotamian archaeological record, see Kathryn A. Kamp and Norman Yoffee, 'Ethnicity in Ancient Western Asia during the Early Second Millennium B.C.: Archaeological Assessments and Ethnoarchaeological Perspectives', *Bulletin of the American Schools of Oriental Research* 237 (1980), 85–104.

# 6

## Urban Government: King, Citizens, and Officials

Every community requires a governmental organization, a means by which social interactions can be regulated. The complexity of such an organization greatly depends on the size and diversity of the community, and the city by definition shows a high degree of both: of necessity, then, there existed a structure within the Mesopotamian city with governmental powers. We can recognize two poles in the power relations in the Mesopotamian city: on the one side were the king and the public institutions that supported his rule, on the other the citizenry who held certain ill-described powers. Arranging contact between the two poles was a group of officials. These three elements, crown, citizenry, and officialdom, all played a role in the urban government. The relationship between crown and citizenry varied over time, and depended on the general political situation. It is my contention that the powers and independence of the citizenry increased over time in Mesopotamian history, rather than the other way around as has been commonly suggested.

The king has always been regarded as *the* political power in Mesopotamian society, or even as the only element within society with any political power. Finley stated that politics did not exist in the ancient Near East, because discussions of policy by citizens or royal advisers were neither open nor binding, and the king made all decisions on his own, allowing for some persuasion by courtiers. Finley called the system government by antechamber.[1] This is surely an overstatement inspired by orientalist stereotypes, as vague traces of political debate within the court are visible in the

[1] M. I. Finley, 'Politics', in M. I. Finley (ed.), *The Legacy of Greece: A New Appraisal* (Oxford, 1981), 22–36.

omen literature and in some historiographic literature.[2] Yet all decisions of a political nature known to us were indeed promulgated by the king who never acknowledged influence by his citizens in the matter. In the discussion of his powers we have to distinguish, however, between his role as a 'national' leader and as the head of the palatial organization, his own household. As national leader he was king of all the subjects of his state, be it a single city-state or a widespread empire. These subjects showed a lot of variation in their status. They included those people dependent upon the palace, to be discussed presently. But they also comprised members of the village and tribal communities and many city residents, who were not part of the palace organization, for whom the king's powers may have been absolute, but limited to certain restricted aspects of life. A Mesopotamian king had obligations to his people, likened in the ancient sources to the responsibilities of a shepherd to his flock. He had to ensure that they were fed and protected from enemies. The king led in war, guaranteed the fertility of the land by digging and maintaining irrigation canals, provided justice, and averted divine wrath against his people by promoting the cult. His power in these matters was seemingly unlimited. In return for this protection and care, the citizens were obliged to provide the king with two things: they had to pay taxes, and render services either in agriculture or in war. The king acknowledged the influence of the gods, who had selected him for kingship or inspired him in establishing justice in the land, and he never seems to have taken his people's opinions into account. But the areas of government he controlled were limited to matters of general policy, concerning security, the cult, and the agricultural conditions. They excluded the details that were important in a citizen's daily life.

One might object that certain kings, such as the famous Hammurabi, are known to have been concerned with trivia, to such an extent that they have even been regarded as petty rulers.[3] The king was indeed involved in the daily affairs of some of his subjects, but this was not in his role as national leader. He was the head of

---

[2] See Mario Liverani, 'Model and Actualization: the Kings of Akkad in the Historical Tradition', in M. Liverani (ed.), *Akkad: The First World Empire* (Padua, 1993), 52.

[3] See e.g. C. J. Gadd, 'Hammurabi and the End of his Dynasty', *The Cambridge Ancient History*, 3rd edn. 2: 1 (Cambridge, 1973), 184–7.

the palace organization, which at times could be extensive, incorporating a large segment of the population. In that role, he was like a *pater familias*, one among many heads of households. He took care of the details of the lives of his dependants, and as such he was involved with what might seem to us petty matters. But the unaffiliated households existed next to the palatial one, and many of the urban citizens were not dependants of the crown. For these citizens the king's influence was limited, and they retained substantial freedom in the running of their daily lives.

In support of his role as national leader the king could rely on an elaborate palatial organization that provided him with administrators and warriors. Palaces were among the most prestigious buildings of all Mesopotamian cities, and the palatial sector was at times of utmost prominence in society. At certain times the temples also formed a major part of the ideological foundations of kingship, but this relationship to the crown did not remain constant throughout Mesopotamian history. As a political organization the temple has to be regarded separately from the palace. Indeed, from the mid-first millennium on, temples became a bulwark of the citizens' power in the Babylonian city.

How did the citizenry that was not attached to the palace organize its own government? This question can only be studied with respect to the urban citizenry, as the members of village communities and tribes remain almost entirely outside the written record. When we try to study the matter of urban government in detail we are confronted with a severe shortage of information. Scholars have used their imagination to complete the details, and the validity of their reconstructions can neither be confirmed nor denied. The lack of evidence does not result from the accident of recovery, but from the nature of the written documentation in general and from the character of political representation among the citizenry. As I stated earlier, Mesopotamian records are primarily concerned with the transfer of property. No such transfers took place between the citizenry and its government. The cities most likely did not have the power to levy taxes, as such tax levies would have been recorded. Yet, a governmental structure is revealed by references in private contracts that attribute the transaction described to the decision of the government, as well as references to governmental actions in private letters, and statements in the so-called 'law-codes' about the duties of officials. These data are almost all of a juridical nature. The courts often forced the transfer of property between two citizens, and such transfers and their justification were put down in writing.

The basis for a study of the citizens' role in government in general will thus by necessity be the juridical organization. It demonstrates certain patterns in the decision-making process that possibly may be expanded to other areas of government as well. Yet the available documentation does not allow the affirmation or denial of whether this was indeed the case. For instance, we see frequently that courts settled disputes over the ownership of land, which indicates that citizens accepted the decisions of a governmental body. But can we extrapolate from that observation that citizens also submitted to a higher authority in other aspects of life? Such a conclusion cannot be drawn on the basis of the available evidence, and becomes a matter of the scholar's intuition.

As I pointed out in the previous chapter, the Mesopotamian city was regarded as a unit, but within this unit several subdivisions existed. The cities were geographically divided into city quarters; they contained various professional associations, such as those of particular craftsmen or of merchants, and several international communities were allowed to maintain a separate identity. Juridically, the entire city and each of its subdivisions had their own courts, which were referred to as 'assemblies'. Texts from the entirety of Mesopotamian history show the existence of these assemblies and their activities as courts of law. A Mesopotamian seems to have had the basic right to be judged by his or her peers, and this principle seems to have been taken so far that when citizens of two different cities were involved in a legal dispute, judges from both towns had to be present. Cases were brought to trial in public, either before the entire city or before one of its subdivisions. The study of the institution of the assembly is complicated by the fact that in the Akkadian language, as in English, the term for assembly, *puḫrum*, refers both to an institutionalized assembly and to any informal gathering of a group of people. When the Code of Hammurabi states that a judge who alters a verdict is removed from his office (§ 5) it can be interpreted as an expulsion from the assembly, as well as a punishment meted out in public. There are no documents that describe the activities of the institutionalized assembly in detail, and we are faced with many questions regarding the composition, the procedures, and the areas of competence of these institutions.

The first difficulty is determining who sat in the assembly.

Scholars who have written on the matter tend to state that membership was limited to 'free male citizens', although the terms free and citizen cannot be easily defined. Obviously, the comparison with classical Greek assemblies has influenced this view. The evidence concerning which individuals had the right to participate in the assembly's discussions is very vague. The surviving record of a trial for homicide, dating to the early second millennium, is an exception. The document has been found in several copies in the scribal quarter of Nippur, and was most likely used as an exercise text for teaching students legal terminology. But there is no reason to assume that it does not reflect a real court case.

Nanna-sig, son of Lu-Sin, Ku-Enlila, son of Ku-Nanna the barber, and Enlil-ennam, slave of Adda-kalla, the gardener, killed Lu-Inanna, son of Lugal-urudu, the priest. When Lu-Inanna, son of Lugal-urudu had been killed, they told the wife of Lu-Inanna, Nin-dada, daughter of Lu-Ninurta, that her husband had been killed. Nin-dada, daughter of Lu-Ninurta, opened not her mouth, covered it up.

Their case was taken to Isin before the king. King Ur-Ninurta ordered that their case should be decided by the assembly of Nippur.

Ur-Gula, son of Lugal-ibila, Dudu the bird-catcher, Ali-ellati the commoner, Puzu, son of Lu-Sin, Eluti, son of Tizkar-Ea, Sheshkalla the potter, Lugalkam the gardener, Lugal-azida, son of Sin-andul, and Sheshkalla, son of Shara-HAR addressed ⟨the assembly⟩: 'They have killed a man, thus they are not live men. The three men and the woman are to be killed before the chair of Lu-Inanna, son of Lugal-urudu, the priest.'

Shuqalilum, the soldier of Ninurta, and Ubar-Sin the gardener addressed ⟨the assembly⟩: 'Did Nin-dada, daughter of Lu-Ninurta, kill her husband? The woman, what did she do that she should be put to death?'

The assembly of Nippur answered as follows: 'A man's enemy may know that a woman does not value her husband and may kill her husband. She heard that her husband had been killed, so why did she keep silent about him? It is she who killed her husband, her guilt is greater than that of the men who killed him.'

In the assembly of Nippur, after the case had been solved, Nanna-sig, son of Lu-Sin, Ku-Enlila, son of Ku-Nanna, the barber, Enlil-ennam, slave of Adda-kalla, the gardener, and Nin-dada, daughter of Lu-Ninurta, wife of Lu-Inanna, were given up to be killed. Verdict of the assembly of Nippur.[4]

---

[4] Thorkild Jacobsen, 'An Ancient Mesopotamian Trial for Homicide', *Analecta Biblica* 12 (1959), 134–6; trans. after J. N. Postgate, *Early Mesopotamia* (London and New York, 1992), 278.

The text shows some of the professions of some of the men who spoke out in the assembly: a bird-catcher, a potter, two gardeners, and a soldier. Ali-ellati's name is followed by the statement that he is a commoner, *muškēnum* in Akkadian,[5] seemingly indicating his social status rather than his profession. The professional designations have no other purpose than to identify the men involved; often the patronymic was used instead. But they are highly informative to us. They show that a wide variety of professions not only had the right, but also the time, to sit in the assembly. No trace of élitism is visible: most of the men were manual labourers, while one of them was a soldier in the service of the temple of the god Ninurta. The fact that they appear here as participants in a debate during a murder trial raises several questions. Where did they find the time to do so? In classical Athens, for instance, only well-off, landowning citizens had the leisure to join in the assembly's debates. Nominal payments were given to juries in trials and, from the late fourth century onward, for participation in the general assembly as well. Were Mesopotamians rewarded similarly? It seems unlikely, although impossible to determine. If there was no financial compensation for time spent with assembly business, it may suggest that meetings were rare or that participation was casual, but none of this is clear to us.

An entirely different source of information on the assembly in early Mesopotamian history is the Sumerian literary composition of Gilgamesh and Agga. Although the tale is presented to us as a historical account of an actual combat, it is clear that it relates a literary *topos* of conflict and resolution. The preserved manuscripts of this composition date to the early second millennium, but the text was probably composed in the late third millennium. It depicts a situation of crisis confronting the city where Gilgamesh ruled. Troops of the city of Kish were laying siege to Uruk and the king had to decide whether or not to fight them. He consulted two assemblies: one of the 'elders of the city' and one of the 'men of the city'. They provided opposing answers, the elders to yield, the men of the city to fight. Did Gilgamesh turn to the general assembly of men because the elders had given him advice he did not like? Could

[5] For this enigmatic term and a survey of published interpretations, see F. R. Kraus, *Von Mesopotamischen Menschen der altbabylonischer Zeit und seiner Welt* (Mededelingen der Koninklijke Nederlandse Akademie van Wetenschappen, afd. Letterkunde, N.R. Deel 36, No. 6; Amsterdam and London, 1973), 95–117.

all men overrule the recommendation of the elders, or was it common practice for the king to consult with both bodies? The text does not provide answers to these questions. In any case, it may indicate that two separate bodies of citizens were in existence: the élite, restricted body of elders, and a wider one of the men in general.[6] Similarly, for the assemblies of the Assyrian colonies in Anatolia of the early second millennium, a distinction between 'big' and 'small' men is attested. But, in the mother city, Assur itself, such a differentiation was not made. This discrepancy has been interpreted as an indication that the 'small men' were excluded from the assembly in larger towns, but that is a mere guess.

Both the terms 'elders' and 'men' appear in other contexts as well, but their interpretation is very difficult. 'Elders', *ab.ba* in Sumerian, *šibūtum* in Akkadian, seems to refer to a select group of men within various communities, such as cities, tribes, temple and palace hierarchies. They are commonly seen to have been the heads of families, whose influence was a survival of tribal practices, and their prominence in texts from the early second millennium has been associated with the arrival of the west-Semitic Amorites in the late third and early second millennia.[7] But this interpretation relies entirely upon the unproven model of gradual sedentarization of nomads in Mesopotamian history, and does not explain the common appearance of 'elders' in texts pre-dating the second millennium. In the Ur III administration high officials could be designated 'elders' to distinguish them from common personnel,[8] and surely no tribal remnants can be assumed for that practice. Hence an interpretation of these men as 'élite' or 'high-ranking', seems more appropriate than as heads of families. These 'elders' did not compose the entire assembly, as many contexts talk about 'the elders and the assembly'. Their exact relationship to the assembly is difficult to determine, however. Possibly they acted as an

---

[6] Dina Katz, 'Gilgamesh and Akka: Was Uruk Ruled by Two Assemblies?' *Revue d'assyriologie et d'archéologie orientale* 81 (1987), 105–14, suggests that the assembly of the men of the city was a literary fiction, while the elders' assembly was historically accurate. I do not see the basis for such a conclusion.

[7] H. Klengel, 'Zu den *šibūtum* in altbabylonischer Zeit', *Orientalia* 29 (1960), 357–75.

[8] See e.g. the grain account G. Reisner, *Tempelurkunden aus Telloh* (Berlin, 1901), no. 111, where ab.ba.ab.ba are set apart from overseers of ploughmen and common workers.

executive committee within it, and they determined what matters would be considered by the entire body.

The Sumerian word for the 'men of the city', *guruš* in the Gilgamesh text, is also too vague to allow us to determine which people constituted that group. The term often refers to palace dependants in the late third millennium, and if this were the right interpretation for the word in this context, it would negate the interpretation of the assembly as an independent body representing the citizenry. The same term can also be used to indicate 'able-bodied men' in general, and this was probably the meaning intended in the context of the assembly. Whether any restrictions existed as to which men were allowed to join the assembly is again unclear. The Gilgamesh episode is equally unclear about how many men sat in the assembly of Uruk.

The question of whether women could sit in the assembly is usually either totally ignored by scholars, or the assumption is simply made that they could not. None of the evidence discussed above attests to their participation, but that may just be a result of the general obscurity of the data. A Babylonian omen of the early second millennium contains the statement that 'a woman will reveal the business of the assembly'.[9] This could indicate that she had been present during the discussions, but, obviously, the woman could have informed herself of what went on in many other ways as well. The question of women's participation in the assembly must thus remain unanswered.

The assemblies I have discussed so far seem to have represented entire towns, but subdivisions of cities had similar organizations. The city wards had legal authority and it is clear that their inhabitants gathered at certain moments to make decisions. For instance, in the Code of Hammurabi the city ward had to determine whether a woman had remained chaste after starting divorce procedures (§ 142), or could warn a man that his animals presented a public danger (§ 251). As with the popular representation for the entire town, we are also here uninformed about the membership, the competence, and the procedures of the gatherings of the inhabitants of a city quarter. Other subdivisions of the towns, such as the associations of merchants or of craftsmen, had their meetings as well, and spoke out with one voice. Assemblies were not limited to

---

[9] See André Finet in *La voix de l'opposition en Mésopotamie* (Brussels, 1973), 18.

native Mesopotamians: in the fifth century, we find evidence of an assembly of Egyptian settlers and other aliens in Babylon. We do not know how many people were needed before they could convene an assembly, but the right to congregate seems to have been unrestricted.

The record of the trial for homicide cited above is interesting as it shows some of the procedures of the assembly. The case was referred to this court by the king. Similar texts from the early second millennium state that the assembly was convened by the king,[10] a statement that casts some doubt on the independent nature of the assembly at that time. There seems to have been no debate about the guilt of the three assassins, but only about the responsibility of the victim's wife, who did not reveal that her husband had been murdered. Nine men argued that she was guilty of murder, while two stood up in her defence. The text is phrased as if we hear statements by both parties, but must be a fictitious rendering of the discussion, as all the accusers and all the defenders speak in unison. Finally the entire assembly pronounced a verdict against the woman, and the record states that she and the assassins were handed over to the executioner.

From the Old Assyrian trading colony at Kanish in Anatolia we have three very unusual, but also extremely fragmentary, texts that originally may have contained instructions on how the assembly there needed to consider a lawsuit. The reconstruction of the procedures remains highly tentative because of the poor condition of the documents. It seems that a lawsuit was first considered by the council of the 'big men' to see whether it needed to be dismissed or to be passed on to the full assembly.

Without ⟨the consent of⟩ a majority of the big men one single 'man of accounting' cannot ask the secretary to convene the assembly of the big and small men. If the secretary convened the assembly of the big and the small men without ⟨the consent of⟩ the big men, at the request of one single person, the secretary will pay 10 shekels of silver.[11]

Seemingly the council was divided into three groups in order to facilitate the deliberations. When a majority was in favour of con-

---

[10] See Stephen J. Lieberman, 'Nippur: City of Decisions', in Maria de Jong Ellis (ed.), *Nippur at the Centennial* (Philadelphia, 1992), 132.

[11] Ferris J. Stephens, 'The Cappadocian Tablets in the University of Pennsylvania Museum', *Journal of the Society of Oriental Research* 11 (1927), 122 no. 19, ll. 6–14, trans. after Mogens Trolle Larsen, *The Old Assyrian City-State* (Copenhagen, 1976), 284.

sidering the case, the secretary was ordered to convene the entire assembly. This assembly may have been divided into seven groups. Its decisions required a majority as well. We do not know how it was determined what the majority felt. Was a vote taken, and, if so, how? Further information about the proceedings of the assembly is not available, unless we take into consideration the literary descriptions of meetings of gods. Those divine meetings show little evidence of discussion, except when they were limited to a small number of prominent gods, who really debated the issue at hand. It has been stated that the proceedings of the assemblies were secret. This conclusion was based on the above-mentioned omen, but such secrecy seems rather unlikely to me. The proceedings were not written down because they were of no importance. It was only the final verdict that was considered significant enough to be recorded.

The participant in the assembly clearly took on a public profile, and was vulnerable to humiliation by his fellow citizens. Fear of this is expressed in prayers to gods:

> Do not abandon me, my lord, to the assembly where there are many who wish me ill.
> Do not let me come to harm in the assembly.[12]

In the famous poem of the Righteous Sufferer the central character's downfall includes the fact that 'my slave cursed me openly in the assembly ⟨of gentlefolk⟩'.[13] One gets the impression that intrigues were rife in the assemblies and that a citizen's good name could be destroyed by gossip, even by that of a slave.

The areas of competence of the assembly are again an extremely difficult matter to discuss. Almost all the records we have deal with legal decisions. The assemblies, both of the entire city and of the city quarters, acted as courts of law, next to those staffed with judges appointed by the king. In the homicide trial cited above, the king assigned the case to the assembly, but it is far from clear whether or not he did so for all cases. The cases heard were most commonly of a civil nature, but sometimes a criminal case was considered as well. We have a record from the mid-first millennium, for instance, describing how the assembly of Uruk examined

---

[12] Trans. Alasdair Livingstone, *Court Poetry and Literary Miscellanea* (Helsinki, 1989), 30–2, reverse ll. 11 and 13, quoted by permission.

[13] Trans. by Benjamin R. Foster, *From Distant Days* (Bethesda, 1995), 301 l. 89, quoted by permission.

the circumstances of a murder attempt on the royal commissioner of the Eanna temple. In this case the assembly only did the preliminary investigation, while the sentencing was passed on to royal judges. Civil cases usually involved disputed property, divorce, and other situations where the main stress lies on the fact that property needed to be transferred from one party to another according to the decision of the court. Hence, it should come as no surprise that these cases predominate in our records.

Was the assembly competent in other matters? A single letter from the Old Assyrian correspondence to the merchant colony in Anatolia, dating to the early second millennium, suggests so. The letter contains an order of the city of Assur to the colony to provide funds for the building of fortifications.[14] In the Old Assyrian correspondence in general 'the city' and 'the assembly' are used as synonyms, suggesting that a great deal of power was located in the assembly, comparable to the situation in classical Greece. Some optimistic scholars have therefore suggested that the assembly's areas of competence were all-encompassing in urban government. There is just not enough information to deny or confirm this view, in my opinion. Jacobsen even stated that the assembly originally had the powers to grant and to revoke kingship, a statement I will investigate below.

The image we thus obtain of the assembly is tantalizing, but at the same time exceedingly vague. We could see in it a meeting of citizens discussing widely ranging topics from lawsuits to the selection of their leaders. Participation can be seen as an act of public prominence, but also as a way of exposing oneself to intrigue and scorn. There is obviously nothing unusual about that, as public behaviour is always judged by others. But was the assembly a place where ambitious men and women, or men alone, gained public recognition? Were participants involved in debates using their rhetorical abilities to convince others of the correctness of their opinion? This is all open to our imagination, as no information for or against such conclusions is available to us.

The palace and the citizenry formed two separate political elements in the Mesopotamian city. Channels of communication between the two needed to exist, and these were the responsibility of a number of officials. The study of these officials is, again, very

---

[14] See Larsen, *Old Assyrian City-State*, 163.

difficult, because of the large numbers of titles we encounter and the vagueness of the duties each official had. We are overwhelmed by a mass of titles when we look at urban administration. For instance, in her study of the city of Sippar in the early second millennium, Rivkah Harris talks about the mayor, the chairman of the assembly, the overseer of the merchants, the governor, the *rabi sikkatim* (Akk.), the *sussikku* (Akk.), the *šakkanakku* (Akk.), the bailiff, the overseer of the barbers, the barber, the gatekeeper, the gateman, and the doorkeeper. She herself notes that 'officials bearing a disturbing variety of titles appear as chief administrators'.[15]

It is virtually impossible to determine the responsibilities of most officials with any accuracy, as a few examples will make clear. Two officials who seemingly played an important role in the government of the Mesopotamian city were the chairman of the assembly and the mayor. The first, chairman of the assembly, owes his English title to the Sumerian designation, *gal.ukken.na*, which literally translates as 'great one of the assembly', a wording that continued to be used even when the texts were written in Akkadian. He rarely appears in our sources, however, in connection with the assembly. Instead, he seems to have had the authority to hold people prisoner, and to have acted as an intermediary between the palace and the citizens. Therefore some scholars have insisted that the reference to the assembly in his title is inconsequential, and that he has no relationship at all to this institution.

Another common Akkadian title, *rabiānum*, bears very little resemblance to our image of a mayor, although we usually translate the Akkadian term as such. In Sippar the *rabiānum* appeared as the chairman of the court and as a witness. In the latter capacity he was almost always listed first, which seems to reflect his prominence. According to the Code of Hammurabi, the *rabiānum*, together with 'the city', was responsible for prosecuting robberies which took place in his city's territory (§§ 23–4), indicating that he was a high official, but without revealing much about his other functions. In Old Babylonian documents, the *rabiānum* often appears as a middleman in hiring contracts of harvest labourers. It seems that he acted as the intermediary between the palace and the townspeople

---

[15] Rivkah Harris, *Ancient Sippar: A Demographic Study of an Old Babylonian City (1894–1595 B.C.)* (Istanbul, 1975), 57–86.

who worked its lands. More than one *rabiānum* could function in a city at the same time, most likely because each ward had one. A recently excavated, and unfortunately not yet fully published, Old Babylonian text provides a less stereotypical view on the *rabiānum*. In Haradum, a Babylonian outpost on the Euphrates, some tablets were excavated in the house of the mayor located in the centre of town. The mayor, Habasanu, seems to have embezzled some of the funds his citizens had paid.

Concerning the silver, which Habasanu during his tenure as mayor had made the town pay, the entire town assembled and spoke in these terms to Habasanu: 'Of the silver which you made us pay, a great amount has stayed in your house, as well as the sheep which we gave on top as voluntary gifts.'[16]

This text suggests that the mayor collected the payments due by his citizens to pass them on to a higher authority, but that he had omitted to do the latter. Still, despite the numerous attestations of the title *rabiānum* in Old Babylonian documents, we can say very little with certainty about the office.

The title did not survive the end of the Old Babylonian dynasty, but a lesser authority, the *ḫazannum* (Akk.), seems to have taken over the duties of the *rabiānum*, and the translation 'mayor' is commonly used to render this title when it appears in texts written after 1500. A unique letter dating to the middle of the second millennium, found in the northern city of Nuzi, describes the duties of this office in some detail. It is a letter from the king of Arrapha to the mayor of Tashuhhe:

Thus says the mayor of Tashuhhe: 'The king has issued an order as follows: "Every mayor is responsible for the outlying territory of his city, and if there is a fortified settlement in the countryside around his city, he is also responsible for it. In the area of his city there should be no robbery, nor enemies murdering ⟨people⟩, nor the taking of booty. If it happens that there is a robbery, or enemies take booty and murder ⟨people⟩ within the territory of his city, the mayor shall pay damages. If a runaway from Arrapha runs away from the territory of his city and enters another country, the mayor shall pay damages. And if a fortified settlement within the territory of that city is abandoned, the mayor shall pay damages."'[17]

---

[16] Francis Joannès, 'Haradum et le pays de Suhum', *Archéologie* 205 (1985), 58.

[17] Ernest R. Lacheman, *Excavations at Nuzi* 6: *The Administrative Archives* (Cambridge, Mass., 1955), no. 1; trans. after A. Leo Oppenheim *et al.*, *The Assyrian Dictionary* 6, H (Chicago, 1956), 164–5.

This man's responsibilities were thus not limited to the confines of his city, but also extended to the surrounding countryside. He seems to have been personally answerable for crimes in his territory, and somehow had to prevent 'refugees' from escaping the area. Moreover, he had to ascertain that small fortified settlements surrounding the city were occupied. As he seems to have had to pay the damages out of his own pocket, the office must have come with pecuniary rewards to make it worth his while.

A unique, unofficial, glimpse at the mayor's status in the city is provided by a Babylonian folk-tale of the first millennium, 'The Poor Man of Nippur'.[18] The tale relates how a poor man, Gimil-Ninurta, was so tired of his lack of decent food that he decided to spend all he had on a goat to cook himself a fine meal. But then he remembered how he would not be able to provide a proper feast for his neighbours, family, and friends, and that he would incite their wrath if he did not invite them all. Thus he decided to go to the mayor of Nippur, offer him the goat, and hoped that in return he would be asked to join him in a nice dinner. But instead the mayor kept the good meat for himself, and gave Gimil-Ninurta the bones and gristle and some third-rate beer. The poor man decided to take a threefold revenge. The first trick he played on the mayor gives us some idea of that man's role in a city. Gimil-Ninurta went to the king and, without explanation, asked to be fitted out as a gentleman with fine clothes and a chariot, for a future payment in gold. He loaded a sealed box in his chariot and rode to Nippur where he was greeted by the mayor.

> He we[nt off] to the gate of the mayor of Nippur,
> The mayor came o[utside] to meet him,
> 'Who are you, my lord, who have travelled so la[te in the day]?'
> 'The king, your lord, sent me, to [    ]
> 'I have brought gold for Ekur, temple of Enlil.'
> The mayor slaughtered a fine sheep to make a generous
>     meal for him.[19]

In the middle of the night Gimil-Ninurta cried out that the box had been opened and the gold in it stolen, thrashed the mayor, and extorted payment in gold and fine clothes.

---

[18] For the most recent English trans. of this tale, used here, see Foster, *From Distant Days*, 357–62.

[19] Trans. ibid. 359, quoted by permission.

The text indicates that the mayor was the representative of the town who was in charge of greeting and entertaining royal emissaries on official business. It also shows again that he was held accountable for thefts in his territory. Obviously this does not tell us much about his daily duties. Yet, his status within the city seems clear: he acted as the intermediary between the palace and the citizenry. Many of the other officials we find attested in the texts played the same role. The contacts between the town communities and the crown were mediated by individuals acting as representatives. This practice was not limited to mayors for cities; nomadic tribes were also represented by their sheikhs in their contacts with the crown.

It is unclear who was responsible for the appointment of these representatives. Suggestions that they held their office only on an annual basis, and that they were elders of the town selected by their peers, have been shown to be false. In later periods mayors were seemingly appointed by the king; but was the king rubber-stamping a communal decision, or did he make the choice himself? The concept of a higher authority channelling its contacts with segments of the community through representative individuals was applied on other levels in the hierarchy of urban government as well. The subdivisions of the city mentioned above had the ability to discuss matters in their own assemblies, and to speak with one voice in their contacts with higher authorities. These contacts were mediated by a representative, be he elected by the people or selected by the king. Thus the mayor may have consulted with representatives of different city wards, while he acted as the representative of the entire city in its contacts with the king. When the palace demanded labour service from the citizens, it was the mayor's duty to gather the people; he probably relied on the representatives of the different wards to find the individual labourers. The only people who fell outside this structure were the so-called refugees, who were either new foreign arrivals, or people who had fled their social unit for whatever reason. The mayor was responsible for them as individuals.

The hierarchy of people representing segments of the population explains, in my opinion, the lack of information on urban government. This government was a very decentralized affair. Most of the responsibilities such as sanitation, policing, or the regulation of marriages and divorces, were not administered by the central power, but by the subdivisions of the towns. As problems were dealt with on a highly personal basis in groups of restricted sizes, they were not registered in writing. Only when a decision resulted in the transfer of property was a record needed, hence the predominance of the legal aspects of the urban government in our documentation.

Despite the citizenry's ability to congregate and debate matters of interest to them, they were not guaranteed the right to make decisions against the will of the king, whose powers were seemingly absolute. The relative powers of the citizenry and the king most likely varied with the nature of the state, and these variations obviously affected the decision-making process concerning urban affairs. The relationship between citizens and the king when city-states were standard would seem likely to have been different from when the city was just a minor part of an empire spreading over most of the Near East. It is my opinion that, with the progressive territorial expansion of the political units in Mesopotamia, the cities and their representatives gained increased political independence and influence. This is the reverse of the currently predominant view that Mesopotamian history evolved from 'primitive democracy' to a totalitarian state headed by an all-powerful king.

The concept of 'primitive democracy' was developed some fifty years ago by Thorkild Jacobsen. Observing the existence of assemblies with judicial powers in early second millennium Assyria and Babylonia, Jacobsen sought to determine whether they were the survival of an older tradition or the indication of something new. He discarded the second possibility 'since the entire drift of Mesopotamian political life and thought in the historical periods is wholeheartedly in the other direction. Throughout we find no signs of growing democratic ideas.'[20] He decided thus that the assembly was an old institution. Indeed he thought that it existed prior to the development of secular kingship in Mesopotamia.

Based primarily on literary material of the second millennium, Jacobsen painted an almost Biblical picture of the rise of kingship in the third millennium. After a period when the assembly elected a military leader in times of crisis, a period of 'primitive democracy', this power was usurped by the elected leader who forced the

---

[20] Thorkild Jacobsen, 'Primitive Democracy', *Journal of Near Eastern Studies* 2 (1943), 165.

citizens to appoint him king for life. This evolution perfectly parallels the depiction of the rise of kingship in the book of Samuel in the Bible. There the last judge, Saul, refused to relinquish his temporary powers, and thus introduced kingship among the Israelites. Jacobsen never pointed out this parallelism, perhaps because in Mesopotamia kingship was portrayed as a benefit to mankind, while the Bible always maintained a strong anti-royalist attitude.

Jacobsen's reconstruction relied extensively on a Babylonian literary text, usually referred to as the 'Epic of Creation'. The text was apparently composed in the twelfth century and celebrated the rise to kingship over the universe by Marduk, the god of Babylon. When the gods were threatened with annihilation by Tiamat, enraged by the murder of her husband Apsu, the wise Ea pushed forward his favourite son Marduk to counter the threat. Marduk offered his services on the condition that he would be accorded supreme powers. The gods agreed to grant his wish during an assembly meeting, which was more a banquet with limitless supplies of beer and wine than a serious discussion of the problem at hand, and Marduk was crowned king before he dealt with Tiamat. After his victory he organized the universe, and finally demanded the building of Babylon as his reward. The events depicted are thus not exactly a usurpation by an elected leader of powers only granted temporarily, but crucial to Jacobsen's thesis is the fact that Marduk had been originally elected as king by the assembly of the gods. Combining this with information from other pieces of literature, Jacobsen pictured the existence in early Mesopotamia of a popular assembly with extensive powers, including the election of the king. By the mid-third millennium the assembly's powers were greatly restricted by life-long rulers, according to Jacobsen, and the subsequent history of Mesopotamia showed an increased totalitarianism. Emperors such as Assurbanipal, who ruled an area from Iran to Egypt, did not need to consult with their citizens.

Leaving aside the issue of the origins of kingship, difficult to study due to the lack of contemporary documentation, the underlying view of Jacobsen's entire argument is that the original, and wide powers of the citizenry were eroded and replaced by the absolute rule of an individual. Although Jacobsen never indicated his own awareness of it, his reconstruction resembles the Marxist model where the communal mode of production is thought to have been replaced by the slave-owning mode of production; from a society where the community was of supreme importance to one where a despotic king was in charge. Their discussion has been framed in the context of the perceived dichotomy between the community and the palace, a dichotomy that does not take into account the private citizens as members of individual households.

Can we discern an evolution from 'primitive democracy' to an absolute monarchy in the Mesopotamian record? I believe not, and wish to postulate instead the reverse: as the territory ruled by Mesopotamian kings became larger and the population more diverse, the urban citizenry gained importance in its relationship to the king. Instead of searching for vague clues of citizens' power in the records of the third millennium, it is more useful to study the status of urban residents in the first millennium, when records are more abundant. We see that these residents were granted a large degree of independence, especially exemptions from royal taxation, corvée, and military duties, which were the primary areas of interaction between the king and his subjects. Also, the physical integrity of citizens was guaranteed, and their blood could not be shed by the king or his representatives. The freedom from taxation and service was thought to be the result of divine protection over the cities, indicated by the Akkadian word *kidinnu*, a divinely enforced security which was probably symbolized by an emblem set up in a prominent place in the cities. We have a list of declarations from Assyrian kings stating that they granted or re-established this status to various cities. The beneficiaries were mostly ancient cult centres in Babylonia: Babylon, Borsippa, Nippur, Sippar, and Uruk. In Assyria the old capital and cult centre Assur commonly received this status, and Harran was occasionally mentioned. One king extended the practice to cities of the state of Urartu in Anatolia, but this seems to have been a special occurrence.

The protection was taken very seriously: the most illustrative example of it is perhaps found in a letter written by the assembly of Babylon to the Assyrian king Assurbanipal and his brother Shamash-shuma-ukin, who was the king of Babylonia. In the letter the citizens requested that the protection granted to them be extended to all residents of the city, even those of foreign origin. They alluded to an earlier statement of the king that 'whoever enters

Babylon is assured permanent protection . . . Even a dog who enters it will not be killed.'[21] An Assyrian preceptive text of the first half of the first millennium, 'The Advice to a Prince', makes a great deal of the preservation of the protected status of Babylonian cities. It states, for instance,

If ⟨the prince⟩ took money of citizens of Babylon and appropriated ⟨it⟩ for ⟨his own⟩ property, ⟨or⟩ heard a case involving Babylonians but dismissed it for triviality, Marduk, lord of heaven and earth, will establish his enemies over him and grant his possessions and property to his foe . . . If he called up the whole of Sippar, Nippur, and Babylon to impose forced labour on the peoples aforesaid, requiring of them service at the recruiter's cry, Marduk, sage of the gods, deliberative prince, will turn his land over to his foe so that the troops of his land will do forced labour for his foe. Anu, Enlil, and Ea, the great gods who dwell in heaven and earth, have confirmed in their assembly the exemption of these ⟨people from such obligations⟩.[22]

The importance of these protected status grants in the imperial policy of the Assyrians has long been recognized. Cities were used by the Assyrian kings to act as outposts of their rule in an often hostile countryside, including enemies from Egypt to the Chaldean tribes in the marshes of southern Iraq. The isolation of the urban centres in ill-secured territory is clearly visible in a letter by an official of Nippur to the Assyrian king Esarhaddon: 'The king knows that all countries hate us because of the land of Assyria. We cannot set foot in any country. Wherever we go we will be killed, as people say "Why did you submit to Assyria?" So now we have locked our gates, and do not go out at all.'[23] The Assyrian kings needed to maintain good urban contacts, especially with the cities of Babylonia, in order to secure their rule over the area. They needed to negotiate with the citizens, and could not simply impose their will upon them, as is clear from this letter written to King Tiglath-Pileser III by two of his officials:

On the twenty-eighth we came to Babylon. We took our stand before the Marduk-gate ⟨and⟩ talked with the *man* of Babylon. X, servant of Mukin-zēr, the Chaldean was at his side. When they came out they were standing

---

[21] Robert H. Pfeiffer, *State Letters of Assyria* (American Oriental Series 6; New Haven, 1935), no. 62, ll. 9 and 11.

[22] Trans. Foster, *From Distant Days*, 391–2, quoted by permission.

[23] Pfeiffer, *State Letters*, no. 123, ll. 11–20.

before the gate with the Babylonians. We said this to the Babylonians: 'Why are you hostile to us for the sake of them? Their place is with the Chaldean tribesmen [ ] Babylon indeed shows favour to a Chaldean! Your privileges (*kidinnūtu*) have been firmly established.' I kept going to Babylon: we used many arguments with them. The Five and the Ten were present. They would not agree to come out, they would not talk to us: they ⟨just⟩ kept sending us messages . . .[24]

The privileged status of certain cities indicates the power of the urban citizenry in general; this is not contradicted by the fact that only a small number of cities in Babylonia are attested as having received the exemptions from royal taxation and service. We have to keep in mind that Babylonia in the early first millennium was sparsely urbanized, and that few cities, other than those mentioned by the Assyrian kings, existed at that time.[25] The fact that few Assyrian cities received privileges is a reflection of the reality that Assyria was securely held by its rulers. But the situation in Babylonia was different: because of its distance from the heartland of Assyria—and its unruly countryside—the Assyrians needed outposts where the allegiance of the people was assured. Those were the ancient cities, which were given special privileges in return.

The special status of citizens was neither new to the early first millennium, nor did it end when the Assyrian empire collapsed. From the mid-second millennium onward, divine protection of the citizens of certain urban centres is attested, and the use of the Akkadian term *kidinnu* coincided with the growth of the territorial state in Mesopotamia. With the end of the Assyrian empire in the late seventh century, the institution of the *kidinnu* disappeared, except for what may have been a nostalgic revival under King Nabonidus (ruled 555–539)—but that did not mean that the rulers felt secure enough to ignore the urban populations. The rulers of the neo-Babylonian dynasty (625–539) did not boast in their inscriptions about their far-flung and successful foreign campaigns,

[24] ND 2632 ll. 5–22, H. W. F. Saggs, 'The Nimrud Letters, 1952—Part I', *Iraq* 17 (1955), 23.

[25] For the low level of urbanization, see J. A. Brinkman, *Prelude to Empire: Babylonian Society and Politics, 747–626 B.C.* (Philadelphia, 1984), 3–10. Brinkman proposes, however, that areas outside the former core area of Babylonia show an increased level of urbanization. B. Landsberger, *Archiv für Orientforschung* 10 (1935–6), 142, suggested that the cities mentioned were representative of Babylonia in general.

but commemorated the fact that they restored temples in their homeland. This work was not done for purely pious reasons, but to ingratiate the kings with the local populations. At that time, the temple organization and the citizenry can be regarded more or less as the same thing. The important families of Babylonian cities divided the temple offices up among themselves, and profited extensively from the temple income. They expressed their views in powerful temple assemblies. As Dandamaev stated, 'a characteristic feature of these cities was self-rule by free and legally equal members of society united in a popular assembly (*puḫru*) around the principal temple of the city'.[26]

The privileged treatment by rulers did not end when Mesopotamia lost its independence to rulers from Iran and Greece. The Hellenistic rulers respected the rights of Babylonian cities, and exempted them from taxes and duties, while allowing them to continue Babylonian administrative practices. The temple continued to play a central role in the city administration, and its head, assisted by a council, became the chief authority in the city. Royal supervision was maintained through a number of officials. This does not need to be regarded as the introduction of the Greek *polis* system into Mesopotamia, but can be explained as the continuation and intensification of older practices whose roots went back for many centuries. The Seleucid city was an autonomous community, centred around a temple where most leading citizens held offices, and with a self-governing body, the assembly. Royal power was absolute in matters of national importance, but it did not interfere with the daily problems of urban life.

It cannot be denied that prior to the mid-second millennium, cities could have been treated with special respect by kings. But before that time the city really was the state, and the palace organization was more pervasive in the urban context. Control of urban population and affairs was much simpler under such conditions. Even when the ruler of one city-state temporarily controlled other cities, the system of government by the local palace was not abandoned. Governors rather than independent rulers continued to fulfil the role of head of the local palace organization, with close citizen interaction. That urban favours had to be bought at times is

---

[26] Muhammed A. Dandamaev, 'Neo-Babylonian Society and Economy', *The Cambridge Ancient History*, 2nd edn. 3: 2 (Cambridge, 1991), 252–3.

shown by the example of King Ishme-Dagan of Isin (ruled 1953–1935), who claims to have freed the inhabitants of Nippur from taxes and military service. But the practice was much less common than in later centuries, when it was a necessity for rulers to curry the favour of urban residents. In the first millennium the empires of Assyria and Babylonia were so large in extent and diverse in nature, with numerous uncontrollable tribes present even in the heartland of Mesopotamia, that the kings needed the cities as pillars for their control of the area. It was necessary to obtain the support of the urban population to effect government policies against those non-urban elements. In order to placate the cities, the kings awarded them numerous special rights.

When we try then to answer the question of who governed an ancient Mesopotamian city, I think we can say that the citizenry itself was most often in charge. Citizens had certain obligations to the king—primarily supplying taxes, corvée labour, and military service—but for the rest, they were mostly left alone. Representatives of the citizenry played the role of ambassadors to the king: they provided the vital contacts needed and bore a lot of the responsibility when things went wrong. They may have been elected by their peers or designated by the palace from among the prominent citizens. The power and the independence of the citizenry seems to have grown over the centuries with the increase in size of the political units in Mesopotamia. Obviously, this was not a simple progression, and at times rulers must have clamped down on urban freedom, but a general tendency towards greater autonomy for the citizens is visible. The palace maintained a hands-off attitude and did not meddle with urban affairs. Such a situation is not unique in the history of the Middle East. The Ottoman emperors also used such an approach towards their urban subjects.[27] On the one hand, it helped preserve the rights of the free citizens, on the other hand it facilitated transactions between the state and its subjects. This lack of intrusion resulted, however, in a failure to record urban governmental matters. A modern-day scholar exposed to extreme government interference in daily life may pine for such independence, but it clearly does not help in the search for a glimpse into the daily life of an ancient Mesopotamian.

[27] See Abraham Marcus, *The Middle East on the Eve of Modernity* (New York, 1989), 76–7.

BIBLIOGRAPHY

Discussions about kingship in Mesopotamia have focused on its relationship to divinity or on royal titulary; for example, Henri Frankfort, *Kingship and the Gods* (Chicago, 1948); C. J. Gadd, *Ideas of Divine Rule in the Ancient Near East* (London, 1948); and M.-J. Seux, *Épithètes royales akkadiennes et sumériennes* (Paris, 1967). Some useful papers on kingship in various periods of Mesopotamian history can be found in Paul Garelli (ed.), *Le Palais et la royauté* (Paris, 1974).

The assembly in Mesopotamia has been studied by numerous authors, in particular Thorkild Jacobsen's fundamental article, 'Primitive Democracy in Ancient Mesopotamia', *Journal of Near Eastern Studies* 2 (1943), 159–72, which reflects many of the topics discussed in this chapter. He also discussed primitive democracy in 'Early Political Development in Mesopotamia', *Zeitschrift für Assyriologie* 52 (1957), 91–140. Both studies were reprinted in *Towards the Image of Tammuz* (Cambridge, Mass, 1970). An attempt at elucidating some of the questions left unanswered by Jacobsen, by using parallels from ancient Sparta and Rome, was made by Geoffrey Evans, 'Ancient Mesopotamian Assemblies', *Journal of the American Oriental Society* 78 (1958), 1–11, 114–15.

A special volume devoted to 'political opposition' in Mesopotamia, which considered this to be opposition to royal power, was published by André Finet (ed.), *La Voix de l'opposition en Mésopotamie* (Brussels, 1973). It contains a number of interesting papers, but is very hard to find. The assembly in Assur and its colony Kanish in the early second millennium has been thoroughly investigated by Mogens Trolle Larsen, *The Old Assyrian City-State and its Colonies* (Copenhagen, 1976), 160–92. Mid-first-millennium Babylonian assemblies have been studied by Muhammed A. Dandamaev, 'The Neo-Babylonian Popular Assembly', in P. Vavroušek and V. Souček (eds.), *Šulmu* (Prague, 1988), 63–71. The most recent treatment of this topic is by Mario Liverani, who is the first to look at the institution in a broad temporal perspective: 'Nelle pieghe del despotismo: Organismi rappresentativi nell'antico oriente', *Studi Storici* 34 (1993), 7–33.

For the final periods of Mesopotamian history, the discussion of the role of the assembly has been marred by the issue of whether or not it showed any resemblance to that of the Greek *polis*, ignoring the earlier history of this institution in Mesopotamia. See, for instance, G. Kh. Sarkisian, 'City Land in Seleucid Babylonia', in I. M. Diakonoff (ed.), *Ancient Mesopotamia: Socio-Economic History* (Moscow, 1969), 312–31, who wants to see Greek-styled *poleis* in Babylonia; for the opposing view see R. J. van der Spek, 'The Babylonian City', in Amélie Kuhrt and Susan Sherwin-White (eds.), *Hellenism and the East* (London, 1987), 57–74.

For the study of officials and their roles, see primarily investigations of specific titles. For early second millennium Babylonia, Arnold Walther, *Das altbabylonische Gerichtswesen* (Leipziger Semitische Studien VI; 1917), is still a fundamental study. For Assyria in the first millennium, a handy article is Jana Pecirková, 'The Administrative Organization of the Neo-Assyrian Empire', *Archiv Orientální* 45 (1977), 211–28; this study is heavily based on J. V. Kinnier-Wilson, *The Nimrud Wine Lists* (London, 1972).

For a review of the material on *kidinnu*, see W. F. Leemans, '*Kidinnu*: Un symbole de droit babylonien', in *Symbolae Van Oven* (Leiden, 1946), 36–61. Hanoch Reviv, '*Kidinnu*: Observations on privileges of Mesopotamian Cities', *Journal of the Economic and Social History of the Orient* 31 (1988), 286–98, provides a recent survey of the same data.

The relationship between the king and the citizenry has been regarded in the context of community rights versus royal power by Marxist scholars. See the work of I. M. Diakonoff, for instance, 'The rise of the despotic State in Ancient Mesopotamia', in I. M. Diakonoff (ed.), *Ancient Mesopotamia: Socio-Economic History* (Moscow, 1969), 173–203; and that of his student N. B. Jankowska, 'Communal Self-Government and the King in the State of Arrapkha', *Journal of the Economic and Social History of the Orient* 12 (1969), 233–82.

Discussions of the preceptive text 'Advice to a Prince' have focused on the date of the piece, which now seems to have a precursor in the late second millennium. Its relevance in practice is clear from a letter addressed to King Esarhaddon, see Erica Reiner, 'The Babylonian Fürstenspiegel in Practice', in J. N. Postgate (ed.), *Societies and Languages of the Ancient Near East: Studies in Honour of I. M. Diakonoff* (Warminster, 1982), 320–3.

# 7

# Feeding the Citizens

Any city requires an economic base for its survival, enabling its residents to feed themselves and remain in the same place all the year round; the Mesopotamian city is no exception. As I pointed out before, the city played a central role in the entire economic organization of Mesopotamia, permitting the exchange of goods among various groups: farmers, fishermen, herders, and so on. Moreover, the city was the only place where people not involved in primary food production, such as specialist craftsmen, administrators, and cult personnel, could be supported thanks to an available agricultural surplus. Today, we distinguish between three sectors in our economy: primary food production, secondary manufacture, and tertiary services. In the following three chapters I will discuss these in turn. A lot of information is available on Mesopotamian economic activity, as it often involves the transfer of goods which needed to be put down in writing. Not surprisingly, the textual data are not of a descriptive character, but provide small details of long chains of interactions leading to a finished product, be it food item, manufactured object, or financial settlement. These details need to be placed in a larger context to be properly understood, and in the following chapters I will try to provide a context for the information available to us about various economic activities, rather than give an overview of what we know about them.

In a pre-industrial society agriculture is the most important economic activity, and without an agricultural base no city could survive. Despite our inability to estimate urban population sizes with any reasonable degree of certainty, we can state beyond doubt that many ancient Mesopotamian cities relied on non-urban resources for their food provisions. While certain city residents were involved in agricultural production, and the existence of fields within city walls is attested in some texts, the produce from these sources was insufficient to feed all inhabitants. In the survey of urban origins I argued that agricultural exchange was one of the determining factors in the rise of cities in the south. The provisioning of cities with food was thus the most important sphere of interaction between cities and their hinterlands. It concerned multiple steps in a process that was influenced by geographical, social, and political conditions along the way. A tentative outline of that process can only be sketched, but will reveal some of the complexity involved.

### HOW DID THE HARVESTS REACH THE CITIES?

As usual we do not have at our disposal a text, or even a string of texts, that describes what happened, for instance, with a barleycorn from the moment it was harvested to when it was consumed as the beer of an urban resident. In order to reconstruct these events we have to put together a jigsaw puzzle with most of its pieces lost, and even whose general outline is missing. Therefore, I will use here, as a guide, a purely theoretical article, written by a specialist in modern-day agricultural management, yet published in a volume devoted to ancient Near Eastern bureaucracies.[1] In this article Robert Hunt reconstructs the sequence of actions that led to the provisioning of cities, and focuses especially on the role of bureaucrats in that process. His reconstruction can be used to provide a framework to the information given in the ancient Mesopotamian sources, and will enable us to outline the process of urban provisioning.

In order to describe the setting of this process, it is perhaps useful to summarize first the food resources which were available to Mesopotamia's urban civilization. These included not only products grown in fields, orchards, and gardens, or acquired through herding, but also food gathered through fishing, hunting, and plant collection. Enormous amounts and varieties of salt- and fresh water fish were caught, as well as other water creatures, such as crabs and turtles; these were to be found in the Persian Gulf, the southern marshes, and the rivers and canals. The hunting of water-fowl,

---

[1] Robert C. Hunt, 'The Role of Bureaucracy in the Provisioning of Cities: a Framework for Analysis of the Ancient Near East', in McGuire Gibson and R. D. Biggs (eds.), *The Organization of Power: Aspects of Bureaucracy in the Ancient Near East* (Chicago, 1987), 161–92.

birds, and game, such as gazelles, mountain goats, and wild pigs was common, as was the collection of bird and turtle eggs. The roots, bulbs, berries, and nuts of wild plants, rushes, and trees were collected, and all found their way into the kitchen. Salt, used as a condiment and for pickling, was washed from rivers and marshes.

The staple of the Mesopotamian diet was made up of cereals, primarily barley and, to a lesser extent, emmer and wheat. An abundance of terms for grain appears in the native terminology, not all of which we can match up with actual species, and the preference for crops varied according to region and probably also time period. Sesame was grown for oil production. The plant was imported, probably from the Indus Valley, in the mid-third millennium and thrived in Mesopotamia from that time.

Orchards were composed of a large variety of trees, but the date-palm was always of primary importance. In Babylonia this tree was ubiquitous along waterways, and formed dense palm groves around the cities. In Assyria, however, the climate was insufficiently hot to expect high yields from date palms, and therefore the tree was less common there. Other fruit trees were cultivated all over the region in various settings: among date palms, in special orchards, and in the mountains. Fruits harvested from these trees included pomegranates, apples, figs, and grapes. Vines were native to many regions and wine was pressed from the earliest periods. A variety of vegetables was grown in special gardens or within orchards using the trees for shade: onions, garlic, lettuces, cucumbers, beans, lentils, peas, and many more.

The last major sector of agriculture was herding, especially the herding of sheep and, to a much lesser extent, of goats. Immense flocks were kept on the fringes of the cultivated zones throughout Mesopotamia. Cattle were rarer and were kept closer to home due to their need for fodder to supplement grazing. It is important to keep in mind that herds of cattle, sheep, and goats were kept primarily for their renewable resources—milk, wool, and hair—not for their meat. As only cows and goats were milked, the innumerable sheep in Mesopotamia were not a major source of food, but reared for their wool. On the other hand, analyses of excavated bones show that the domesticated pig was commonly eaten. Finally, besides these larger animals, bees were kept for the production of honey.

The Mesopotamian could thus potentially rely on a highly varied diet. The ingredients were derived from a wide range of sources and some could have been home-grown by urban residents: a cow could be kept in the courtyard, for instance, or a vegetable plot could be maintained near the house. Most foods were produced in the countryside, however, and certain segments of the urban society needed to obtain them from producers to whom they were not related. These producers were not only villagers permanently residing in the countryside, but also nomadic and seminomadic herdsmen. Of all food products, bread and beer were the most basic in the Mesopotamian's mind, and were considered to be synonymous with food and drink in general. Hence, I will investigate how bread and beer were produced, from the growth of the cereal to the baking of the bread or the brewing of the beer. The production processes of bread and beer are entirely similar until the final stages; therefore their progress from the producer to the consumer can be studied jointly. For other foods, the sequence of steps needed to bring them to the consumers was most likely somewhat different, but documentation about them is scarcer, and we can surmise that the procedures were as equally complex as they were for cereals.

Cereals were grown primarily in fields located outside the cities. A basic—and very thorny—question concerns the matter of ownership of agricultural land in ancient Mesopotamia, which affects the access of urban residents to the produce. It is now certain that, throughout the history of the region, both privately and institutionally owned land existed. Detailed knowledge of the situation in various periods and regions escapes us, however, and different conclusions can be drawn from the scarce source material.

Ownership of land appeared in various forms in Mesopotamia. There is a general lack of documentation on the communal ownership of land, owing to the fact that work on land of this type was part of the subsistence economy, not of the redistributive economy which dominates our textual sources. Members of the commune farmed it for their own needs, and very little, if any, surplus was produced for the benefit of urban residents or institutions. Therefore little or no evidence on this type of land is found in the written records of the cities, and its role for urban provisioning was minimal. Individually owned private land is another matter. It could conceivably be of two types: first, that of individuals who remained in villages and had full control over the land they worked, and second, absentee-owned land, either acquired by urban residents from villagers or retained by people who had migrated to the city. The first type is part of the subsistence economy and, for that reason, is scarcely documented. The second, however, was very important for the provisioning of urban residents. From very early on in Mesopotamian history, the written documentation contains sales of landed property, and investment in rural real estate by wealthy citizens is a constant feature of subsequent history. Limitations on this practice seem to have been imposed in certain periods and places, such as Arrapha in the middle of the second millennium where land seemingly could be transferred only to a family member. How common and successful these restrictions were is hard to say. Several means of circumventing them, such as fictional adoptions, were used and the lack of land sales in our documentation need not be interpreted as the result of such legal restrictions. The migration of large landowners to cities can be postulated on the basis of comparisons with more recent practices in the Middle East, although such moves are not detailed in our sources. Yet it is safe to suggest that many urban residents who had acquired fields, or landowners who had left their fields for a city life, did not work the land personally. Arrangements for the exploitation of the fields and the distribution of its produce had to be made. These issues will be addressed presently, after a discussion of palace and temple ownership of agricultural land.

The extent of palace and temple holdings of land varied considerably in different periods, and at times there must have been little or no difference between the two types of land. As we have seen, the temples were the first central institutions in Babylonian society and their resources were enormous in the early third millennium. But, with the rise of secular kingship, the palace obtained a greater importance in the economy, and certain kings may have merged the temple and crown lands under their control. In later periods in Assyria the crown seems to have had ultimate authority over most of the fields, and with widespread foreign conquests and the development of marginal areas by deported populations, crown domains must have been enormous. Meanwhile, in first-millennium Babylonia the temples seem to have been the major landowners, while the palace acted only as a large private household. But temple administrations were closely supervised by the palace and the crown thus managed these temple assets as well. When the Persians conquered Mesopotamia, royal administrators were granted large domains by the king and the latter was the ultimate proprietor of much of the land, a practice continued by Hellenistic Seleucid rulers. Interestingly, the latter donated some of it to cities, perhaps reviving the practice of communal land ownership. Private land continued to exist, however. When the Seleucids started to tax the sale of such property around 270 BC, the deeds of these transactions had to be written in Greek on perishable parchment, and henceforth land disappears from our documentation.

Land held both institutionally and by the urban gentry was not farmed by its owners. Different methods were used in order to assure that it was worked with the least possible trouble for the landlords. Three arrangements were common throughout the history of the region, and were often used simultaneously. Some agricultural labourers were directly dependent on the proprietors, while many estates were worked by tenant farmers. Finally, people were granted land by their employer as a reward for their service. The last agreement was often made with administrators of palaces and temples, who thus joined the ranks of urban landlords, if not legally, at least in practice.

Exploitation by personnel dependent on the owner seems to have been the least desirable. The large landlords, especially palaces and temples, were confronted with the task of managing, guarding, and rewarding with rations and sometimes salaries, an enormous labour force. These workers were the owners' responsibility in years of bad as well as good harvests. They had to be housed and fed when there was no agricultural activity, which was a large part of the year, and they had to be guarded. The latter required an army that, in the Bronze Age at least, would have been scarcely better equipped than the workmen who handled hoes and sickles. In the third millennium the southern Mesopotamian kingdoms still exploited many of their fields directly, but in the early second millennium such arrangements became rarer, as the palace and private landowners began to avoid the use of full-time dependants on their estates.

Instead, the second arrangement, work by tenant farmers, was much more convenient for the landowners, and probably also more rewarding for the labourers. Tenant farmers were allowed to work the land in return for a share of the yield, or a payment in kind or in silver. Many different arrangements were worked out, and the tenants' rewards depended on factors such as amount of labour invested, quality of the field, and the relationship to the landlord. When a new field was developed by a farmer, he was not required to pay any dues in the first year, and paid only a reduced rate in the second year. We have to remember that labour was not always abundantly available, so we cannot imagine a system that was based on the absolute exploitation of farmers by the landlords. The use of tenant farmers was beneficial to the owners, who were guaranteed a certain income from their land without having to supervise or support the tenants year round. It was a popular arrangement throughout Mesopotamian history.

The third way in which the palaces and the temples used their land holdings was by awarding their usufruct to people who provided the institutions with rents or labour. The labour could be quite varied in nature, and included military and administrative services, craft production, and agricultural work such as fishing, herding, and even farming. Hence, someone who ploughed palace lands could be given the use of a field as a reward, and the beneficiaries of these land grants were not necessarily urban citizens. The land was awarded to the individual who provided the services, and withdrawn at his death or when he defaulted on his obligations. But in practice we see how frequently the land passed on from father to son without the ability of the owner to reclaim rights to the property. By receiving the usufruct of these demesnes the urban beneficiaries obtained direct access to land, and needed to organize its exploitation as if they were the legal owners. Hence, they became hardly distinguishable from other urban landowners.

In addition to these full-time arrangements for the cultivation of institutional lands, additional resources could be enlisted through hirings or the levying of corvée labour in times of intense demand for manpower, such as during the harvest. Throughout Mesopotamian history we find evidence of such arrangements, but it seems improbable that the institutions ever relied on them as their main supplies for manpower. Obviously all harvests had to be collected in the same season, and free labourers had to worry about their own fields. Hence, the institutions had to lure them with sufficiently high salaries to make it worth their while. Also the levying of substantial numbers of workers would be counter-productive, as other harvests would be left uncollected.

The way in which the cereals reached the cities depended on the manner of exploitation of the fields. Some means of provisioning are entirely undocumented: an urban landowner probably had food delivered by farmers from his estate, a transaction that took place completely within the household and did not need to be put down in writing. Small independent farmers possibly peddled some of their produce in the cities, again not leaving a trace in the written record. But large landowners, both individuals and institutions, needed a more elaborate system of organization. We see here an evolution in Mesopotamian history from close supervision to a reliance on intermediary agents.

The system of direct control can be described most easily, as it involves more bureaucratic supervision which required record keeping. In the third millennium, the palace and temple administrations supervised every step of agricultural production on their estates. We find documentation from these institutions about the preparation of fields, seeding, irrigation, and harvesting. After the harvest, which took place in the months April and May, the cereals needed processing for preservation, and preparation for consumption. The work included threshing, winnowing, sieving, and storing. All these activities were overseen by palace or temple bureaucrats, and could probably be studied by a close examination of, for instance, the texts of the state of Ur in the twenty-first century. Strict control was of the utmost importance, and the barley had to be well preserved: if a moist batch ended up in the storage house, it could cause the destruction of the entire harvest.

Tenant farmers had to pay their rents in cereals on the threshing floor, where the entire yield of the field was openly visible to all interested parties. At that moment the share owed to the landlord joined his other grain, and probably from then on the owner took full responsibility over it. The tenants took their share back home with them. The threshing floors were probably in the possession of the large organizations, and worked with their own labour force, both human and animal. The tenant had to pay a fee for its use. When animals were not readily available, they were hired for the occasion. An early second-millennium letter from northern Babylonia gives some details on this matter:

To my commander say, thus speaks Mannum-mēshu-liṣṣur: . . . 'The oxen and slave-girls of the house are well. 12,880 litres of barley have been produced on the threshing floor of the city Egaba. Excluding the expenditures for the threshing floor, I have measured and recorded the barley, and they have taken it to Egaba. At the threshing floor of Lammaja we will be finished with the threshing on the seventh day of the month Simânu (May–June). We have threshed it with hired oxen and workmen' . . .[2]

It is likely that threshing floors were spread throughout the countryside. Assyrian texts often refer to them in the description of an agricultural estate, and each village had one or more threshing floors. They needed to be close to the fields, as it is doubtful that unprocessed barley was transported over long distances.

After the cereal was treated, it was stored until needed for the preparation of bread or beer. Substantial storage was probably located near the threshing floor. Farming animals required fodder, and seed needed to be kept for the next year's planting. Dependent farmers were probably also provided with their rations from a local storage house. Numerous small magazines, named after the person who administered them, are attested around Ur in the late third millennium. They were not only used for cereals but for keeping an amazing variety of goods: '[from] metal utensils, weapons (maces), furniture, cartwheels, balances, boxes, vats, querns and supplies of linens, wool and cloth, to various woods, aromatics, oils, and foodstuff such as grains, milk and cheese, honey, dates, wine, etc. In almost all cases small quantities are kept in stock.'[3] Due to the absence of archaeological evidence from the Mesopotamian countryside, we have little idea what these storage houses could have looked like. The only information presently available is from small rural sites, in the middle Habur region in northern Syria, such as Tell ʿAtij. They were equipped with silos and food-processing facilities such as mills, ovens, and cooking vats, used for processing the grains, parching them, and boiling them into foods such as bulgur. These sites were located at a great distance from the urban centres they served, including the city of Mari, some 250 kilome-

---

[2] R. Frankena, *Tabulae Cuneiformes a de Liagre Böhl collectae* IV (Leiden, 1965), no. 54 ll. 1–3, 6–15; trans. after R. Frankena, *Briefe aus der Leidener Sammlung* (Altbabylonische Briefe 3; Leiden, 1968), 42–3.

[3] Thorkild Jacobsen, *Towards the Image of Tammuz and other Essays on Mesopotamian History and Culture*, (Cambridge, Mass., 1970), 424 n. 18.

tres away, but this was an unusual circumstance, as I will show later.

The grain needed for urban residents was shipped to the cities to be stored there. Boats were used for this purpose, because they provided a cheap means of transportation and could easily navigate the canals connecting the cities with the fields. These vessels are attested in the Babylonian texts as having a capacity of up to 36,000 litres. Chariots and pack animals were also utilized for grain transport but to a lesser extent. Obviously theft during the trip must have been a concern to the owner. The case of the embezzlement of enormous amounts of grain in his care by captain Khnum-nakht in twelfth-century Egypt is famous, but in the Mesopotamian sources we do not find anything comparable. In Egypt the institutional landowners protected themselves against such dangers by having the amount of grain checked by scribes both on the threshing floor and before it entered the granary, but again no known Mesopotamian sources include such accounts. This is all the more surprising since we know that theft from the granaries was not uncommon. An explanation for this silence may be found in the fact that most trips were of a short distance. The Egyptian case involved travel from the Delta to the first cataract, a journey of some 1,000 kilometres. In early Mesopotamia, most food was grown locally, as I hope to show later, thus minimizing the occasion for theft by shippers.

Where canals entered the cities, it was probably possible for the boats to moor near the urban storage facilities. All of the monumental palaces and temples appear to have contained magazines. Yet these cannot have been the only storage facilities in town. A study of third- and second-millennium palaces concludes that the store-rooms in them were too small to contain more than what was immediately used for the feeding of the palace personnel.[4] The only urban granaries excavated so far were discovered in the mid-third-millennium city of Shuruppak in central Babylonia. In the northern sector of the city more than thirty silos were found, dug some 8 metres deep into the ground, and with diameter of about 4 metres. They were lined with two courses of bricks, and there is some

[4] Jean Margueron, *Recherches sur les palais mésopotamiens de l'âge du bronze* Tome 1, Texte (Paris, 1982), 549–55.

evidence that they were roofed. Each of them would have had a capacity of about 100 cubic metres. It has been calculated that the contents of all of them could have fed 20,000 persons for a period of six months, and that may have been the total population of the city.[5] A few iconographic representations permit us to visualize grain silos, although of a different type than those excavated in Shuruppak. Sealings from western Iran, dated around 3000, represent domed buildings, in one case clearly built upon a wooden infrastructure (Fig. 7.1). The image shows ladders placed against these domes and men climbing to the top with jars to pour the contents into the building.

The difficulties facing a man or woman in charge of the storage of grain were numerous. Moisture, insects, and rodents could all cause damage; omens, for instance, foresee the infestation of granaries by insects or by 'black spots'. But human predators also existed. The physical barriers that could be put up against thieves were not strong. Doors were made of reeds or low quality wood, and no great effort was needed to break through them. Moreover, there were no locks that could resist a break-in. The system used to secure the doors was very simple: a hook or rope attached to the door was latched to a knob stuck in the adjoining wall. Then, a small amount of clay was pressed over the knob, and the official in charge of the magazine rolled a seal over it. When the door needed to be opened, the clay sealing was broken off, a process that did not require any strength or special tools. Still this system seems to have been quite efficient. It provided a psychological barrier rather than a physical one. The thief knew that a forbidden act was performed when the seal was broken, and an unsealed door was one that had been opened illicitly. Only the officials in charge could break the seal as only they were able to reseal the door, a privilege that gave them and their office much prestige and power. The device was not flawless, however, and evidence for theft from granaries appears.

Oppenheim has stated that, in the late Babylonian period, grain was stored in communal piles covered with mats,[6] and indeed a

[5] See H. P. Martin, *Fara: A Reconstruction of the Ancient Mesopotamian City of Shuruppak* (Birmingham, 1988), 42–7; and Giuseppe Visicato, 'Archéologie et documents écrits: les "silos" et les textes sur l'orge de Fara', *Revue d'assyriologie et d'archéologie orientale* 87 (1993), 83–5.

[6] A. Leo Oppenheim, *Ancient Mesopotamia: Portrait of a Dead Civilization* (Chicago and London, 1977), 314–15.

(a)

(b)

(c)

FIG. 7.1 Sealings representing grain silos

number of texts from Babylon locate heaps of grain in various places in the city. It seems unlikely, however, that piles would have been used to keep grain all year round, as they would have been exposed to rain, groundwater, insects, and animals. Probably these heaps were only used temporarily, just before the grain was consumed, due to lack of storage space in the palace. According to the texts from Babylon, important people were fed from these piles, and it seems unlikely that they were given contaminated grain.

Once the cereals were in the city, they had to be passed on to the consumers. In the redistributive economy of the public institutions, this procedure was carried out in two ways: a large group of palace and temple dependants was issued rations of unprepared food, while a smaller number of people were provided with cooked meals. Rations were the hallmark of the early Mesopotamian economy. The great organizations, the temples and palaces, supported the majority of their personnel with amounts of food and wool. Such rations were not only issued to urban dependants, but to all personnel. The rural workers were probably supplied by the regional store-rooms mentioned above. The basis of the food ration was barley, issued in monthly set amounts, the quantity determined by the worker's gender, age, and position in the hierarchy. For instance, in twenty-first-century Babylonia, a basic barley ration for an adult man was 60 litres a month, for a woman 30 litres. The practice was common throughout southern Mesopotamia and western Syria in the third millennium; later the ration system broke down and was replaced by a system of wages. It should be clearly understood that rations in no sense at all compare to the free distribution of grain to the urban proletariat of the late Roman Republic and the Empire. Ration recipients had to work for them, and probably worked hard. Perhaps only in old age may they have been granted something without labour in return.

Two characteristics of the rations are important for our consideration of urban provisioning: the food provided was limited to cereals, with some oil, and the food was unprepared. First, no one can live on cereals alone, so we have to imagine that the recipients of the rations either had access to gardens and orchards to supplement their diets with vegetables and fruits, or that they used part of their grain rations to barter it for other food. These activities are not documented in the sources, yet either or both of them must have taken place. It has been suggested that, at least in the early third millennium, most of the recipients of rations were also granted subsistence fields that could have provided them with vegetables and fruit. If barter took place, the fresh products were most likely delivered by independent farmers, and institutional and private economies must have intersected here. Second, the food was unprepared: the ration recipients still had to grind and cook the cereals before they could consume them. This was most likely done in the house, and required the presence of family members who were free to perform these time-consuming tasks.

Some people were provided with finished food products rather than rations, and this custom remained constant throughout Mesopotamian history. There is a unique passage in an inscription by Assurnaṣirpal II (ruled 883–859) where he describes how he fed 69,574 men and women from all over the kingdom for ten days at the inauguration of his new capital city, Kalhu. The menu is unfortunately not given, but the ingredients are listed. They include oxen, calves, sheep, lambs, deer, ducks, geese, pigeons, birds, fish, jerboa, eggs, bread, beer, wine, sesame, greens, grains, pomegranates, grapes, onions, garlic, turnips, honey, ghee, seeds, mustard, milk, cheese, nuts, dates, spices, oils, and olives.[7] This was of course a special banquet, and worthy of boasting. But all kings, as well as the temples, provided select personnel with daily meals. We do not have to imagine that all these people were fed in communal dining halls, although the royal table probably had many guests. Numerous texts from all periods of Mesopotamian history list loaves of bread, jugs of beer or wine, onions, fish, oils, fats, and dates that were probably taken home. Food could also be obtained through the temples. All Mesopotamian temples had kitchens for the preparation of the gods' repasts. Obviously, the statues representing the gods did not consume the food; instead it was distributed to the temple personnel according to strictly established quotas.

Bread and beer had to be produced by the institutional workshops. First the cereals had to be ground. This was a labour-intensive enterprise, as the typical mill was a flat slab of stone on which the grain was ground by rubbing it back and forth with a long and narrow stone. Grinding was mainly done by women, who

---

[7] A. Kirk Grayson, *Assyrian Rulers of the Early First Millennium BC. I (1114–859 BC)* (The Royal Inscriptions of Mesopotamia. Assyrian Periods 2; Toronto, Buffalo, and London, 1991), 292 3.

laboured very hard. They worked year-round in the mills, and daily quotas were set for them, such as 10 litres of ordinary flour or 20 litres of coarse flour. When needed, workers were pulled from the mills and set to work at agricultural tasks such as harvesting, threshing, winnowing, or transport. The enormity of this task in the large institutions of third-millennium Babylonia cannot be underestimated. Milling was extremely strenuous work with a low rate of productivity.

When flour was available, the preparations of bread and beer took separate paths. Bread could be baked immediately by making thin unleavened loaves that were placed in clay ovens, very similar to the *tanurs* still in use in the Middle East, and found throughout excavated monumental and domestic buildings. In addition to the simple loaf of bread, fancier types and cakes with dates or the like were also produced. Beer took longer to prepare, as several stages made up the brewing process. The length of time this required is not known to us, although we do know much about the ingredients and the processes involved. Brewing required careful supervision at certain times; for instance, at the stage when the barley was allowed to sprout to become malt, the humidity and temperature needed to be carefully controlled. It is interesting that, at first, most brewers were women, and their patron deity, Ninkasi, was female as well. After the middle of the second millennium men took over as brewers, and it has been suggested that by the turn of the millennium the drink they produced had nothing in common with the original product as it was no longer made from barley, but from dates.

None of the information given above has been quantified, and with reason. We are unable to determine the percentages of institutional land issued for tenancy, or of palace employees receiving meals rather than rations, or even of palace and temple dependants as compared to other citizens. We have the impression that, throughout Mesopotamian history, large groups of people depended on the institutions for part of their food supplies, with variations by period and region. But the exact numbers and their importance within the total populations remain unknown. It also has to be kept in mind that many people may have had several sources of income simultaneously. A high temple administrator, for instance, received food from the employer, and was rewarded with the usufruct of temple land. Moreover, he or she may also have been a private landowner at the same time, drawing income from estates. These various sources of income were accounted for in different ways and by separate offices, or not accounted for at all, so it is unlikely that we will ever be able to reconstruct the entire picture.

We can say with certainty, however, that the institutions were weary of providing all the services expected from them. It took a lot of manpower and administrative control to make the system work smoothly. Thus we see how, starting in the early second millennium, much of the labour and supervision was contracted to private businessmen who became involved in all aspects of the sequence described above. Their services to the institutions were managerial and financial, and will be discussed in a later chapter. Important here is the fact that their inclusion in the sequence of urban food provisioning caused changes in the ways food was distributed. No longer were the central institutions in a position to provide for a substantial part of the population, since these institutions collected silver rather than agricultural products. Moreover, the private businessmen needed a way of converting the produce they gathered into silver, part of which they paid to the institutions.

This could only be accomplished through market mechanisms, in my opinion. The entrepreneurs who acted as intermediaries between landowners and agricultural producers had excess food supplies on their hands. Meanwhile certain products needed to be acquired by urban residents, either from institutions, from fellow citizens, or from the farmers. It seems likely that these city-dwellers became the clientele of the entrepreneurs. How this was accomplished is entirely undocumented, but this should not lead us to conclude that the marketing of food did not take place. There was no need to record these retail sales of food, as all sales were final, and no later claim could be made on either the products or the payment. The only way we could find information about them would be if the entrepreneurs had kept inventories of their stock or records of their expenditures, but these are not available to us.

The existence of a market does not exclude the possibility of the exchange of goods through reciprocity or redistribution. The three modes of exchange coexisted, and all played an important role in the economy. We should not relate a mode of exchange with a particular sector of society either. Although the great organizations often relied on redistribution, they are also known to have acquired goods on the market. Some private citizens may have relied on numerous sources for their food: cereals from the institutions, vegetables and milk from their own households, and fish or meat from the market. The market transactions were seemingly all *ad hoc* and needed no recording. Therefore they remain entirely undocumented in our sources.

### SOURCES OF DRINKING WATER

The survey above has indicated some of the difficulties facing an urban society that needs to provide food for its citizenry. A related question involves the supply of drinking water to cities, a problem that has been rarely discussed by scholars. The rivers and canals could obviously provide a source of drinking water, especially in Babylonia where all cities needed to be located at their banks and where canals entered their walls. In the suburbs of Tell Taya in Upper Mesopotamia a number of streets led to the Wadi Taya in order to give access to its water. Kings made certain that such water remained available; Nabopolassar (ruled 625–605) boasted that he redirected the water of the Euphrates into a canal with bitumen and baked brick lining when a shifting of the river branch had made it too remote to be drawn.[8]

Yet there are problems connected to a reliance on this type of water supply. First, these rivers and canals were not always easily accessible. Even if they ran through the city, many neighbourhoods were not near them. The Nippur map, for instance, shows only one canal within the city walls and people had to walk several hundred metres to reach it. The height of the *tell*s caused these canals to be quite a distance below the city level, and it must have been difficult and even dangerous to reach the water. This problem was more acute in Assyria where the rivers and canals were fewer and their banks even steeper. Assur is located on a cliff overlooking the Tigris and to reach the river one has to climb down a precipitous slope. War conditions could make access very difficult. A letter most likely written to king Esarhaddon by the governor of Nippur,

---

[8] Stephen Langdon, *Die neubabylonische Königsinschriften* (Vorderasiatische Bibliothek 4; Leipzig, 1912), 64–5.

a Babylonian city that collaborated with the Assyrians and that was under considerable local pressure, depicts a dire situation:

> The king knows that all countries hate us on account of Assyria . . . So now we have closed our gates and do not even go out of town . . . Let the king not abandon us to anyone! Our water is gone. Let us not die of thirst! The king, your father, gave us the water rights for the Banītu-canal, saying: 'Dig an outlet from the Banītu-canal toward Nippur.' [The    ], however, refused us the water. The king should write to Ubar, the commander of Babylon, that he should grant us an outlet from the Banītu-canal, so that we can drink water with them and not have to desert the king because of lack of water. All countries should not say: 'The people of Nippur, who submitted to Assyria, became fed up with the lack of water ⟨and deserted⟩'.[9]

Considerable energy must have been spent on fetching water for the household, a task probably assigned to the women, and not documented in our sources as far as I know.

A second problem may have been more serious as it made even abundant water supplies unfit for use: pollution. The rivers and canals were used for many purposes other than the provision of drinking water, such as transport, agricultural irrigation, and industry. Moreover, there was the danger of sewage entering the watercourses. The network of canals was shared by numerous cities and villages, so pollution upstream affected many communities further down. Navigation and irrigation do not necessarily have to foul the water although we can imagine that dirt entered it due to these activities. Various industries used water extensively. Some that readily come to mind are laundering and tanning. The tanning of leather, an evil-smelling enterprise, the primary stages of which took place outside the city, required large amounts of water to soak the hides. Moreover, this water needed to be discarded after use—where else could this be done but in the river or canal? Then there was the problem of human waste. Archaeological evidence of latrines in private houses is lacking, and public toilets do not seem to have existed either. People could defecate in fields and orchards, where there was always the risk of contaminating a water source. The textual material makes little reference to such dangers.

---

[9] Robert H. Pfeiffer, *State Letters of Assyria* (American Oriental Series 6; New Haven, 1935), no. 123, obv. ll. 11–13, rev. ll. 4–22; trans. after A. Leo Oppenheim, *Letters from Mesopotamia* (Chicago and London, 1967), 175.

Although a ritual text prohibits urinating or vomiting in a water-course, acts that were considered as bad as killing one's friend, the relevance of this source for the study of daily life is to be doubted. Considering that the Euphrates is a very slow river and that water levels in the summer were low, it would seem that a lot of the filth thrown in canals feeding from it must have remained in the area. As fuel was quite scarce, the boiling of water before consumption was probably too expensive to be a widespread practice. It appears likely, therefore, that canal water was rather risky to drink in Babylonia, and not to be recommended.

A second source of water was provided by wells. Their existence both in Assyria and in Babylonia is attested in texts and in the archaeological record, but their frequency is less clear. In the south of Mesopotamia, pockets of fresh water within the surrounding water-table existed underneath and at the sides of rivers. This water could be reached by digging vertical wells through the dikes. The presence of wells is attested in such varied sources as the neo-Babylonian laws, where careless use of well water for irrigation was punished,[10] and the Sumerian tale of Gilgamesh and Agga, in which the king rallies his people for war by urging them to protect the wells.[11] Yet for cities located on top of a *tell*, pockets of fresh water were much less accessible as one had to dig through layers of debris. Despite this problem, intramural wells are attested with their sides reinforced with ceramic pipes or with bitumen. In Nebuchadnezar's southern palace at Babylon several of them were found, and this ruler also boasted of his repair of the well in the temple of Shamash at Sippar. Wells in private houses in Babylon are attested archaeologically. For some obscure reason the excavator stated that they were only used for bathing, washing, and household tasks. He based this assertion on a puzzling remark: 'The Babylonians would not have been "Orientals" if they had drunk well water in the neighbourhood of a river.'[12] House sale documents do not mention the existence of such a valuable asset, however, and it is doubtful that they were common. So far no

---

[10] James B. Pritchard, *Ancient Near Eastern Texts relating to the Old Testament*, 3rd edn. (Princeton, 1969), 197 § 3.

[11] Ibid. 45.

[12] 'Die Babylonier hätten keine Orientalen sein müssen, wenn sie in der Nachbarschaft des Flusses Brunnenwasser getrunken hätten', Oscar Reuther, *Die Innenstadt von Babylon (Merkes)* (Leipzig, 1926), 26.

communal wells have appeared in the archaeological record, but their existence is suggested by the fact that a foundling is said to be someone abandoned in a well.

In Assyria more wells are attested both in the texts and in the archaeological record. One of them, excavated at Kalhu, still yielded 5,000 gallons a day in AD 1952.[13] Again kings boasted of their construction: Sennacherib, for instance, rebuilt the pulling system of the wells in his palace, which must have been very deep, considering the height of the mound at that spot. A letter to an Assyrian king relates how a fox entered the city of Assur and fell in a well, indicating that they were easily accessible.[14] Yet very few house sales mention the presence of a well in a house.[15] Well water was less likely to be polluted than that of rivers and canals, although a lot of brackish water in wells is reported in modern Iraq. How common wells were in Assyria, and how much water they produced, remains unknown, hence we cannot determine how important they were for urban residents. It seems safe to say that fresh drinking water was a scarce resource in Mesopotamia, especially in the south, and that diseases could have easily spread through the water supply. These circumstances may explain why beer was such a popular drink.

THE AGRICULTURAL POTENTIAL OF THE
URBAN HINTERLAND

A last issue to be discussed is whether the hinterlands were able to support the larger cities with their agricultural produce. After all, the urban population in Mesopotamia was at times very large, and big cities were common from very early on in its history. This question has important historical repercussions. If some cities were not supported by their immediate hinterland, where did they obtain the required additional food, and how did they manage to guarantee themselves a constant supply? At times the need for

---

[13] H. W. F. Saggs, *The Greatness that was Babylon* (London, 1962), 172.
[14] Pfeiffer, *State Letters of Assyria*, no. 227.
[15] See C. H. W. Johns, *Assyrian Deeds and Documents recording Transfer of Property* 4 (Cambridge, 1923), 9. For examples of houses with wells, see Theodore Kwasman, *Neo-Assyrian Legal Documents in the Kouyundjik Collection of the British Museum* (Rome, 1988), nos. 123, 373.

supplemental food has been used as an explanation for the military expansion by a Mesopotamian power, even to such distant regions as northern Syria in the case of the Old Akkadian dynasty.[16] Such an explanation is only valid if we can demonstrate that nearby food production was insufficient. In order to study whether an adequate supply of food was available near a city to feed its population, we need access to a set of data including size of population, food resources available, cultivated area, crop types and productivity, caloric value of the crops, and caloric consumption. Most of these data are unavailable at the moment and the problems in trying to acquire them are very substantial.

A first problem lies in establishing the size of the hinterland. If we ignore political considerations that would have denied access to fields beyond a certain point, the limits to the hinterland were determined solely by distances to be covered by the producers and by the transporters of the food to and from the urban centre. If all farmers resided within the city and needed to commute to their fields on a daily basis, the remotest fields would probably have been only some 7 kilometres from the city, to be reached after one and a half hours travelling time.[17] We can imagine, however, that a corona of farming villages surrounded the cities, and in that case the hinterland was only limited by the distance the food needed to be transported to the urban consumer. In Assyria most transportation needed to be done overland, which was extremely expensive, and the hinterlands of the cities were thus greatly restricted. Water transport is much cheaper, and was obviously readily available in Babylonia with its numerous irrigation canals. The size of the hinterland was thus much greater there, but impossible for us to establish with accuracy, as we cannot calculate the transportation costs involved. Political considerations may thus have been the primary limiting factor there, with access to agricultural areas restricted either because of the existence of boundaries between political entities or because the urban centres were unable to assert their political control beyond a certain distance.

As I pointed out before, our population estimates are extremely

---

[16] See Harvey Weiss and Marie-Agnès Courty, 'The Genesis and Collapse of the Akkadian Empire', in M. Liverani (ed.), *Akkad: The First World Empire* (Padua, 1993), 131–55.

[17] See David Oates, *Studies in the Ancient History of Northern Iraq* (London, 1968), 44.

unreliable. Even if we are able to determine the exact size of a city at a particular moment in time, we cannot establish how densely inhabited it was. Moreover, we lack data about the population of the surrounding countryside: the villagers that produced the food also consumed part of it. Since the villages were not as continuously inhabited as the cities, their remains are often invisible to us. Hence the total population of a district becomes virtually impossible to appraise.

The types of food available to an urban population obviously varied with the geographical surroundings. Cereals may have been the main source of nutrition, but surely not the only one. Dates, which have a high caloric value, must have been a major part of the diet in Babylonia, and although we have good evidence on the cultivation of dates, we have little information on their consumption. Fish was consumed in great amounts in certain regions of Mesopotamia, but in others it was probably less readily available; again our information is incomplete. Also the importance of the big herds of sheep, goats, and cattle cannot be established. These animals were not only reared by herdsmen dependent upon urban institutions and individuals, but also by semi-nomadic and nomadic groups who almost totally elude us both in the textual and archaeological records. Access to their products must have been seasonal, and how they came to the city is unclear. We know that meat was eaten but not to what extent. Dairy products, which have a high caloric value, were probably readily available to most urbanites, but we know very little about the amounts consumed.

In our calculation of available cereal resources we have many uncertainties, despite the fact that more textual and archaeological data are at hand. In all of Babylonia, agriculture was based on irrigation: access to water was as crucial as the availability of land. Although both textual and survey data can give us information about the location of canals around certain cities, nowhere do we have a complete picture. We cannot assume that there was a continuous band of cultivation around any site. We also have difficulties in determining the productivity of the soil. We have textual data that give the yields of particular fields at a given moment in time, but we cannot extrapolate this information to other areas and periods.

A major uncertainty, for instance, concerns the negative effects of salinization. Irrigation agriculture causes the accumulation of salt upon the fields. This can be counteracted to a certain extent by fallowing, a practice definitely in use in Babylonia, and drainage, something that was very difficult in the area due to its extremely low relief. Yet, how damaging was salinization to cereal agriculture? In the 1950s a very appealing picture of three cycles of exhaustion of the soil throughout the history of Babylonia from 4000 BC to AD 1000 was drawn by Jacobsen and Adams,[18] but their interpretation of the empirical data is now considered equivocal at best, as their statements about declining yields were based on a misunderstanding of the sources.[19] Thus the negative effects of salt, although real, cannot be properly assessed. Moreover, we cannot determine the relative importance of the various cereals cultivated in Mesopotamia—wheat, barley, and sesame—and how much area was devoted to each. Hence the caloric value of the crops cannot be established.

How much food did one person need to survive? We can look at figures from contemporary developing nations to estimate what someone needs to survive at a subsistence level and try to use this data as a guide for what a Mesopotamian would have required.[20] But can we assume that the same caloric requirements existed in antiquity, and what exactly is meant by a subsistence level? Moreover, it seems likely that a certain sector of the population consumed much more than the minimum caloric requirement. How large was that sector, and how much more did it consume? Again we are faced with a high level of uncertainty.

Considering all these limitations on our knowledge, is it even worth asking the question whether or not urban populations could be fed by their hinterland? I think that it is extremely important that we pose the question, and would like to propose an answer that could function as a working hypothesis for further research. It seems to me that most cities were supported by their own hinterlands, and that the long-distance transport of food was rare and unusual. There are only a few cases where cities were not self-reliant and those need a special investigation. The hypothesis that

[18] Thorkild Jacobsen and Robert McC. Adams, 'Salt and Silt in Ancient Mesopotamian Agriculture', *Science* 128 (November 1958), 1251–8.

[19] Marvin A. Powell, 'Salt, Seed, and Yields in Sumerian Agriculture: A Critique of the Theory of Progressive Salinization', *Zeitschrift für Assyriologie* 75 (1985), 7–38.

[20] For such an approach, see Elizabeth C. Stone and David I. Owen, *Adoption in Old Babylonian Nippur and the Archive of Mannum-mešu-lissur* (Winona Lake, 1991), 8–9.

most Mesopotamian cities were fed by the agricultural produce of their own hinterlands is supported by a number of historical facts.

At the time of the foundation of most Babylonian and Assyrian cities, the political situation in the regions was characterized by fragmentation. In the early history of Babylonia, i.e. the late-fourth through mid-third millennia, the most important cities in the region were the political centres of a set of more or less equally powerful city-states. Although conflicts between them could arise over the control of certain agricultural zones, as is exemplified by the border conflict between Umma and Lagash,[21] these cities by necessity had to rely on the resources of their own surroundings to survive. The agricultural potential of Babylonia seems to have been sufficient, however, to support large urban centres. In the early third millennium Uruk grew to an enormous size of at least 400 hectares, a size unsurpassed until two millennia later, yet only a 14-kilometre-wide band of agricultural fields surrounding it was needed to provide for its inhabitants and for the people residing in the neighbouring towns and villages.[22] Between 2300 and 1600, regional powers occasionally developed under the regimes of Akkade, Ur, Larsa, and Babylon. The hinterlands of the Babylonian cities were then no longer restricted for political reasons, and we see that cereals were transported from the provinces to the capital cities. For instance, under the Third Dynasty of Ur in the twenty-first century, the province of Umma provided Nippur, the religious centre, and Ur, the ancestral home of the dynasty, with grain.[23] The logistics of that conveyance were relatively uncomplicated as one could rely on canal transport. The observation that such grain shipments took place should not necessarily lead to the conclusion that they were regularly needed. They may have been taxes levied by the kings of Ur to symbolize their control over the provincial centres of Babylonia. As Ur lost its hegemony over Babylonia, the contributions by the provinces

[21] See Jerrold S. Cooper, *Reconstructing History from Ancient Inscriptions: The Lagash-Umma Border Conflict* (Malibu, 1983).

[22] Robert McC. Adams, *Heartland of Cities* (Chicago and London, 1981), fig. 24. Obviously Adams's reconstruction depends on figures, such as those for population density, that are impossible to establish with certainty, as I pointed out before.

[23] See Tom B. Jones, 'Sumerian Administrative Documents: An Essay', *Sumerological Studies in Honor of Thorkild Jacobsen* (Assyriological Studies 20; Chicago and London, 1975), 41–61.

ceased, and it has been suggested by scholars that this led to a famine within the city.[24] Yet the ruling king, Ibbi-Sin, remained in power in Ur for at least another fifteen years, and it is generally accepted that his final defeat was due to a military invasion by the Elamites. The fact that the city recovered very soon after its military defeat and actually grew in size despite its loss of political importance, suggests that the provincial contributions to its food supply had been a luxury rather than a necessity.

Later in Babylonian history, in the period from the seventh century BC to at least the seventh century AD, the region underwent a process of intense urbanization and a simultaneous intensification of agricultural development. At first the region of Babylon, and later the area some 50 kilometres further north referred to as al Madāʾin, 'the cities', in early Islamic writings, became very densely inhabited by several large urban centres in close proximity to one another. In the sixth century BC, Babylon was expanded to include an area of 890 hectares and within a 40-kilometre radius around the metropolis were located the major cities of Borsippa, Kish, Kutha, and Dilbat, while Sippar was only 60 kilometres to the north. Moreover, in the countryside numerous villages existed. The successive imperial governments colonized the region with foreign people deported from conquered areas, as is well known from the case of the Judaean exiles who were settled in central Babylonia. The density of settlement in northern Babylonia seems to have been enormous, yet the agricultural resources of the area seem to have been sufficient to feed the inhabitants, and even to produce a surplus.

Herodotus (1. 92) stated that one-third of the supplies of the Persian court and army was provided by Babylonia, while the rest of Asia contributed the remaining two-thirds. While this may not have been a very accurate statement, later tax documents show that Mesopotamia was an extremely fertile region into the eighth century AD.[25] The hinterland of the city of Babylon must be considered to have included almost the entirety of Babylonia, and it seems that cereals must have been transported over a distance of up to 200 kilometres from the south to the north of the region. This was

---

[24] Th. Jacobsen, 'The Reign of Ibbī-Suen', in *Towards the Image of Tammuz*, 173–86.

[25] See Peter Christensen, *The Decline of Iranshahr: Irrigation and Environments in the History of the Middle East 500 BC to AD 1500* (Copenhagen, 1993), 34–44.

possible, however, due to the extensive canal system that enabled transport by boat. The neo-Babylonian texts excavated in Babylon describe the activities of certain merchants who supplied the urban residents with food. For instance, one Iddin-Marduk dealt in barley, dates, and onions, which he had transported and stored in magazines in the city and its suburbs. Unfortunately, we do not know how wide an area he had to explore to find sufficient supplies, but the texts of his archive focus upon localities between Babylon and Borsippa, hence close to Babylon. Others may have shipped agricultural goods over longer distances, but we find no evidence of great concerns over the difficulties involved.

Short-term decreases in the water flow of the Euphrates, or loss of political control over the hinterland, for instance, could place a city in a situation where it could not feed itself and would have been under pressure to import food from distant regions. But it is to be doubted that such an option actually existed. Where would that food have been obtained outside Babylonia? Khuzistan to the east of the Tigris could only be reached via a laborious overland route from the Diyala southward, or by boat through the marshes. The north Syrian Jezirah, which has sometimes been portrayed as a bread basket for Babylonia, is located 1,000 kilometres away. The entire transport could have been accomplished by boat over the Balikh, Habur, and Euphrates rivers, but the labour required would have been excessive. It seems doubtful that such long and expensive expeditions would have been relied upon, except in unusual circumstances.

The agricultural situation in Assyria, i.e. the Jezirah between the Euphrates and Tigris and the Mosul plains east of the Tigris, was quite different from the South. On the one hand, most of the area relied on rain-fed agriculture, which has a lower level of productivity than irrigation agriculture, and on the other hand it lacked good water transport along canals. In the early history of the region, from 3000 to 1500 BC, urban settlement never exceeded a 100 hectare limit. It has been convincingly argued that the hinterlands could not support larger cities because only a 15 kilometre radius around them could be exploited under the prevailing political circumstances of small regional powers.[26] Although in the early second

---

[26] T. J. Wilkinson, 'The Structure and Dynamics of Dry-Farming States in Upper Mesopotamia', *Current Anthropology* 35 (1994), 483–520.

millennium somewhat larger political entities developed, whose exact outlines are unknown to us so far, this does not seem to have affected the size of the urban centres. Problems of transport, mostly overland, may have precluded larger urban agglomerations.

We are thus struck by the building activities of the Assyrian kings in the late second and early first millennia, who constructed a set of enormous capitals for themselves: Kar-Tukulti-Ninurta, Kalhu, Dur-Sharrukin, and Nineveh. Not all of these survived for long: Kar-Tukulti-Ninurta and Dur-Sharrukin were more or less abandoned at the death of their founders, which may be an indication of the fact that they presented too many difficulties of food supply.[27] But Kalhu and Nineveh survived for several generations, and as centres of a large imperial bureaucracy they must have consumed the agricultural output of a wide geographical zone. David Oates, who studied some aspects of the agricultural base of these cities, came to the conclusion that they represented 'a highly artificial element in the economy of northern Iraq'.[28] The Assyrian capital cities were too large, too densely packed together, and probably also too wasteful of resources to have been fed by their hinterlands. It has been stated that this is to be expected in an empire.[29] However, this assumes an integration of the conquered areas into the economy of the Assyrian core, something that should be concluded from the insufficient resources of Assyria rather than the other way around. The almost total abandonment of these cities subsequent to the collapse of the Assyrian empire in the late seventh century suggests that residents had to revert by necessity to a village life that could be sustained by the immediate environment.

If the conclusion is correct that the late Assyrian cities required provisions from the empire to survive, this reality had important repercussions on the organization of the food supplies. Transport over long distances and storage near the place of consumption needed to be co-ordinated. Shipping was not easy in the region, as

---

[27] Obviously other considerations may have played an important role. It is usually assumed that these cities were built on the kings' whims at the expense of the existing ancient centres, Assur and Nineveh, and that the aristocracies of the old cities were able to reclaim primacy upon the deaths of those kings.

[28] Oates, *Studies in the Ancient History of Northern Iraq*, 52.

[29] Mario Liverani, 'Review of Oates *Studies*', *Oriens Antiquus* 10 (1971), 157.

the Tigris was a difficult river to navigate. Moreover, little land upstream from Nineveh was available to produce a surplus. Fertile areas certainly were to be found to the east and to the west; these were regions unconnected to the heartland of Assyria by waterways. Thus, transport had to take place overland, a very expensive affair. We lack any data from Mesopotamia itself to assess the costs, but information from the Roman empire, which had a similar technology, can give us some idea of what was involved. It has been asserted that in the late Roman empire the price of a wagon-load of wheat would double in 150 Roman miles, and that famines could occur in cities located as little as 75 kilometres from abundant supplies.[30] The validity of these assertions has been disputed on various grounds, but the stated price of overland transport fits the general pattern of pre-industrial societies,[31] and it can be safely concluded that the overland shipping of bulky items in the Roman empire was usually short-haul.[32]

The Assyrian imperial bureaucracy must have had the ability to organize the conveyance of food products over a certain distance, even at a great expense, but we do not know where the geographical limit was. Strangely, its records scarcely document overland transport of food products. Cereal taxes were standard in the Assyrian empire, but we are not informed about the destination of the grain collected. An unusual letter to king Sargon may refer to a grain shipment to be made to Dur-Sharrukin:

[To the king, my lord]: yo[ur servant] Tariba-Issar . . . Now, I have collected 500 homers (= 100,000 litres) of barley in the city of Kilizi, and would like to deliver it. If the king my lord commands: 'Collect barley for three palaces,' I will collect it in Adian and Arbela as well.[33]

If indeed the man wanted to take the barley to Dur-Sharrukin, he would have had to transport it either by boat from Kilizi down the

---

[30] A. H. M. Jones, *The Later Roman Empire* 2 (Norman, 1964), 841–4. For the recalculation to 150 rather than 300 miles, see Keith Hopkins, 'Models, Ships, and Staples', in Peter Garnsey and C. R. Whittaker (eds.), *Trade and Famine in Classical Antiquity* (Cambridge, 1983), 104 n. 46.

[31] See Richard Duncan-Jones, *The Economy of the Roman Empire: Quantitative Studies*, 2nd edn. (Cambridge, 1982), 368–9.

[32] Hopkins, 'Models, Ships, and Staples', 105.

[33] Simo Parpola, *The Correspondence of Sargon II*, Part I (Helsinki, 1987), no. 160, quoted by permission.

Greater Zab river and then upstream to Nineveh, where it would have to be loaded onto wagons, or overland for the entire distance of about 60 kilometres as the crow flies. Both methods are certainly possible, yet already complicated. The letter may also refer to deliveries to palaces in the three nearby cities mentioned, and then the transport problems would have been minor. It seems thus that the late Assyrian capitals required the produce of an empire for their support, but, strangely, the logistical difficulties that this would have presented are not clear within the textual record at our disposal.

A similar difficult situation seems to have existed at the Middle Euphrates site of Mari. The city, which originally might have been 254 hectares in size, was strategically located on the junction between Babylonia and Syria, and also acted as an intermediary between the nomads of the Syrian desert and the agriculturalists of the Euphrates valley. But its agricultural base was limited. It lies in a zone where there is insufficient rainfall for dry-farming, and the river cuts through a barren plateau on both sides. The valley is only 6–14 kilometres wide in Mari's neighbourhood, and just a narrow section of it could be easily irrigated. Thus a massive and long irrigation canal had to be dug when Mari developed into a major settlement, and this canal had to be carefully maintained. Yet even these irrigated areas were unable to produce sufficient food for the city, and the texts attest to the practice of grain imports from northern Syria. The following letter documents this procedure:

To my lord your servant Yasim-Sumū says as follows: 'With respect to the barley boats which leave the city of Emar, from now on they will not leave any longer. Harvest time has come, but there will be no more boats arriving to load the barley for the palace. And for the next five months there will be no more boats leaving. Now either there are boats ⟨from Mari⟩ on their way that will arrive here; ⟨in that case⟩ we will fill them up so that they shouldn't have to return (to Mari) empty—or, if it pleases my lord, he should send me five minas (= five pounds) of silver; then I, in concert with the merchants living in Emar, will hire ten boats of 300 *ugar* (= 3,600 litres) capacity ⟨each⟩, [co]lle[ct barley] and dispatch thus 3,000 *ugar* (= 36,000 litres) of barley to Mari. One should give either to Idinyatum or to another official 60 *ugar* (= 600 *kor*) of barley for the five minas (= 300 shekels) of silver at a rate of $2\frac{1}{2}$ *kor*-measures per shekel. Then, in order that the five minas of silver return to the palace, the wages for the sixty men of the crew will be $2\frac{1}{2}$ shekels per man, hence $2\frac{1}{2}$ minas of silver which amounts to 300 *kor* of barley. And the balance of 210 *ugar* should go into the palace . . .'[34]

The letter is not easy to understand, and the calculations in it appear mistaken at first glance; a recent study by Durand has elucidated its contents, however. Yasim-Sumū was in Emar, and announced that all cargo ships were chartered, and would be unavailable for five months, indicating that Emar shipped grain to other places that were at a round-trip distance of five months' travel. Now, either he had to hope that ships from Mari would soon arrive and could be loaded with grain, or he had to spend five pounds of silver from the palace to hire other boats from merchants, whose representative in Mari was Idinyatum. These merchants were independent from the palace and needed to be convinced with financial incentives to reassign their boats or to release some boats that they had previously withheld. This was to be done by offering Idinyatum 60 *ugar* (= 600 *kor*) of barley, which was worth five minas (= 300 shekels) of silver in Emar. Yasim-Sumū would recover the additional costs by taking advantage of the differences in the price of barley between Emar and Mari. In Emar he could acquire 2.5 *kor* of barley per shekel of silver, in Mari only 2 *kor*. The 3,000 *ugar* acquired in Emar was worth twenty minas of silver there, but in Mari it would be priced at twenty-five minas. Thus the only transport costs the palace would have to take care of were the salaries for the boatmen. We see here how palace, private merchants, and salaried boatmen all were involved in the process, each of them eager to make a profit.

The cereals in the letter cited above came from Emar, a city upstream on the Euphrates, in the zone where rain-fed agriculture was possible. The region of the upper Euphrates was only accessible to Mari when its political relations with Aleppo were good. Such was not always true, however, and an alternative source for cereals was perhaps the middle Habur area. The grain storage and processing facilities found at sites such as Tell ʿAtij, and mentioned before, may have been established for that purpose. Transport of the grain by boat along the Euphrates was facilitated by a canal on

---

[34] Maurice Birot *et al.*, *Textes divers* (Archives royales de Mari XIII; Paris 1964), no. 35 ll. 1–32; the trans. and interpretation of this letter are based on Jean-Marie Durand, 'Relectures d'*ARMT* XIII, II: La correspondance de Numuš da-Nahrârî', *Mari. Annales de Recherches Interdisciplinaires* 2 (Paris, 1983), 160–3.

its west bank, more convenient and cheaper than the use of overland caravans which are also attested. According to the letter
quoted above, the crew of six men would be paid the equivalent of
450 litres of barley in silver to navigate a 3,600 litre boat over a
distance of more than 300 kilometres. If overland transport had
been used, the teamsters themselves would have consumed the
entire load. Mari was thus most likely unable to feed its citizens
with its own resources, and had to import food. Its location provided the city with much income from trade, however, and this
income could be used for food acquisition.

In conclusion, it seems that Mesopotamian cities were usually
able to support themselves with the food produced in their hinterlands, and that imports of food over long distances indicate
exceptional circumstances. The exceptions could have been caused
by natural disasters, such as droughts, or they could have been
related to political events. Emperors might construct cities that
needed to be supplied by a wide geographical area, or kings might
demand that provinces make contributions to support the capital
city as a political statement. Certain cities always were artificial
foundations, unsustainable by their own surroundings, but ideally
located for trade or other purposes. Yet those were rare cases and
most of the cities were self-reliant with respect to foodstuffs.

The problem of food supply is thus related to many issues
regarding the ancient economy of Mesopotamia. Questions of
land ownership, political and bureaucratic organization, markets
and redistributive centres, land use and agricultural techniques, all
have an impact on our understanding of the ways in which people
obtained their food. As many of these questions are matters of
dispute, the reconstruction provided in this chapter has to be
regarded as provisional and open to debate too.

BIBLIOGRAPHY

Some of the issues addressed in this chapter have been extensively
debated, and the list of publications provided here has to be very
selective. For a survey of the agricultural resources of Mesopotamia
see J. N. Postgate, *Early Mesopotamia: Society and Economy at the
Dawn of History* (London and New York, 1992), 157–72. Armas
Salonen has published several, mainly lexicographical, studies

on aspects of agriculture: *Agricultura Mesopotamica nach sumerisch-akkadischen Quellen* (Helsinki, 1968); *Die Fischerei im alten Mesopotamien* (Helsinki, 1970); *Vögel und Vogelfang im alten Mesopotamien* (Helsinki, 1973); and *Jagd und Jagdtiere im alten Mesopotamien* (Helsinki, 1976).

Seminal articles proving the existence of private ownership of fields in third-millennium Babylonia were written by I. M. Diakonoff, 'Sale of Land in Pre-Sargonic Sumer', in *Papers Presented by the Soviet Delegation at the XXIII International Congress of Orientalists. Assyriology* (Moscow, 1954), 5–32, and I. J. Gelb, 'On the Alleged Temple and State Economies in Ancient Mesopotamia', *Studi in onore di Edoardo Volterra* 6 (Milano, 1971), 137–54. A collection of essays on land ownership in various periods of Mesopotamian history was edited by Burchard Brentjes, *Das Grundeigentum in Mesopotamien* (Jahrbuch für Wirtshaftsgeschichte, Sonderband 1987; Berlin). For varying opinions on the existence of communal ownership of land, see I. M. Diakonoff, 'The Commune in the Ancient Near East as treated in the Works of Soviet Researchers', *Soviet Anthropology and Archeology* 2, no. 1 (1963), 32–46; I. J. Gelb *et al.*, *Earliest Land Tenure Systems in the Ancient Near East: Ancient Kudurrus* (Chicago, 1991), 16–17, 24–6; G. Komoróczy, 'Landed Property in Ancient Mesopotamia and the Theory of the so-called Asiatic Mode of Production', *Oikumene* 2 (1978), 9–26; W. F. Leemans, 'Trouve-t-on des "communautés rurales" dans l'ancienne Mésopotamie?', *Recueils de la Société Jean Bodin* XLI, *Les communautés rurales*, Deuxième partie, Antiquité (Paris, 1983), 43–106; J. N. Postgate, 'Land Tenure in the Middle Assyrian Period: a Reconstruction', *Bulletin of the School of Oriental and African Studies* 34 (1971), 496–520, and '*Ilku* and Land Tenure in the Middle Assyrian Kingdom—a Second Attempt', in J. N. Postgate (ed.), *Societies and Languages of the Ancient Near East: Studies in Honour of I. M. Diakonoff* (Warminster, 1982), 304–13; Carlo Zaccagnini in C. Zaccagnini (ed.), *Production and Consumption in the Ancient Near East* (Budapest, 1989), 1–126.

The need for processing of cereals after harvesting has been extensively illustrated by G. C. Hillman, 'Traditional Husbandry and Processing of Archaic Cereals in Recent Times: Part I, the Glume Wheats', *Bulletin on Sumerian Agriculture* 1 (1984), 114–52, and 'Part II, the Free-Threshing Cereals', *Bulletin on Sumerian*

*Agriculture* 2 (1985), 1–31. Some of the ancient documentation can be found in Armas Salonen, *Agricultura Mesopotamica* (Helsinki, 1968), 263–82. For grain processing sites excavated in the Middle Habur area see Michel Fortin, 'Trois campagnes de fouilles à tell ʿAtij: Un comptoir commercial du IIIème millénaire en Syrie du Nord', *Bulletin of the Canadian Society of Mesopotamian Studies* 18 (1989), 35–56, and 'Tell Gudeda: un site "industriel" du IIIème millénaire av. J.C. dans la moyenne vallée du Khabur?', *Bulletin of the Canadian Society of Mesopotamian Studies* 21 (1991), 63–77; Glenn M. Schwartz and Hans H. Curvers, 'Tell al-Raqāʾi 1989 and 1990: Further Investigations at a Small Rural Site of Early Urban Northern Mesopotamia', *American Journal of Archaeology* 96 (1992), 397–419. Seals with representations of grain stores are reproduced by Dominique Collon, *First Impressions: Cylinder Seals in the Ancient Near East* (London, 1987), 146 nos. 622–3; Salonen, *Agricultura Mesopotamica*, pl. x no. 3.

For the functioning of door locks see Richard L. Zettler, 'Sealings as Artifacts of Institutional Administration in Ancient Mesopotamia', *Journal of Cuneiform Studies* 39 (1987), 197–240. Their psychological importance in Egypt has been described by Barry J. Kemp, *Ancient Egypt: Anatomy of a Civilization* (London and New York, 1989), 113.

Rations have been widely studied. I. J. Gelb, 'The Ancient Mesopotamian Ration System,' *Journal of Near Eastern Studies* 24 (1965), 230–43 was the first systematic discussion of their importance. Some important recent works are: Hartmut Waetzoldt, 'Compensation of Craft Workers and Officials in the Ur III Period', in Marvin A. Powell (ed.), *Labor in the Ancient Near East* (New Haven, 1987), 117–41; and Lucio Milano, 'Le razioni alimentari nel vicino oriente antico: per un'articolazione storica del sistemo', in Rita Dolce and Carlo Zaccagnini (eds.), *Il pane del re* (Bologna, 1989), 65–100.

On millers in the Ur III period see Robert K. Englund, 'Hard Work—Where Will it Get You? Labor Management in Ur III Mesopotamia', *Journal of Near Eastern Studies* 50 (1991), 255–80. On brewers see Louis F. Hartman and A. Leo. Oppenheim, *On Beer and Brewing Techniques in Ancient Mesopotamia* (New Haven, 1950). For a statement that the market was of little importance in the distribution of food products, see Johannes Renger, 'Formen des Zugangs zu den lebensnotwendigen Gütern: Die

Austauschverhältnisse in der altbabylonischen Zeit', *Altorientalische Forschungen* 20 (1993), 87–114.

For drinking-water supplies in Mesopotamia, see the remarks by H. W. F. Saggs, *The Greatness that was Babylon* (London, 1962), 171–2; and H. W. F. Saggs, *Civilization before Greece and Rome* (New Haven and London, 1989), 121–5. Archaeological evidence for wells was summarily described by Valentin Müller, 'Brunnen', *Reallexikon der Assyriologie* 2 (Berlin and Leipzig, 1938), 72–3.

For an example of how one should study the agricultural potential of an area, see Terence N. D'Altroy, *Provincial Power in the Inka Empire* (Washington and London, 1992), 154–63. For southern Babylonia the issue has been studied by Robert McC. Adams, *Heartland of Cities* (Chicago and London, 1981); and for northern Babylonia by McGuire Gibson, *The City and Area of Kish* (Coconut Grove Miami, 1972). For Assyria, see T. J. Wilkinson, 'The Structure and Dynamics of Dry-Farming States in Upper Mesopotamia', *Current Anthropology* 35 (1994), 483–520; and David Oates, *Studies in the Ancient History of Northern Iraq* (London, 1968), 19–66.

For the complex issue of salinization and for information on yields see Thorkild Jacobsen, *Salinity and Irrigation Agriculture in Antiquity* (Malibu, 1982); J. N. Postgate, 'The problem of yields in Sumerian texts', *Bulletin on Sumerian Agriculture* 1 (1987), 97–102; and Marvin A. Powell, 'Salt, Seed, and Yields in Sumerian Agriculture: A Critique of the Theory of Progressive Salinization', *Zeitschrift für Assyriologie* 75 (1985), 7–38.

For the geographical situation of Mari see Bernard Geyer and Jean-Yves Monchambert, 'Prospection de la moyenne vallée de l'Euphrate: rapport préliminaire: 1982–1985', *Mari: Annales des Recherches Interdisciplinaires* 5 (Paris, 1987), 293–344; Jean Margueron, 'État présent des recherches sur l'urbanisme de Mari -1-', ibid. 483–98 and, 'Mari, l'Euphrate, et le Khabur au milieu du IIIᵉ millénaire', *Bulletin of the Canadian Society of Mesopotamian Studies* 21 (1991), 79–100.

# 8

## Crafts and Commerce

The economy of the ancient Mesopotamian city was not restricted to the primary activities of food production and processing. The manufacture of goods, both common utensils and luxury items, found in abundance in the archaeological and textual records, was also a major economic enterprise. Craft production was not limited to cities: village craftsmen produced a variety of goods for the local market as well. But manufacture in cities, or administered by urban institutions, was clearly more extensive, more complex, and of greater importance to the Mesopotamian economy. In this chapter I will investigate how crafts in Mesopotamia depended on the city, and especially how they were intrinsically connected to international trade. Their reliance on cities was threefold: first, the producers could only be supported in an urban economy where a food surplus was available; second, the variety of raw materials needed for manufacture was only available in cities where both local supplies, such as reed and wool, and foreign ones, such as metal ores, were collected; third, the clientele was an urban one, which either used the finished products locally or exported them.

Eight main crafts can be distinguished, primarily on the basis of the material employed: potting, reedwork, weaving, leatherwork, carpentry, stonecutting, metalwork, and jewellery-making. Others, such as glassmaking, had less economic importance. All these crafts are known to have had specialist practitioners, even basic crafts such as the production of pottery. For although simple vessels can be, and most probably were, made in the household by women, there are numerous indications that most pots were manufactured by a specialized group of potters, starting in prehistory. The most direct indicator is the fact that there existed a professional designation of potter, *bahar*, found already in the earliest Sumerian documents from the late fourth millennium. Some scenes carved on cylinder seals of that period seem to represent

FIG. 8.1    Sealing representing potters at work

potters at work (Fig. 8.1). The professionalization of pottery production is also visible in the archaeological record. From early
prehistory on, starting with the earliest permanent settlement in
Mesopotamia proper, pottery was standardized in shape, ware, and
decoration.[1] At times, the standardization for certain types of vessels was so rigorous that something approaching on industrial level
production can be imagined. For instance, in the late fourth millennium, enormous numbers of bowls, now referred to as bevelled-
rim bowls, were produced in moulds of one shape and a limited
number of sizes. The archaeological record also indicates that most
pottery kilns were concentrated in particular areas of towns. Yet
the existence of specialized craft areas in early Mesopotamian cities
is not conclusively proven, as I will discuss presently. Finally, we
have a limited number of accounts listing enormous quantities of
pots produced in specialized workshops. Unfortunately, no archive
of such a workshop has been preserved, but their existence cannot
be denied. The following example derives from the late third
millennium, and lists an enormous number of vessels produced in
a single year. This is just a short excerpt:

> Total: 3 pithoi of 300 litres
>     workdays: 30
> Total: 6 pithoi of 300 litres
>     workdays: [60?]

[1]  See Hans J. Nissen, *The Early History of the Ancient Near East, 9000–2000 B.C.*
(Chicago and London, 1988), 45, who argues that the pottery of the Halaf period
is so refined that it must have been created by specialists.

Total: 9 pointed jars of 120 litres
        workdays: 54
Total: 40 pointed jars of 110 litres
        workdays: 220
Total: 170 jars of 30 litres
        workdays: 170
[Total]: 320 wide rimmed vessels of 30 litres
        workdays: 400

            .    .    .    .    .    .    .    .    .

Total of 2,960.55 workdays.[2]

The need for specialization increased with the level of difficulty of the craft: jewellers obviously needed more training than potters. It is likely that fathers usually passed on their skills to their sons, and that recruits were taught through apprenticeship. From very late in Mesopotamian history we have a small number of apprentice's contracts, drawn up between specialists and the owners of slaves who wanted their servants to learn a craft. This example dates to the second year of King Cyrus (537/6 BC):

Nūpta, daughter of Iddin-Marduk, descendant of Nūr-Sin, has given Atkal-ana-Marduk, the slave of Itti-Marduk-Balāṭu, son of Nabu-ahhē-iddin, descendant of Egibi, to Bēl-eṭir, son of Apla, descendant of Bēl-ēṭiru, to learn the weaver's trade for five years. He must teach him the weaver's trade in its entirety. Nūpta will give to Atkal-ana-Marduk daily bread made from one litre of grain, and his work clothes. If he does not teach him the weaver's trade, Bēl-eṭir will pay six litres of grain as quitrent. Whoever breaks this contract will pay a one-third pound of silver. Witnesses, scribe, place, and date.[3]

Some of the other professions attested in apprenticeship documents are cooking, bleaching, carpentry, seal engraving, leatherworking, shoemaking, and building. The periods of training varied from sixteen months for cooking to eight years for building. We have only one similar text from the early second millennium, not a contract itself but a copy of it in a textbook of legal forms: 'Lu-Inanna, son of Nūr-Kubi, his father Nūr-Kubi gave him to Wusum-bēli for two years, in order to learn the profession of cook,

    [2] H. Waetzoldt, 'Zwei unveröffentliche Ur-III-Texte über die Herstellung von Tongefäßen', *Die Welt des Orients* 6 (1970–71), 28–31, col. iv l. 2–col. v l. 2, l. 29.
    [3] M. San Nicoló, *Der neubabylonische Lehrvertrag in rechtsvergleichende Betrachtung* (Sitzungsberichte der Bayerischen Akademie der Wissenschaften, Philosophisch-historische Klasse; Munich, 1950), 8.

as an apprenticeship . . .'[4] The so-called law code of Hammurabi regulates what happens if a craftsman adopts a child, and teaches him his craft: 'If a craftsman has adopted a child and has taught him his profession, he (the boy) cannot be reclaimed. If he did not teach him his profession, the adopted child may return to his parents' house.'[5]

The specialized class of artisans needed to be exempt from the tasks of primary food production, and this was only possible in an urban economy. It is clear that craft specialization took place in the early stages of the development of urban society, and that the sustainable size of the class of craftsmen was directly related to the size of the urban economy. It is often stated in current literature that, at least until the late second millennium BC, most craftsmen were employed by the central institutions of palace and temples, as only these rich organizations were able to support them; only in the first millennium would artisans have worked privately, both for institutions and for private customers. This reconstruction is based too much on the restricted documentary evidence, which derives primarily from the palaces and temples that possessed workshops.

There are sufficient indications to suggest that craftsmen worked both independently and in institutional workshops throughout the history of Mesopotamia. For instance, the temple workshop at Nippur in the late third millennium did not have metalworkers, and when such delicate tasks as the recasting of a divine statue in gold needed to be done, private goldsmiths were hired.[6] The Code of Hammurabi regulates the fees to be paid to hired craftsmen, unfortunately in a damaged passage:

If someone wants to hire a craftsman, he shall pay per day:

| | |
|---|---|
| as the wage of a [    ] | five grains of silver; |
| as the wage of a felter | five [grains] of silver; |
| [as the wage of] a linen-weaver | [grains] of silver; |
| [as the wage] of a seal-cutter | [grains] of silver; |

---

[4] Claus Wilcke, 'Die Inschriftenfunde der 7. und 8. Kampagnen (1983 und 1984)', in B. Hrouda (ed.), *Isin-Išān Bahrīyāt III* (Munich, 1987), 106 col. ii, ll. 4–11.

[5] Code of Hammurabi §(§ 188 and 189.

[6] Richard L. Zettler, 'Metalworkers in the Economy of Mesopotamia in the Late Third Millennium', in Naomi F. Miller (ed.), *Economy and Settlement in the Near East: Analyses of Ancient Sites and Artifacts* (Philadelphia, 1990), 85–8.

| | |
|---|---|
| [as the wage of] a lapidary | [grains] of silver; |
| [as the wage of a] smith | [grains of] silver; |
| [as the wage of] a carpenter | *four* grains of silver; |
| as the wage of a leather-worker | [  ] grains of silver; |
| as the wage of a reed-worker | [  ] grains of silver; |
| [as the wage of a] builder | [  grains of] silver.[7] |

We are even informed about how artisans were commissioned by their clients to do work. They were provided either with funds to buy the materials needed, or probably more often with the actual materials, as is still common in the Middle East today, and then were expected to perform the work in a timely fashion. That they were not always in a hurry, however, is clear from this letter found at Mari, written by the priestess Bahlatum to the goldsmith Ili-idinnam:

To Ili-idinnam say, thus speaks Bahlatum: 'You have acted towards me as if you and I have never talked, and you are not solving my problem. Earlier, I had given you grain in order to buy stones for a necklace. But you have not yet bought stones for my necklace! It is four years ago that I paid you! Now, while a jeweller did take the gold and silver, these toggle-pins have not yet been made. Now, if you really are like a brother to me, for the sake of all gods, send me that piece at once. Do not hold it back! If that piece does not reach me at once, this commission will no longer be in effect. ⟨If⟩ the two and one-third shekels of gold and four shekels of silver, which were given to you, are not enough for the work, add four shekels of bronze to it, and you will have five shekels of each.'[8]

If craftsmen indeed sold to private customers, why do we lack receipts or sale documents recording these transactions? It is likely that all sales of such items were final: once a finished product was sold, it was not subject to litigation and no records of the sale had to be preserved. Sale documents from Mesopotamia are preserved, but record the sales of real estate, humans, and cattle. The sale of those possessions could be contested in the future: the seller of a house, for instance, could produce witnesses stating his ownership. Thus a written document had to exist to show that the new owner had title to the property. This was not the case for small items that passed from seller to buyer with immediate payment. The private

---

[7] Code of Hammurabi § 274.
[8] Georges Dossin, *Correspondance féminine* (Archives royales de Mari X; Paris, 1978), 162–5 no. 109.

affairs of an artisan are thus quite different from those of an institutional workshop where bureaucrats kept track of the movements of large amounts of materials, products, labour, and payments.

The presence of institutional workshops throughout the history of Mesopotamia cannot be denied. The palaces and temples were large consumers of manufactured goods, and clearly wanted to be guaranteed a supply. Their workshops varied from the private ones in that they employed a concentration of variously skilled artisans. For instance, the palace workshop at Ur in the late third millennium engaged specialists in eight departments: metalworkers, goldsmiths, stonecutters, carpenters, blacksmiths, leather-workers, felters, and reed-workers. This resulted from the fact that many of the desired products required various skills; for example, a chariot for the king was made from wood and leather, contained metal parts, and was perhaps inlaid with semi-precious stones. Leather boots could be lined with felt. As in any pre-industrial economy, component parts were not made separately, but the entire product was manufactured in one location. Hence, various specialists had to collaborate and were active on the same premises. The workshops were entirely owned and operated by the palaces and temples, yet the craftsmen were not necessarily always employed full-time. In the case of an early second-millennium palace workshop in Isin, it is clear that they provided their labour on a part-time basis, having an equal amount of time to work for their own account, an activity that remains undocumented.

The institutions may have had to negotiate with these specialists. A unique document from the sixth century records an agreement between three groups of craftsmen and the administrators of the Eanna temple in Uruk:

Nidinti-Bēl, Chief Administrator of the Eanna, son of Nabû-mukīn-zēr, descendant of Dabibi, and Nabû-ah-iddin, Royal Commissioner ⟨and⟩ Executive Officer of the Eanna to: (5 names, carpenters; 14 names, metal engravers; 11 names, goldsmiths), and to all of the car[penters, metal engravers, goldsmiths], and to the craftsmen of the Eanna, all together, spoke in their midst as follows:
'[You will make the re]pairs and do the work involving silver, gold, bronze, gems, and wood, as much [as there is]. [If] you do not do the work and do not make repairs, or [if someone] does work or makes repairs [in] another temple, [it is an offence.]'

The [carpenter]s, metal engravers, goldsmiths, all the craftsmen of the
Eanna together, by [Bēl, Nabû, and the majesty of Cyrus, king of Babylon]
to Nidinti-Bēl, Chief Administrator of the Eanna, and Nabû-ah-iddin,
Executive Off[icer of the Eanna swore:]
'If someone within his community will do work or make repairs in the
temples of the town, or in the cult-centres, as many as there are, without
our [permission], or if we conceal or keep secret anything when we see or
hear about someone doing work else[where], ⟨may we be damned⟩.' We
swear an oath to Nidinti-[Bēl], Chief Administrator of the Eanna, and
Nabû-ah-iddin, Executive Officer of the Eanna: 'If someone within his
community has seen or heard that someone, without ⟨the permission of⟩
Nidinti-Bēl and Nabû-ah-iddin, has d[one] work or made repairs in another temple, ⟨but⟩ has not told Nidinti-Bēl and Nabû-ah-iddin, the loyalty oath of the king will be violated; he shall be punished by the gods and
the king.'
(Names of 12 witnesses and date).[9]

The craftsmen in this document commit themselves to working for
one temple only in Uruk, which implies that without such a com-
mitment they would have been free to hire themselves out to
whatever institution they chose. It has been stated often that such
professional groups only appeared in the first millennium, when
independent craftsmen became the norm. It seems to me that
earlier craftsmen as well were able to set terms because of their rare
skills. They may have agreed to provide labour to institutional
workshops under special conditions only. Some work could not be
contracted out to them, because the products desired required the
skills of different specialists that could only be brought together in
a central workshop. In such circumstances they may have agreed to
work for the institutional workshop. Other craft activity may have
been commonly institutionalized, because the labour force was not
hard to train. For instance, textile workshops with full-time weavers were often present in palaces, which required large amounts of
finished cloth. It is a mistake, however, to conclude from such
workshops that all craft production was institutional.

The dependence of the Mesopotamian artisan on the central
institutions was thus much smaller than is often suggested, in my
opinion. Craftsmen belonged to a select segment of society with
skills that were in demand by institutions and individuals alike.

[9] David Weisberg, *Guild Structure and Political Allegiance in Early Achaemenid
Mesopotamia* (New Haven and London, 1967), 5–7.

Their distinct status is especially clear in the first millennium, when we find clear evidence for craftsmen's quarters in various cities. Nineveh had its neighbourhoods of goldsmiths, bleachers, and potters. Babylon had a street named after the makers of a particular vat called *ḫuburu* in Akkadian, Nippur had a potters' quarter, and so on. It is thus tempting to suggest parallels with the Islamic cities where one finds *souq*s of goldsmiths, brassworkers, cordmakers, and the like. In the Babylonian material of the first millennium we also see that professional designations were used as the equivalents of our family names: tanner, reedworker, builder, smith, seal-cutter, potter, etc. As the holders of these names may have had other professions, one can say that they were as relevant to some-one's occupation as 'Mr Smith' is today. But this practice indicates that in an earlier period, possibly in the late second millennium, the association with a craft was regarded as a great distinction.

It is hard to determine how far back in time the clearly distinctive social status of craftsmen in Mesopotamian society goes. Evidence for the existence of craft quarters before the first millennium is inconclusive, if not contradictory. Already in the thirteenth century the inner city of Assur had a gate named 'gate of the metalworkers', and one could easily conclude that a concentration of metalworkers lived or at least worked near it. Many archaeologists refer to crafts-men's areas in their discussions of sites, based on surveys that show concentrations of pottery kilns, metal slag, and specific equipment in certain areas of towns. But the archaeological surveys also reveal in most, if not all, domestic quarters evidence of pottery, metal, and lapidary work. Moreover, a unique text from Mari listing the names of craftsmen and the quarters to which they belong, indi-cates that each quarter housed a mixture of various craftsmen, all represented in small numbers. A tabular rendering of this text shows this clearly (see Fig. 8.2). It may thus be best to conclude that all residential quarters had the facilities to generate craft prod-ucts for the basic needs of the inhabitants, although certain crafts were primarily performed in a particular neighbourhood. These specialized areas were probably located where it was easier to get access to resources such as clay and water, or downwind from residential areas in order to avoid the bad smells of the manufactur-ing process. Perhaps only in the first millennium did all the crafts-men limit their activities to certain areas of town.

Throughout the history of Mesopotamia, the skilled craftsmen

| Occupation | Puzur-Dagan | Idin-Itūr-Mer | Zabinum | Dagan-ašrāya | Mut-Ramē | Ana-Ea-taklāku | Total |
|---|---|---|---|---|---|---|---|
| Metalcasters | [3] | 4 | 3 | 3 | 0 | 0 | 13 |
| [ ] | 3 | — | — | — | [ ] | 3 | [ ] |
| Felters | 1 | 2 | 0 | 0 | 1 | 0 | 4 |
| Engravers | 2 | 1 | 4 | 4 | 1 | 0 | 12 |
| Carpenters | 1 | 1 | 1 | 1 | 1 | 1 | 6 |
| Perfumers | 1 | 2 | 0 | 0 | 0 | 0 | 3 |
| Gardeners | 1 | 1 | 0 | 0 | 0 | 0 | 2 |
| Millers | 1 | 0 |  |  | 0 | 0 | 1 |
| [ ] |  | 2 | 2 | 1 | 2 | — | [ ] |
| [ ] | — | — | 1 | — | 1 | — | [ ] |
| Boatmen | 0 | 0 | 0 | 0 | 5 | 0 | 5 |
| Ploughmen | 0 | 0 | 0 | 0 | 1 | 0 | 1 |

FIG. 8.2 'Select men among the craftsmen [   ]'[10]

[10] The names of the individual craftmen, mentioned in the text, have been omitted in this table. [   ] indicates that the passage is broken. A hyphen is entered when it is unclear whether a number was written on the tablet, which is now damaged.

had a distinct and prominent position in society. It is thus logical that they would feel an affinity for their colleagues, and that they would form professional associations. From the early second millennium onward such organizations are attested in the texts. It has been stated that these groups depended on the palace or the temples because they were headed by an overseer, but this common and broad title can also indicate that one of the members was selected to represent the group in its interactions with the government authorities, as I discussed in an earlier chapter. The strength and cohesion of these associations is hard to define. They have been called 'guilds' by a minority of scholars, usually under severe criticism. In a sense, the issue whether or not it is appropriate to use that designation boils down to one of terminology, and to what one has in mind when talking about guilds. Many of the characteristics of a medieval European guild cannot be documented in Mesopotamia, including the crucial element that only guild members could perform a particular craft. But their absence also cannot be proved, and I think that we should not underestimate the power of these professional associations. In any case, the existence of highly specialized artisans, organized in associations with undefined powers, cannot be denied. Such specialists could only be supported in an urban setting.

Crafts were dependent on the city in other ways as well, especially because of their reliance on trade. Many Mesopotamian crafts could not exist without trade, both for the procurement of materials, and for the marketing of finished products. Only in the city was the variety of materials needed in manufacture available. These materials could come either from the city's hinterland or from distant regions. Examples from two crafts will show the various processes involved.

The textile industry relied upon locally produced materials and shows a close interaction between rural and urban economies. Its organization can be reconstructed from a group of texts from the late third millennium, found in the southern city of Ur, and probably deriving from the palace administration. In this region enormous herds of sheep and, to a lesser extent, goats were reared on the steppe by professional herdsmen. Once a year they brought the animals into villages for shearing, and great quantities of wool and hair were collected by the 'wool office', an accounting bureau keeping its records in the city. The wool was not necessarily brought into the city, but could have been kept in storage houses in the countryside, from which it was issued by the wool office to the weaving institutions that were located in villages around Ur. The texts are not clear on what exactly took place there: although we call them weaving workshops, it is likely that the wool was also washed, combed, and spun there. Yet this is not explicitly stated, since it was of no interest to the accountants who were only concerned with amounts delivered and produced. The location of the mills in the villages provided them with easier access to water, which was needed in abundance for the washing of the wool and the finished cloth. The time spent on single pieces of cloth seems exorbitant to us. For instance, three women could weave about 25 centimetres of a third-rate cloth in one day, or about 33 centimetres of a fourth-rate cloth. This has been interpreted as a sign of low productivity, but it could just as easily indicate that production standards were very high, and that extreme care was used in the weaving of these pieces. We know that certain weavers specialized in the production of a particular type of cloth, and the skills involved should not be underestimated. As mentioned above, it took five years for an apprentice to learn the craft.

The labour force active in the textile industry was enormous: it has been calculated that some 13,200 weavers operated around Ur in the late third millennium, and, in other cities of southern Babylonia, similar numbers were likewise engaged. In this period the weavers were mostly women, employed full-time by these institutions, and entirely dependent on them for their support. They received food and cloth rations, yet they probably returned home to their families after work as they are known to have borne children. Young children were taken to work. This was partly caused by the natural need to take care of them, including breast-feeding babies, but older children were able to do work requiring particularly keen eyesight, as they still do among Middle Eastern carpet-makers. The workers were most likely inhabitants of the villages where the weaving mills were located.

After the cloth was woven, it was passed on to the fullers for further processing. Their work was as important as that of the weavers, but it is much less documented in our sources. An exception is a long text from the early second millennium providing a detailed account of numbers of days spent for the work on very fine garments. Unfortunately, most of the technical wonds used can only be given a conjectural translation. For instance,

> One second quality *šētum* garment, (weighing) three and a half
> kilograms:
> three months and six days: twisting
> two days: cleaning
> two days: trimming
> one month: sewing up
> two days: pressing
> one month and twenty days: teaselling
> four days: scraping and levelling
> one month: sewing, teaselling, and finishing
> six days: beating
> two months: picking the threads from the front
> twenty days: picking the threads from the back
> ten days: stretching and pressing
> one month and eighteen days: untwisting
> one month and ten days: blowing
> 400 ⟨workdays of⟩ textile workers,
> quota for one second quality *šētum* garment, ⟨weighing⟩ three and a
> half kilograms.[11]

Most likely the fullers were also located in the countryside with easy access to water. Thus the labour was provided by the villagers, the wool by the rural herdsmen, and the administration by the city bureaucrats. The finished textiles became the property of the institution whose records we have, which was also the largest consumer, as it clothed its numerous dependants. The textile industry at Ur is the only one that we can reconstruct in detail, but other palaces and temples had similar weaving mills.

Work with leather, reed, and clay probably functioned along similar lines as that with wool, as all of them relied primarily on locally available resources. Other crafts depended on imported materials, however: carpentry for its hard woods, stone-cutting for stone other than the local soft limestone, metalwork for its ores, and jewellery for its gold, silver, and gems. The access to these materials was restricted, as they could only be obtained through trade or conquest. Bronze metallurgy, for instance, relied entirely

---

[11] Sylvie Lackenbacher, 'Un texte vieux-babylonien sur la finition des textiles', *Syria* 59 (1982), 131–2, § e.

on supplies gathered from various remote sources. Although from early prehistory onwards trade contacts between Mesopotamia and other regions are evident, and international trade did not necessarily require an urban environment, the procuring of two metal ores from various directions could only be organized by a central institution supported by an urban infrastructure. In the mid-third millennium, for instance, copper was imported from Oman, tin from Afghanistan. As the latter metal was used only in alloy, its import was senseless unless it was certain that it could be combined with copper. Hence, the need for central planning which could only be provided by a central institution supported by an urban economy.

We know surprisingly little about the organization of metallurgy. As mentioned above, cuprous slag is found in domestic areas of towns, indicating the production of metal objects within private households. The textual evidence of the third and second millennia shows, however, that domestic use of metal was very limited, though not entirely absent. The archives from palaces and temples contain most of the information on metallurgy, but, again, they only record the materials handed to the smiths and the finished products received, without details of what happened in between. In the first millennium, there was a marked increase in the amount of metal available in Mesopotamia. Besides copper and tin, iron gradually became more common, although the growth of its use was a very slow process. Assyrian military expansion gave direct access to mines in Anatolia; additionally large quantities of metals were commandeered from subject regions. Over the centuries, a substantial accumulation of various scrap metals must have developed in Mesopotamia, permitting the temporary suspension of new supplies. Worries about the interruption of supply routes are not attested in the sources, as far as I know. But the dependence on the exterior world never disappeared, and the increased demand for base metals documented in our sources always had to be satisfied by new imports. These could only be co-ordinated in an urban setting. The centres of production for metal objects were always located in the cities, and the idea of the itinerant smith spreading ironworking techniques is not at all supported by our sources.

There was thus a need for an urban society with the facilities to procure the varied resources used in manufacture. These resources were not only the raw materials collected from different sources, both local and foreign, but also labour and administration. The labour force needed for the large weaving mills of the late third millennium, for instance, could only be gathered near an urban environment. And, when the manufacturing process became complex, because of the needs for a large variety of materials and for highly specialized craftsmen, an appropriate administrative structure to organize this was crucial. Again, only in cities could such an administration be found. If they were to flourish, crafts also needed an urban environment to provide them with suitable markets. This is not to imply that all craft products were locally consumed: even if they were intended for export, the mechanisms of trade to accomplish this were only available in cities.

The domestic market varied enormously according to craft, time period, and even city. The clientele becomes more exclusive when the craft product becomes more valuable. Private citizens owned only a few metal objects, and jewellery or seals of semi-precious stone were even rarer. Reed mats, leather bags, and cooking vessels certainly had a broader market. Demand varied over time as well. Metal objects became much more common in the first millennium than ever before. In the early first millennium Babylonia had hardly any luxury products, while in the sixth century there was an abundance.

The presence of large institutions in a city greatly influenced what products were needed. The palatial organizations of Babylonia in the late third millennium required large amounts of products for their dependants, especially cloth, issued as a ration. The Uruk bevelled-rim bowls, mentioned above, may have been used to distribute barley rations, which could explain why they are nearly ubiquitous in sites of this period. The quantity of bowls required led to a highly standardized production method in moulds. Palaces provided their messengers with leather sandals and water-skins, and so on. The demand for luxury products such as jewellery was dictated by the presence of palaces, temples, or courtiers, and goldsmiths could only work in cities where these existed. All these needs determined what was produced.

Many craft products were locally consumed but, as already indicated, they could also be exported. This is the second point where crafts and trade were essentially related: trade procured some of the materials needed, while crafts provided goods needed for export. It is quite clear to us what things were imported into Mesopotamia; however, we are ill-informed about the goods used to obtain them, and the issue has received little attention. Mesopotamian agricultural surplus undoubtedly was bartered in certain cases: cereals, dates, sesame oil, and dried fish were available in abundance. By ship, large quantities of these could be cheaply transported to such places as modern-day Oman. But when overland transport was required, cargoes of this nature would become prohibitively expensive. The often-repeated idea that grain was shipped from Uruk to Afghanistan in order to acquire lapis lazuli is ludicrous. By the time the human or animal carriers had completed their journey of over 2,000 kilometres, they would long have consumed their entire load. More valuable and less bulky items needed to be used.

Information about the exported items is rare. Unique is the documentation on the trade that took place between Assur and central Anatolia in the twentieth and nineteenth centuries, due to the chance find of the Assyrian traders' correspondence in their Anatolian colony at Kanish. Assur sent two products to Anatolia: tin and textiles. The first was obtained from an unknown source in the east and Assur only acted as a place of transit for it. Textiles were either local products of a standard quality, or high quality imports from Babylonia. Caravans were assembled with donkeys and asses each carrying loads of about 90 kilograms in total, made up from textiles only or from a mixture of textiles and tin. The 800-kilometre voyage lasted some fifty days. In Anatolia the loads were traded for gold and silver. Even after deducting expenses for food bought along the way and transit taxes, for which five kilograms of loose tin were taken, profits averaged at least 50 per cent. The preserved records document exports of about 17,500 textiles and about 13.5 tons of tin from Assur to Kanish over a period of forty to fifty years; the total transfer of goods during this time has been estimated to have amounted to at least 100,000 textiles and 100 tons of tin. These would have been worth between twelve and thirteen tons of silver on the market in Assur, which must have been approximately the amount of the precious metal imported by the Assyrian merchants.

It is certain that the Assur–Kanish network was not unique, and trade in many areas was conducted along similar lines. Mesopotamia's crucial resource in all its international trade was its manufacture of craft products, desired abroad by suppliers of raw materials. The latter could be re-exported to third parties for a substantial profit, but they could not have been acquired in the first place without Mesopotamian craft products. These derived from the most basic crafts, primarily the textile industry, but probably also leather and reed work. There is no evidence for the export of fine jewellery or the like, and these luxury goods were seemingly only made for a local clientele. The exchange between Mesopotamia and its neighbours clearly was not an even one: basic finished products were traded for valuable raw materials. There was no need for a military threat to enforce such an exchange. We have here a clear example of a technologically advanced society dominating the market of more primitive societies surrounding it. Yet we should not imagine that the Mesopotamians dumped low-quality merchandise on foreign markets. The exported textiles were fine products and were made by specialized weavers. They did not prevent the existence of local textile manufacture. That the abundant wealth displayed in the so-called royal tombs at Ur, for instance, was funded by something as basic as the city's textile industry, need not surprise us. Similar situations where textiles of one area were in high demand internationally and provided the basis for great economic development are familiar elsewhere in history. One needs only to think of Flanders in the Middle Ages, for instance.

Mesopotamian trade and crafts were thus intrinsically connected: one provided the materials without which certain crafts could not function, the other the goods without which these materials could not be obtained. Mesopotamia was technologically more advanced than its neighbours, and this enabled it to obtain the goods that were locally absent. The idea that it was a bread basket for the Near East has to be rejected as the transport of bulky items over long distances was unfeasible except over the Persian Gulf. The main centres of manufacture were located in the cities where the materials, labourers, and markets were available both to produce and to sell the goods. I do not want to exclude the likelihood that some basic manufacture took place outside cities. Villagers must have produced pots, baskets, bags, and so on, for their own use, and even to exchange locally. But their main occupation involved food production, and there did not exist a cottage industry providing goods for an urban market. If villages existed that specialized in the manufacture of a certain product, such as pottery, as we sometimes find today in the Middle East, they could not have survived without an urban market nearby. Moreover, they would not show the necessary diversity of products from various crafts to equal the production in the urban centres. Urban manufacture was thus something unique, yet poorly documented. We cannot determine, for instance, what percentage of the urban population was involved in manufacture. Since a substantial part of these activities took place in an undocumented private sector, we will always be denied detailed knowledge of this part of the urban economy.

An important group of ancient historians holds firmly to Max Weber's idea of the ancient city as a centre of consumption, in contrast to the medieval European city where manufacture provided the goods that enabled a very lucrative trade. The specialized craft workshops that can be discerned in the historical record are regarded by these scholars as having catered to a local market, and the importance of trade in craft products, such as Attic painted pottery, is downplayed.[12] The Mesopotamian city has never been considered from this point of view. In fact, most scholars who have dealt with issues of trade portray the ancient Mesopotamian city pretty much like a medieval European one, and comparisons with places like Genoa have been made without hesitation. The Mesopotamian cities lack Guildhalls, as do the Graeco-Roman ones, and the political powers of craftsmen and traders are unclear to us, but probably less than those of their medieval counterparts. However, some cities, like Assur, may have been established primarily for trading purposes,[13] and Mesopotamia's location on the junction of numerous trade routes from Asia to the Mediterranean world strongly suggests that long-distance trade flourished in the region. The image we get of certain cities, such as Assur and Ur, as centres of trade may obviously be false, and generated by the relative abundance of documentation dealing with that activity. In general the Mesopotamian written sources on trade are relatively rare, yet

---

[12] For instance, M. I. Finley, *The Ancient Economy*, 2nd edn. (Berkeley and Los Angeles, 1985), 134–9, 191–6.

[13] See David Oates, 'The development of Assyrian towns and cities', in Peter J. Ucko, Ruth Tringham, and G. W. Dimbleby (eds.), *Man, Settlement and Urbanism* (London, 1972), 799–804.

well studied. Since we cannot quantify the entire urban economy, we cannot estimate the importance of any of its component parts. We have to be careful not to exaggerate the significance of trade, and not to be misled by later European parallels. On the other hand, we cannot deny that long-distance trading activities were common, and that, in Mesopotamia at least, they required manufacture for their survival: that intrinsic connection between trade and manufacture was a crucial aspect of the urban economy.

BIBLIOGRAPHY

No history of Mesopotamian crafts exists at the moment, but the recent book by P. R. S. Moorey, *Ancient Mesopotamian Materials and Industries: The Archaeological Evidence* (Oxford, 1994), provides a gold-mine of information on the materials of archaeologically recovered objects and good surveys of the textual sources for the crafts involved. A very useful discussion of Ancient Near Eastern crafts in general is by Carlo Zaccagnini, 'Le tecniche e le scienze', in S. Moscati (ed.), *L'alba della civiltà* 2: *L'economia* (Turin, 1976), 291–421. For late third-millennium Babylonia see Hans Neumann, *Handwerk in Mesopotamien* (Berlin, 1987); for early second-millennium Babylonia, Marc Van De Mieroop, *Crafts in the Early Isin Period* (Orientalia Lovaniensia Analecta 24; Louvain, 1987); and for the late first millennium, David Weisberg, *Guild Structure and Political Allegiance in Early Achaemenid Mesopotamia* (New Haven and London, 1967).

Some records from pottery workshops were published by H. Waetzoldt, 'Zwei unveröffentliche Ur-III-Texte über die Herstellung von Tongefäßen', *Die Welt des Orients* 6 (1970–71), 7–41; and Dietz Otto Edzard, *Altbabylonische Rechts- und Wirtschaftstexten aus Tell ed-Der im Iraq Museum, Baghdad* (Munich, 1970), 192–9 text no. 198. For the textile industry in the Ur III period, see Thorkild Jacobsen, 'On the Textile Industry at Ur under Ibbī-Sîn', in *Towards the Image of Tammuz and other Essays on Mesopotamian History and Culture*, (Cambridge, Mass., 1970), 216–29; and Hartmut Waetzoldt, *Untersuchungen zur neusumerischen Textilindustrie* (Rome, 1972). For metallurgy, see P. R. S. Moorey, *Materials and Manufacture in Ancient Mesopotamia:*

*The Evidence of Archaeology and Art. Metals and Metalwork, Glazed Materials and Glass* (Oxford, 1985); Henri Limet, *Le Travail du métal au pays de Sumer* (Paris, 1960); F. Joannès, 'Metalle und Metallurgie A.1: In Mesopotamien' (in French), *Reallexikon der Assyriologie* 8 (Berlin and New York, 1993), 96–112; and J. D. Muhly, 'Metalle B: Archäologisch', (in English), ibid. 119–36. The latter contains an extensive bibliography on discussions of the metal trade.

For the location of craft areas in second-millennium Babylonian cities, see Elizabeth C. Stone, 'The Spacial Organization of Mesopotamian Cities', *Aula Orientalis* 9 (1991), 235–42. More theoretical discussions of the identification of craftsmen's quarters are provided by Luca Mariani, 'Craftsmen's Quarters in The Proto-urban Settlements of the Middle East: The Surface Analysis', in B. Allchin (ed.), *South Asian Archaeology 1981* (Cambridge, 1984), 118–23; and by Maurizio Tosi, 'The Notion of Craft Specialization and its Representation in the Archaeological Record of Early States in the Turanian Basin', in Matthew Spriggs (ed.), *Marxist Perspectives in Archaeology* (Cambridge, 1984), 22–52.

For the apprenticeship contracts of the late period, see M. San Nicolò, *Der neubabylonische Lehrvertrag in rechtsvergleichender Betrachtung* (Sitzungsberichte der Bayerischen Akademie der Wissenschaften, philosophisch-historische Klasse; Munich, 1950/ III); H. P. H. Petschow, 'Lehrverträge', *Reallexikon der Assyriologie* 6 (Berlin and New York, 1980–3), 556–70; and Muhammad A. Dandamaev, *Slavery in Babylonia* (DeKalb, 1984), 279–307. The last work also contains important insights on the relative importance of free and slave artisans in the late Babylonian period, concluding that slave labour in crafts was very limited.

The specialization of crafts during the development of urbanism in Mesopotamia was stressed by V. Gordon Childe, 'The Urban Revolution', *Town Planning Review* 21 (1950), 3–17. Robert McC. Adams, *The Evolution of Urban Society*, (Chicago, 1960), is more nuanced in his appreciation of the role of craft specialization in the general context of labour specialization.

The argument that guilds existed in ancient Mesopotamia has most recently been posed by David Weisberg, *Guild Structure and Political Allegiance* (1967). A. Leo Oppenheim, *Ancient Mesopotamia*, (Chicago and London, 1977), 79–81 talks about guild-like

associations already in the early second millennium. Criticism of
Weisberg's thesis has been extensive; see, for instance, Johannes
Renger, 'Notes on the Goldsmiths, Jewelers and Carpenters
of Neobabylonian Eanna', *Journal of the American Oriental Society*
91 (1971), 494–503; and Hans M. Kümmel, *Familie, Beruf und
Amt im spätbabylonischen Uruk* (Berlin, 1979). The latter also men-
tions the existence of professional designations as 'family names',
which were discussed briefly by W. G. Lambert, 'Ancestors,
Authors and Canonicity', *Journal of Cuneiform Studies* 11 (1957),
1–14.

Trade has been the subject of numerous books and articles; most
have focused on the early history until *c.*1500 BC. A survey placing
trade in the context of the exchange of goods in general is provided
by Carlo Zaccagnini, 'La circolazione dei beni', in S. Moscati (ed.),
*L'alba della civiltà* 2: *L'economia* (Turin, 1976), 425–582. W. F.
Leemans provides a good historical survey of international trade
throughout Mesopotamian history in 'Handel', *Reallexikon der
Assyriologie* 4, (Berlin, 1972–5), 76–90. In two earlier books he
studied aspects of third- and early second-millennia trade in detail:
*The Old Babylonian Merchant*, (Leiden, 1950) and *Foreign Trade in
the Old Babylonian Period* (Leiden, 1960). Several interesting articles appeared in the Proceedings of the XXIII Rencontre
Assyriologique International, published in the journal *Iraq* 39
(1977). A lengthy review of the issues raised in this volume and of
prehistoric trade has been written by Norman Yoffee, *Explaining
Trade in Ancient Western Asia* (Malibu, 1981). Important problems
concerning the early trade between Mesopotamia and Iran are
addressed by P. R. S. Moorey, 'Iran: a Sumerian el-Dorado?', in
John Curtis (ed.), *Early Mesopotamia and Iran. Contact and Conflict
3500–1600 BC* (London, 1993), 31–43. Old Assyrian trade has
been well studied in books by K. R. Veenhof, *Aspects of Old
Assyrian Trade and its Terminology* (Leiden, 1972); Mogens Trolle
Larsen, *Old Assyrian Caravan Procedures* (Istanbul, 1967), and *The
Old Assyrian City-State and its Colonies* (Copenhagen, 1976). See
also a popularized account by Larsen, 'Caravans and Trade in
Ancient Mesopotamia and Asia Minor', *Bulletin of the Canadian
Society of Mesopotamian Studies* 4 (1982), 33–45, and his 'Commer-
cial Networks in the Ancient Near East', in Michael Rowlands *et al.*
(eds.), *Centre and Periphery in the Ancient World* (Cambridge,

1987), 47–56. For exports from Babylonia in the third millennium see H. E. W. Crawford, 'Mesopotamia's Invisible Exports', *World Archaeology* 5 (1973), 231–41. For later periods, the literature on trade is much smaller. Late second-millennium exchange of goods is studied by Carlo Zaccagnini, *Lo scambio dei doni nel Vicino Oriente durante i secoli XV–XIII* (Rome, 1973). For first millennium Babylonia, see A. Leo Oppenheim, 'Essay on Overland Trade in the First Millennium B.C.', *Journal of Cuneiform Studies* 21 (1967), 236–54; and Muhammed A. Dandamaev, 'Die Rolle des *tamkārum* in Babylonien im 2. und 1. Jahrtausend v.u.Z.', *Beiträge zur sozialen Struktur des alten Vorderasien* (Berlin, 1971), 69–78.

# 9

# Credit and Management

The most commonly recorded transaction in Mesopotamian contracts is the loan. Thousands of documents detailing the receipt of goods or silver and the obligation for their repayment, with or without interest, are preserved from the late third millennium on in Babylonia and Assyria. The format of the loan contracts varied enormously. The creditor could be an individual, several persons, an individual together with an institution, or an institution by itself. The debtor could be a single person or a group of people. The commodities loaned could be silver, consumables such as corn or dates, or a mixture of both. The loans could be repaid in kind, consumables could be given for silver, or silver could be paid for with agricultural produce. The repayment period could vary from a few days to, on rare occasions, several years. Interest rates also fluctuated considerably, despite statements in the so-called law-codes, usually proclaiming a 20 per cent rate for silver and a $33\frac{1}{3}$ per cent rate for grain. Interest-free loans were quite common; sometimes interest was only charged when the debtor failed to repay the loan on time; or rates charged could amount to 50 per cent and more.

Although the formulary and legal significance of the loan contracts have been studied extensively from the moment they became known to us, their role in the economy of Mesopotamia has not been investigated. Due to their number and variety this would be an enormous project to undertake, but one that promises important results. Some significant points have to be remembered before one can undertake such a study. The documents we have are evidence of loans that were not repaid; we can only study the bad loans issued by moneylenders. When a loan was repaid in full, the document on which it had been recorded was destroyed, as it had no further use. Moreover, many of the loans in our documentation were not simple transfers of effects for a set period of time to be

used by the debtor for whatever purpose. Many of them were
fictitious, arranging a sale on credit or a payment of dues to be
refunded with goods at a later point in time.

The loan, as known to us, was essentially an urban phenomenon;
urban residents or institutions provided it to one another or to
residents of the countryside. The ability to issue loans required
access to silver, a commodity not widely available in Mesopotamia,
and most likely only present in cities; moreover, one needed to be
within reach of a substantial number of people in order to be able
to conduct money-lending as a routine business activity. Obviously, one cannot discount the possibility that villagers made
loans to one another, but to provide credit on a regular basis to a
varied clientele would almost certainly have been beyond their
capability.

In this chapter I wish to focus attention on the role of credit in
two aspects of the Mesopotamian urban economy: international
trade and the procurement of agricultural resources for the urban
consumer. In both areas, city residents with access to liquid capital
provided funds to entrepreneurs who used them to acquire goods
to be brought into town. Although international trade and local
trade in agricultural produce were two entirely separate businesses
and most likely undertaken by different people, they show a similar
organization with respect to financing. Both required substantial
funds which were raised from various sources. The two businesses
may have diverged, however, in their contacts with the producers
of the goods obtained. Credit played an important role in the
interaction with farmers, but it seems unlikely that it was issued to
the producers of the raw materials imported into Mesopotamia.
The latter were probably not forced to provide set amounts of
copper ore, or the like, and were thus not in danger of falling
behind in production.

International trade required funds to pay for the expenses of the
expeditions and for the acquisition of goods abroad. These funds
could be raised in a variety of ways and from different sources.
Both private citizens and institutions are known to have invested
their capital in international trade. One of the most common
procedures was the gathering of an investment purse from various
financiers through partnership agreements. One example of such
an agreement was drawn up in Assur in the early second
millennium:

(Fourteen names with amounts of gold) Total: fifteen kilograms of gold, the investment purse of Amur-Ishtar. Starting from the eponym-year of Susaja he will trade for twelve years. Of the profit he will receive one-third. He will take responsibility for another third. He who withdraws his money before the end of his term, shall take two kilograms of silver for each pound of gold. He will not take any of the profit. (Seven witnesses).[1]

The procedure was simple: fourteen wealthy Assyrians put a sum of fifteen kilograms of gold at the disposal of Amur-Ishtar to enable him to conduct trade with Anatolia for a twelve-year period of time. This was a substantial sum to work with, and allowed Amur-Ishtar to acquire in Assur tin and textiles to be exported to Anatolia, where they would be traded for silver and gold. An average gain of 50 per cent could be expected from such an expedition, a third of which would go to Amur-Ishtar. The investors could thus still expect a 33 per cent profit on their investment.

These partnership agreements were not limited to Old Assyrian trade. There is evidence for them in Babylonia at the same time period. They provided funds for trade over the Persian Gulf, with the difference, however, that the partnerships lasted only for the duration of one expedition rather than for several years. The reluctance to conclude long-term agreements may reflect greater risks and political instability in the Persian Gulf than in the Assur-Kanish trade. Late in Babylonian history such partnerships were still in use, at that time seemingly for prolonged periods of time.

Partnerships were not the only way in which a trader could raise funds. He could also turn to numerous investors who each contributed small sums. We have, for instance, records from Ur in the early second millennium, where the merchant Ea-naṣir collected small amounts of goods, baskets, textiles, and silver from his fellow citizens:

1 silver ring: Uqâ-Shamash
1 silver ring: Sin-ēmāni, son of Dakullum
1 silver ring: Sin-nāṣir
1 silver ring: Nidnat-Sin
1 silver ring: Sin-bēl-apli
1 silver ring: Ikun-pīsha

---

[1] B. Landsberger, 'Vier Urkunden aus Kultepe', *Türk Tarih Arkeologya ve Etnografya Dergisi* 4 (1940), 20–1 no 3; trans. after Mogens Trolle Larsen, 'Partnerships in Old Assyrian Trade', *Iraq* 39 (1977), 125 and n. 16.

1 silver ring: Gullubu, son of Belashu
1 silver ring: Nanna-mansum
1 silver ring: Nawīrum-ili, son of Ishi-ili
1 silver ring: Dumuzi-mansum
1 silver ring: Ibni-Ea, son of the carpenter
1 silver ring: Erībam-Sin
1 silver ring: Appa, son of Ludingira
1 silver ring: Sin-muballiṭ
1 silver ring: Appan
Responsibility of Ea-nāṣir.[2]

The merchant could also take out loans. The various agreements he concluded with his creditors included the equivalent to the bottomry loan, the primary source of funding available to the maritime traders of fourth-century Athens and later.[3] Bottomry loans were taken out with the promise of a very high return, which was only to be repaid, however, when the trade mission was a success. Thus the trader was not liable for repayment in the event that his cargo was lost at sea. The investors took a higher risk, as they could lose their entire contribution, but on the other hand their gains were greater if the expedition was successful. Similar agreements existed in Mesopotamia. For instance, the following contract records an agreement between two traders and one investor in which the latter provides silver and goods for an expedition to the island of Dilmun, modern Bahrain in the Persian Gulf:

Lu-Meslamtaë and Nigsisa-nabdiri have received from Ur-Ninmarkika one kilogram of silver ⟨in the form of⟩ 1,500 litres of sesame oil and thirty garments for an expedition to Dilmun in order to buy copper there, capital of a partnership. At the safe return of the expedition, the creditor will not recognize losses. By mutual agreement the debtors will satisfy Ur-Ninmarkika with the just price of two kilograms of copper for each eight grams of silver. They have sworn together by the king. Witnesses. Date: 1795 BC.[4]

The contract stipulates that the investor will only receive a return on his investment if the expedition is successful, which is an agree-

[2] H. H. Figulla and W. J. Martin, *Letters and Documents of the Old Babylonian Period* (Ur Excavations, Texts 5; London and Philadelphia, 1953), no. 554 ll. 1–16.

[3] See P. C. Millett, 'Maritime loans and the structure of credit in fourth-century Athens', in P. Garnsey, K. Hopkins, and C. R. Whittaker (eds.), *Trade in the Ancient Economy* (London, 1983), 36–52.

[4] Figulla and Martin, *Letters and Documents of the Old Babylonian Period*, no. 367.

ment similar to the bottomry loan. The contract also states that the investor will not be held responsible for any losses incurred by the traders, but will receive a guaranteed payment of two kilograms of copper for each eight grams of silver he invested, thus totalling 250 kilograms. The investment by Ur-Ninmarkika is substantial but undoubtedly insufficient to finance an entire expedition. We see a clear attempt to distribute the risks for both the investors and the traders. No individual or firm was the sole investor in an expedition, nor did a person invest his or her entire capital at one time. This practice was wise, considering the dangers confronting the long-distance trader.

That the merchants were not always able to obtain the investments on their own terms is clear from the following letter. In it, Pushuken, who became one of the most successful Old Assyrian traders, complains about the unwillingness of his financiers to advance him money on his terms. He would prefer an arrangement over a three-year period, while his creditors are talking about five years. Why the shorter period would have been better for Pushuken is unclear, unless he wanted the chance to dissolve the partnership at an earlier stage in order to renegotiate it at that time:

To my investors, Shu-Hubur, and my representatives speak: thus says Pushuken: 'I asked the god for three full years saying: "Let me go and clear my working-capital and deposit before them as much as there is." Shu-Hubur spoke about five years, and you were in agreement, but I did not agree to this. I said: "I will not wait for five years. For as much time as I asked from the god, I shall come and clear my working-capital." Two or three of the financiers on whom I depend do not have common sense. A lot of money has escaped me because they are not favourably disposed towards me. I will not tell you their names. I thought: "They will come later; the financier will give them every shekel needed and they will give me as much as they can." May Assur and your god be witnesses! I have lost no less than sixty kilograms of silver. But enough! You are my lords. If you please, consider how many commissions have been levied in the house of my investors, so do certify a tablet for me, stating that for three years my deposits will come and the money will not be seized; and send your good message with my servant so that I can collect every last shekel of silver of my working-capital before harvest-time.'[5]

---

[5] A. T. Clay, *Letters and Transactions from Cappadocia* (New Haven, 1927), no. 32, trans. after Paul Garelli, *Les Assyriens en Cappadoce* (Paris, 1963), 233–4. The trans. of ll. 4–17, and 28–39 is based on Larsen, *Iraq* 39 (1977), 130 and 143. Garelli suggests that the debate over the duration of the agreement may have

Investments in trade were not only made by individuals, but also by public institutions. The palaces and the temples were the primary consumers of imported materials, and thus were greatly interested in the procurement of supplies. However, their role has been overly emphasized, in my opinion. As almost all third-millennium records regarding international trade derive from institutional archives, it has been commonly stated that such trade was only undertaken by merchants as palace or temple dependants. Any contact between a trader and an institution has been interpreted as evidence that the institution employed the trader. It is equally possible that the merchants were private citizens who received most, if not all, their funds from the crown or a temple for one or more trading expeditions. The independent status of the merchant was to his benefit. In the contentious world of Mesopotamia, trade embargoes were an appealing weapon, and the lack of a clear affiliation with a political power allowed the autonomous trader to go where palace officials would be barred. This is nothing unusual, of course, and the most famous traders throughout world history have often been based on the fringes of the major political and military powers rather than in them: the Genoans, Venetians, and Dutch, for instance. A collaboration in international trade between the private and institutional sectors of the Mesopotamian economy would have been mutually beneficial. Thus, long-distance trade relied heavily on credit, which was provided to the merchants by investors who wanted to make a profit with their assets. The loans they issued were for productive purposes.

A prominent school of ancient historians claims that, in Greece, maritime trade was the only area of the economy where credit was provided for such objectives.[6] The possibility that the same was true in Mesopotamia has not been investigated.[7] There are strong indications, however, that this was not the case, and that liquid

resulted from the fact that the temple issued credit for three years (op. cit., 248–9), while Larsen thinks it involves the extension of an existing contract (op. cit., 130–1).

[6] M. I. Finley, *The Ancient Economy*, 2nd edn. (Berkeley and Los Angeles, 1985), 141–2, 196–8; Paul Millett, *Lending and Borrowing in Ancient Athens* (Cambridge, 1991).

[7] The only time this question has been asked is in a recent statement by J. Renger, 'Zu aktuellen Frage der Mesopotamische Wirtschaftsgeschichte', in P. Vavroušek and V. Souček (eds.), *Šulmu* (Prague, 1988), 306–7. He presumes that the Greek situation applies to Mesopotamia as well.

assets were used in other profit-making credit operations as well. The best documentation for this is found in the area of the procurement of agricultural produce by urban entrepreneurs. Credit played a crucial role there, enabling the exchange of goods in a massive agricultural economy without developed market mechanisms. It was provided to entrepreneurs by landowners who granted them the right to collect agriculture produce in return for a payment in the future, or by financiers who subsidized the acquisition of produce by entrepreneurs. At the same time the entrepreneurs provided loans to farmers, who repaid their debts at harvest time with produce. Thus credit was issued both to and by the intermediaries who organized food provisioning for the urban citizenry.

Many of the large landowners in Mesopotamia did not reside on their properties. The public institutions centred in the cities owned agricultural estates in a wide geographical area. Rural landowners often lived in town, while prominent administrators and the like, who were granted fields as a reward for their services, could not work that land themselves. Large numbers of tenant farmers lived and worked on these estates, each assigned a plot of land which would support his family, as well as provide the landowner with an income. Rents were due to the owners, and in certain circumstances taxes were to be paid to the palace. Tenants had access only to the products of their labour as a method of payment, while the owners had only a limited use for such food products. These problems not only arose on grain-producing lands: herds were similarly assigned to shepherds and their milk products had an even shorter shelf-life. The enormous amounts of wool produced by the herds owned by palaces and temples were bulky, and hard to store. Fishing rights in the marshes and on the rivers could only be paid in easily spoiled fish, orchards provided an abundance of dates, and gardens huge amounts of vegetables. The owners could consume only a fraction of these goods through redistribution to their dependants. Surpluses could only be stored at a high cost, and the demand for these goods did not guarantee total consumption. Marketing surplus foodstuff was a time-consuming affair, requiring an extensive network.

Instead, it was easier to sell the rights of collection to people who would pay for it with easily storable silver. These entrepreneurs became the managers of the agricultural estates for the urban landowners, and interacted directly with the farmers. After what seems to have been a highly centralized and direct bureaucratic management of these affairs in the third millennium, the remainder of Mesopotamian history—in Babylonia at least—shows the extensive involvement of private entrepreneurs in these matters. Their activities are documented to us through the credit transactions that were involved: records of payments owed by the entrepreneurs to the owners, or by the farmers to the entrepreneurs. They allow us to reconstruct how the system worked in Babylonia, as the following three examples will show. For Assyria we lack the data, or at least an analysis of them, to determine whether similar systems were in use.

The earliest clear evidence of the use of private entrepreneurs in the collection of dues and taxes derives from the southern Babylonian kingdom of Larsa during the eighteenth century. In advance of the harvest, the palace sold the rights to collect the produce owed to it for only a third of its value. The staples involved were barley, fish, legumes, and wool, and after they had been gathered and sold, another third of the price had to be paid to the palace. All the latter wanted was easily storable silver, and in return the collectors were granted the possibility of a substantial return on their investment. Moreover, the palace was rather lax in the collections of its dues, again to the benefit of the entrepreneurs. But the entrepreneurs had to work hard: not only did they need to organize collection of the staples, they also needed to transport them, preserve them when necessary, store them, and finally sell them at a profit. The last activity is entirely undocumented in our sources, but there is no doubt that it must have taken place as the entrepreneurs could certainly not have consumed all the goods. The reason for this absence from the documentation is similar to that regarding the sale of manufactured goods: all sales were final. There was no possibility of non-payment resulting in court action, and no records of the transactions needed to be kept.

The persons who were involved in the collection and marketing of the staple goods grouped themselves into an organization that was almost self-governing, and with the conquest of Larsa by Hammurabi in 1762 they acquired an important role in state affairs by becoming tax-farmers. How they bid for the contracts, if they did so at all, is unclear to us. But they had the right to collect for the crown in Babylon the taxes owed to it, and, although they paid for this right, their payments were often made after long delays. A question remains about where the entrepreneurs found the funds to engage in this business. A payment needed to be made to the palace for the right of tax collection; this could have been a substantial amount. It is possible, although undocumented so far, that investments were sought for this enterprise in the same way that an international trader raised funds.

The opportunities of the entrepreneurs were not limited to buying at a low price and selling at a much higher one. They could also provide interest-bearing loans to farmers. Tenant farmers probably lived precariously. Dues were often collected at one-third or one-half of their entire harvest, when they were not calculated in set amounts enforced in lean as well as fat years. The size of the average tenant plot is not known to us, thus we are unable to determine whether or not the income from it was sufficient to feed a family after the dues were paid. We do know, however, that many farmers were often in trouble and required help to tide them over until harvest time. They could only turn to entrepreneurs for credit, and these men were willing to provide it for a price. For instance, when grain was needed to feed a farmer's family in the month preceding the harvest, or to allow the farmer to sow his fields, its value was calculated with its silver equivalent at the current market price. As it was generally in short supply at that time, the price was high. The farmer had to repay the grain at harvest time, when prices were low and he had to give much more of it than he had originally received, even if we ignore the interest charged. In this way, the creditor benefited from variations in market price, as well as from the interest charged. The calculation of the latter depended on the formulation of the original loan: when it was entirely calculated with the silver equivalents of the barley it amounted to 20 per cent; when the quantity of barley originally granted in the loan was recorded in the contract the interest was calculated at $33\frac{1}{3}$ per cent, as the creditor could not benefit from varying market prices.

As a guarantee for the loan, the borrower provided a pledge. Often this was a term of service supplied by a member of the family—a wife, son, or daughter—to the creditor. Alternatively, the farmer might pledge a tool or a boat, which then needed to be rented from the creditor. The debtor could even agree to pay a rent for the land he already worked for another proprietor. In any case, the farmer's expenses increased substantially, as did the likelihood that he would need another loan the following year. He was sucked into a spiral of increasing indebtedness from which escape was unlikely. His final resort was flight, but because this had so many negative social repercussions and reduced him to the status of a brigand, this alternative was, it seems, rarely used.

The situation was often so bad that the palace intervened and declared all consumer debts null and void. The annulment of debts by the king became a common occurrence in Babylonia in the eighteenth–seventeenth centuries, restoring the tax base by freeing farmers from the debts to their creditors, including those for outstanding taxes. This is an excerpt from the most famous of these edicts, the one issued by Ammiṣaduqa of Babylon (ruled 1646–1626): 'The arrears of the tenant-farmers, shepherds, flayers, herders, and crown tributaries are remitted in order to strengthen them and to treat them justly. The collector may not act against the household of the crown tributary.'[8] A very precarious situation was thus created by the landowners' use of entrepreneurial middlemen. On the one hand, the owners were freed from the daily worries about managing their properties, and instead were guaranteed an income in silver which was easily storable and useful for other purposes. On the other hand, the middlemen could acquire such a firm grip over property, by controlling the tenants, that the owners lost all influence. Only the palace seems to have had the power to restore the original balance by absolving all tenants of their debts, but the repetition of these debt cancellations shows the kings' inability to redress the basic injustice of the system.

Another well-documented instance of the crucial involvement of private entrepreneurs in the interactions between cities and countryside appears in Babylon in the sixth century. At that time, the city was at the height of its urban expansion and the capital of a great empire. Food was needed in abundance. The countryside around Babylon was extremely fertile, extensively cultivated, and probably provided sufficient supplies for the large urban population. The mechanisms used to bring the food into the city are demonstrated by an archive found in Babylon, documenting the activities of Iddin-Marduk. The preserved texts record his acquisi-

    [8] F. R. Kraus, *Königliche Verfügungen in altbabylonischer Zeit* (Leiden, 1984), 168–9, § 1.

tions of very substantial amounts of barley, dates, and onions in three localities to the south-west of Babylon, located on a canal that gave direct access to the city: Shahrīnu, Bīt-Ṭāb-Bēl, and Til-Gula. The techniques used by Iddin-Marduk to acquire the food products were threefold. He could buy them outright. Sometimes only one or two weeks were needed to pack and sort the products according to quality, but acquisitions several months before delivery are attested as well. As the amounts involved were sometimes too large to have been produced by a single farmer, it seems likely that another middleman had already gathered the goods before they were sold to Iddin-Marduk. These sales are most often expressed as statements of amounts of produce owed to Iddin-Marduk in the future.

3,960 litres of barley and 9,000 litres of dates, ⟨claim⟩ of Iddin-Marduk, son of Iqīsha, descendant of Nūr-Sin, over Līshiru, son of Etel-pî, descendant of Bēl-napshāti. In the month Simânu (May–June) he will deliver the barley in the harbour at Til-Gula, in the month Kislimu (November–December) he will deliver the dates in the harbour at Til-Gula. This is in addition to the 2,088[+ *x*] litres barley [   ]. Witnesses, ⟨document drawn up in⟩ Babylon. The month of Ajaru (April–May), second day, year 41 of Nebuchadnezzar, King of Babylon. (i.e. 10. 4. 564 BC)[9]

The second means of acquisition revolved entirely around credit. Tenant farmers in need of funds before the harvest turned to men such as Iddin-Marduk for credit, and promised a share of their harvest as repayment. The land they worked was pledged as a guarantee for these loans, most of which were granted three to six months before the harvest. Iddin-Marduk thus acquired produce long before it was harvested. The price he paid must have been based on a low estimate of the value of the staples, as the loans were issued to farmers who had no other way of obtaining credit.

192 grams of silver and a sheep worth 16 grams ⟨of silver⟩, Nabû-shuma-ibni, son of Nabû-shuma-iddin owes to Iddin-Marduk, son of Iqīsha, descendant of Nūr-Sin. In the month Addar (February–March) he will repay the silver in its principal amount (i.e. interest free). He will repay it entirely from his onion-patch (i.e. with produce). Witnesses, scribe,

---

[9] Cornelia Wunsch, *Die Urkunden des babylonischen Geschäftsmannes Iddin-Marduk: Zum Handel mit Naturalien im 6. Jahrhundert v. Chr.* 2 (Groningen, 1993), 32–3 no. 36.

⟨document drawn up in⟩ Shahrīnu. The month of Ajaru (April–May), eleventh day, year 4 of Nabonidus, King of Babylon. (i.e. 4. 6. 552 BC)[10]

A third method of buying food at Iddin-Marduk's disposal was the acquisition of rents and dues from temple and palace officials. These officials collected harvest shares and fees for the use of canals and the like, paid by the farmers with staples which were of limited use to the collectors. Iddin-Marduk paid silver for the right to collect the fees, and thus acquired more produce, probably at a low price. All the staples he procured in these three ways were transported by him to Babylon over the Borsippa canal, and marketed in town. Again the sale of produce is not documented in our sources, although it must have required an elaborate system of distribution.

Iddin-Marduk needed a lot of capital for his work, capital he lacked at the start of his career. He raised it by concluding partnership agreements with other Babylonian businessmen. The agreements were simple: one or more businessmen assigned silver or goods to an enterprising man with few assets for a specific purpose whose nature they determined jointly. The arrangements were thus similar to the partnership agreements found in international trade, but their purpose was to enable the entrepreneur to acquire produce. Both the profits and the losses were shared by all parties involved. Soon Iddin-Marduk acquired enough capital of his own to act as an investor, as well as a person receiving funds. The agreements concluded by him became thus more complicated. It remained beneficial to him to raise credit from others for activities which he seemingly could have financed himself, and at the same time he may have invested his funds into enterprises undertaken by others. How and why he combined these financial arrangements is still unclear to us.

Iddin-Marduk promised his investors a return of 40 per cent on their capital. The loans he granted to the farmers had only a 20 per cent interest, if interest was charged at all, so a profit had to be made in addition to the interest rates charged. This profit was made by taking advantage of two price differentials. First, the sales and loan agreements were mostly concluded before the harvest when prices were higher than at harvest time. Thus a loan expressed in silver, but granted in produce, would have to be paid

[10] Cornelia Wunsch, 103 no. 124.

back with a much larger amount than was originally given. Second, there must have existed a difference of price between city and countryside that ensured a profit to the entrepreneur bringing the produce into the city. The size of that profit depended on the market rates, however, which did fluctuate as is shown by the astronomical diaries that register not only planetary phenomena, but also matters such as weather and prices. According to one of these diaries one shekel (i.e. 8 grams) of silver could buy the following amounts of produce in the 37th year of king Nebuchadnezzar (i.e. 567–566 BC):

| month | barley | dates | mustard | sesame |
|-------|--------|-------|---------|--------|
| 10 | 192 litres | 240 litres | 180[+] litres | [ ] |
| 11 | 180 litres | 240 litres | 216 litres | 24 litres[11] |

Although the differences may seem minor in this example, they affected Iddin-Marduk's profits. The 3,960 litres of barley he acquired in the first example I gave, would have been worth 165 grams of silver in the tenth month, while the 176 grams it was worth in the eleventh month represent a 6.6 per cent price increase. So the moment of sale and the market price at that time were of importance to Iddin-Marduk.

We can compare the situation to the futures market in farm produce, still very active today. Investors took risks by buying up agricultural products long before their harvest, when their sale price was uncertain. There were obviously avenues open to men like Iddin-Marduk for improving their profit margins by manipulating prices. They could withhold supplies until the price was right, or they could form a cartel that set prices. None of these actions are attested in the sources, but we should not therefore simply discount the possibility of their occurrence.

Thus credit played a double role in Iddin-Marduk's affairs: he received it from investors for making his business possible, and he provided it to farmers (at much less favourable terms) to help them meet their basic requirements. After two successful decades (573–553 BC), Iddin-Marduk changed the organization of his business as it became possible for him to rely on his own funds. No longer did

---

[11] See Abraham J. Sachs and Hermann Hunger, *Astronomical Diaries and Related Texts from Babylonia* 1 (Vienna, 1988), 49–51. Later diaries have more extensive records of market prices, but I selected this example because it dates to the period when Iddin-Marduk was active.

he need to find partners for his enterprise: he could send his representatives to the countryside, where he had now such an extensive network of contacts with farmers and officials that he may have had a monopoly. When his daughter married Itti-Marduk-balāṭu of the powerful Egibi family, the business was passed on to the new son-in-law.

Iddin-Marduk was not the only Babylonian involved in this business, nor was it limited to the city of Babylon. The large temple estates of Sippar and Uruk are known to have made arrangements with private entrepreneurs for the management of their agricultural lands, which were enormous in size. These rent collectors were responsible for certain predetermined amounts of income to the temples, but received from them, in addition to the rights to the land, farming instruments, draught animals, and seed grain. A contract written in Larsa in the year 555 records that two men rented 7,410 hectares of land. In the first year of the lease they were given 540,000 litres of barley as seed, 300 kilograms of iron for ploughshares, 400 farm labourers, 400 oxen, and 100 'large' cows to replace the oxen in case they were unable to continue work. As rent they were obliged to pay to the temple 4.5 million litres of 'high quality' barley and 1.8 million litres of dates yearly.[12]

Nor did this system disappear after Babylonia became part of the Persian empire. The Persian noblemen of the crown, often residing in distant parts of the empire, needed local people to administer their demesnes. They employed the services of firms such as the Murashû family, which was active around the city of Nippur. The Murashû family enterprise was to rent land from the landowners and sublease it to small tenant farmers. The firm also had acquired from the state the right to irrigation water, which it sold to the same tenants. Moreover, it provided, at a price, seed, equipment, and livestock to the tenants. In return, the landowners allowed the firm to keep a percentage of the rents and taxes due. As in earlier periods, the Murashûs were willing to advance taxes to the tenants and to give them loans of silver, demanding the land they worked as collateral. Seemingly many farmers had to use this service, and soon lost the title to their land. It is possible that the state intervened with debt cancellations similar to those attested in the early

[12] Muhammed A. Dandamaev, 'Neo-Babylonian Society and Economy', *The Cambridge Ancient History*, 2nd edn. 3: 2 (Cambridge, 1991), 267–8.

second millennium,[13] but no solid evidence for them exists so far.

The use of private entrepreneurs and tax farmers for the management of agricultural estates in the well-documented periods of Babylonian history is thus clear. We are not as well informed about these issues in other periods of Babylonian history. In Assyria, the state as the largest landowner seems to have been directly involved in the collection of taxes and rents. The privatization of services in Babylonia, after the highly centralized management in the third millennium, contradicts Finley's 'iron law of absolutist bureaucracy that it grows both in numbers and in the expensiveness of its life-style'.[14] Instead of an increase in the size and competence of the bureaucracy, as Finley's law would have it, we observe an eagerness to 'privatize' some of its duties. I am not suggesting that the Babylonian bureaucracy was anxious to make itself redundant. An opposite trend, centralizing power in the hands of the bureaucracy, can be observed in certain periods. Seventeenth-century Babylonian monarchs, for instance, tried to curry favour with the leading urban families by giving them bureaucratic offices. Centralizing forces were at work throughout the history of the region. But, simultaneously, the inability of any state to control every step of agricultural production and exchange is obvious. The concurrent use of different systems in the exploitation of resources—direct supervision by bureaucrats and use of independent managers—intimates that the opposing trends of centralization and decentralization coexisted.

Credit was central to all the transactions described above; without it the entrepreneurs could not have financed their business. The arrangements made by Iddin-Marduk particularly show this to have been the case, and in other periods investments were possibly collected in a similar way. The farmers may have depended on the credit for their survival. In contrast to the funds raised by the entrepreneurs, the loans taken out by the farmers were not for productive purposes but only for consumption. They did not

---

[13] Their existence has been suggested by G. Van Driel, 'Continuity or Decay in the Late Achaemenid Period: Evidence from Southern Mesopotamia', in Helene Sancisi-Weerdenburg (ed.), *Achaemenid History I. Sources, Structures and Syntheses* (Leiden, 1987), 175–6. He entertains the possibility that such an act was responsible for the large number of bad debts held by the firm dated to the first year of Darius II.

[14] Finley, *The Ancient Economy*, 90.

attempt to upgrade their farms with the borrowed funds. They consumed whatever they borrowed. People who wanted to raise funds for the purpose of a profit-making enterprise were able to do so, primarily through partnership arrangements. Besides funding for international trade and the acquisition of farm produce, enterprises that were financed in this way included the production of beer and date-wine, herding, perhaps even the running of a brothel!

Another way for wealthy individuals and institutions to make profits without doing much work was to assign large sums of silver to moneylenders who parcelled the funds in small-scale loans to numerous debtors, while taking on the burdens of collecting and managing the loans. They also bore most of the risks. For instance, when temples made loans, they most often did so in conjunction with a private moneylender in whose house the documentation of the transactions was kept.

Promissory notes became negotiable. From the early second millennium on we can document the transfers of loans from one creditor to another. The transferability of debt extended beyond city limits: there are many cases where a debt incurred in one place was to be refunded elsewhere. Old Assyrian traders travelled with promissory notes to Kanish. All these are sophisticated credit operations that we usually associate with early capitalist societies. Perhaps we are overestimating their importance, but they allow us to say that Mesopotamia had a more complex financial organization than did ancient Greece.

The fact that productive credit was common in Mesopotamia does not exclude the existence of loans granted to help out neighbours, friends, or family members. It has been convincingly argued that such loans were a normal and important part of the social relations of the ancient Athenians,[15] and it is likely that in Mesopotamia this was also often the case. Many of the records preserved describe interest-free loans. We lack, however, the documentation to enable us to ascertain the prevalence of this practice, as interest rates by themselves are insufficient to determine whether or not the loan was intended to help someone out.

Many questions about credit remain unanswered. How many people were involved in the business and how large were their

---

[15] Millett, *Lending and Borrowing*.

enterprises? A study of one neighbourhood at Old Babylonian Ur has shown that something resembling a financial district existed there. But most of the inhabitants may have been small-time moneylenders who held onto contracts detailing their outstanding loans. It is also not clear what percentage of the rural economy, for instance, relied on credit for its functioning. Many farmers may have paid their rents and taxes on time. Even if a receipt was given upon payment, we would never know of it until a Mesopotamian farm is excavated—an overlooked task.

Then, there is the question of how urban residents obtained access to silver. Unlike the ancient Athenians, no Mesopotamian had a stake in silver mines, which were too far away. Long-distance trade brought the metal into Mesopotamia, as is clearly shown by the Old Assyrian documents. But long-distance traders are not to be identified with local entrepreneurs and moneylenders. The ability of moneylenders, as private citizens, to deal with silver from the early second millennium on shows that earlier in history sufficient supplies of the metal were imported to enable its internal circulation. In the third millennium the profits of long-distance traders—be they independent or subject to the public institutions—must have been reinvested in the local economy so that other citizens could gain access to silver. An increased monetarization of the economy over the centuries took place, with silver acquiring the role of a currency. Finally, there is the question of why Mesopotamians wanted to invest their assets in interest-bearing loans. Were they interested in profit for its own sake, or did they want to attain a particular goal? A man like Iddin-Marduk is known to have acquired land when his business started to go well, as a means of consolidating his wealth. But he may also have had the ambition to be a landowner, perhaps providing him with a certain prestige. Such motives are not revealed to us. We can only observe moneylenders who bought land, but we will never know whether they hoped in this way to fulfil the 'Mesopotamian dream'.

BIBLIOGRAPHY

A survey of the history of lending in Ancient Mesopotamia was provided by Raymond Bogaert, *Les Origines antiques de la banque de dépôt* (Leiden, 1966). The book does not distinguish between the different purposes for which loans were taken, and is primarily interested in determining whether or not banks existed in the ancient Near East.

The role of credit in international trade has not been investigated in a separate study. For Old Assyrian trade the works mentioned in the previous chapter are very informative. See also Mogens Trolle Larsen, 'Partnerships in Old Assyrian Trade', *Iraq* 39 (1977), 119–45. For Old Babylonian Trade, see A. Leo Oppenheim, 'The Seafaring Merchants of Ur', *Journal of the American Oriental Society* 74 (1954), 6–17.

For the financial role of urban entrepreneurs in the Babylonian economy of the early second millennium see Marc Van De Mieroop, *Society and Enterprise in Old Babylonian Ur* (Berlin, 1992); and J. N. Postgate, *Early Mesopotamia* (London and New York, 1992), 191–205. Iddin-Marduk's archive has been carefully studied by Cornelia Wunsch, *Die Urkunden des babylonischen Geschäftsmannes Iddin-Marduk: Zum Handel mit Naturalien im 6. Jahrhundert v. Chr.* (Groningen, 1993). For the Murashû family in Persian Nippur see Matthew W. Stolper, *Entrepreneurs and Empire* (Instanbul, 1985); and the important review by G. van Driel, 'The Murashûs in Context', *Journal of the Economic and Social History of the Orient* 32 (1989), 203–29. The increase in the number of bureaucrats in seventeenth-century Babylonia was analysed by Norman Yoffee, *The Economic Role of the Crown in the Old Babylonian Period* (Malibu, 1977).

For partnership agreements in the late Babylonian period see Hugo Lanz, *Die neubabylonischen ḫarrânu-Geschäftsunternehm* (Berlin, 1976). For the Old Babylonian period there is only a badly outdated study by Wilhelm Eilers, *Gesellschaftsformen im altbabylonischen Recht* (Leipzig, 1931).

# 10

# Cities as Centres of Religion and Learning

It is something of a truism to state that the centres of culture in Mesopotamia were the cities, since I started this book by saying that Mesopotamian culture as known to us was an urban culture. Yet it is remarkable that there is no trace at all of an awareness or recognition of culture outside the cities. Non-urban people had a culture; oral tradition, religion, and art are found universally among villagers and nomads. In Mesopotamian tradition there is no acknowledgement of the fact that they had or could have influenced the urban culture. This is especially true with regard to religion and literacy, where the urban bias is absolute.

All the temples we know from Mesopotamia were located in cities. There is no indication at all in the archaeological and textual records that cult activity took place outside the cities. No sanctuaries or cult objects existed in the mountains or in the steppe, according to our records. There were no sacred trees or rocks, no rivers, lakes, or seas that had cultic significance. This is in stark contrast to what we see in surrounding areas such as Palestine and Anatolia where cult objects in the countryside were common. A partial explanation for this phenomenon may be found perhaps in the natural conditions of Mesopotamia, especially in the South where most of the religious traditions had their roots. This region lacks the natural features that drew the focus of cults in other places: prominent mountains or enormous trees such as the cedar. But other aspects of the natural environment such as rivers, the lifelines of the region, could easily have become objects of veneration. The only rivers to be deified were those used in the river ordeal, a practice where an accused person was thrown into the water to determine guilt or innocence. Usually the river involved remained nameless in the texts, but when identified it was located outside Babylonia and probably associated in the people's minds with the waters of the underworld.[1] In Assyria mountains and trees were present, some of them quite conspicuous in shape or size, but none of them became an object of a cult. There was perhaps an awareness that natural features could be objects of veneration in areas outside Mesopotamia. The Epic of Gilgamesh seems to condemn the felling of trees in the cedar forest as a sacrilege; but the text is not very consistent in the matter as the same act was recommended by the sun god earlier in the story. The manuscripts in which the condemnation is preserved derive from Anatolia and may reflect a local ideology. Mountains in the periphery were considered to be the dwellings of Mesopotamian gods, but again this may have been a borrowing of foreign traditions. In Mesopotamia proper such sacred elements of nature did not exist, and all gods were thought to dwell in temples within cities.

Yet, many of the gods had their origins in natural phenomena. The sun, moon, planet Venus, heaven, earth, grain, flax, and so on were gods. It appears that, even in the countryside, these gods were venerated as anthropomorphic deities, not as animist spirits. They were 'domesticated'; their cults were enshrined in a temple in the city. When the king attempted to promote the fertility of the land, he did not go out to the fields to perform rituals, but visited the goddess Inanna in her city temple. The gods rarely left their cities, and, if they did, it was a cause for great concern. Once a year Marduk's statue was taken out of Babylon for a short stay outside the city walls in the New Year's house. The purpose of his departure was to re-enter the city triumphally to mark the beginning of the new year. The urban setting of the cult was of primary importance.

There did exist a god of the nomads, named Martu in Sumerian and Amurru in Akkadian, who posed a special problem in this respect. How could he become integrated in an urban pantheon, while his adorers by definition lived outside the cities? The problem seems to have been solved by marrying him to an urban goddess, Adnigkidu, daughter of the god Numushda, as described in the mythical text, 'The marriage of Martu'.[2] His status as a relative

---

[1] Jeremy Black and Anthony Green, *Gods, Demons and Symbols of Ancient Mesopotamia* (London, 1992), 155–6.

[2] See Jean Bottéro and Samuel Noah Kramer, *Lorsque les dieux faisaient l'homme* (Paris, 1989), 430–7.

newcomer in the pantheon seems to be reflected in the fact that he was not the tutelary deity of a particular city.[3]

We can thus say that the institutionalized cult in Mesopotamia was entirely an urban phenomenon. Even if gods had powers over elements outside the cities, they could only be venerated in an urban setting. This seemingly contradictory situation derived, in my opinion, from the original role that temples played in Mesopotamian society. They were not primarily centres of cult, but centres of administration. They were economic rather than religious institutions. I have argued that cities arose in southern Mesopotamia as places of redistribution for variously obtained local resources. Some power structure needed to exist to organize such redistribution, and religion provided the authority required to formalize the transactions. The temple building was not only a place of cult, but also of administration and storage. Contributions could be portrayed as offerings to the god, distributions as divine rewards. There was no place for organized religion outside this system, as it could not perform its redistributive role without an attachment to a city. Later in history when a secular power structure had grown up, the temples lost their role as the sole agents of economic exchange, but by that time the urban roots of official cults were so firmly established that all new cults, even those of nomadic peoples, were integrated within that pattern. Gods required temples, and temples needed to be located in cities.

Scribes made up a vital segment of the temple hierarchy. Writing in Mesopotamia, after all, was developed for accounting purposes by temple bureaucrats. Soon afterwards, the use of writing was expanded to non-administrative contexts, including literature, yet throughout the history of the region the most common documents remained administrative records. Both the public institutions of palace and temple and the private urban entrepreneurs required writing for the recording of their transactions, because these reached a level of complexity that precluded other means of accounting. The variety and numbers of economic documents are enormous. The public institutions required the equivalents of laundry lists: records of their transactions concerning their holdings of

---

[3] See D. O. Edzard, 'Martu, A. Gott', *Reallexikon der Assyriologie* 7 (1987–90), 433–8.

goods and livestock, lists of payments of rations and salaries, accounts of contributions, and so on. Businessmen had notes of their outstanding loans, receipts of payments, rental agreements, and many more. Domestic arrangements such as inheritance divisions, marriage contracts, and dowries were put down in writing when they involved valuable property. Moreover, letters were important means of communication both for businessmen and their customers or partners, and for various departments of public institutions. These texts were indispensable due to the complexity of the urban economies of Mesopotamia. As I pointed out before, the hinterlands of the cities were integrated in these economies. Agriculture, fishing, and herding were practised outside the city walls, and certain industries were located in villages. Yet these only functioned at a high level of complexity because of their urban connections. The records made up there were intended for an urban administration.

Consequently, other forms of writing were equally city-bound. The literature of Mesopotamia was composed, copied, and preserved in the cities, under the auspices of the palaces and the temples. The royal library of Assurbanipal at Nineveh has been our main source of Mesopotamian literature, and the recently discovered temple library of Achaemenid Sippar may yield equivalent riches. Sumerian literature is primarily known from manuscripts found in houses of early second-millennium Nippur and Ur. Mesopotamia's literature is one of city-people, who were afraid of what was to be found outside their walls. It reflects urban concerns and ideologies, not those of people living in the countryside.

Some of the literary output had a practical use in the official cult and in private lives. Hymns, prayers, and rituals were composed and preserved for cultic purposes. The 'Epic of Creation' was recited during the New Year's festival, and possibly other so-called myths and epics played similar roles. Those were thus integrated in the urban setting of the official cult. The most voluminous part of Mesopotamian literature relates to the reading of omens. Enormous lists of observations of phenomena in nature, the stars and planets, and every aspect of daily life, along with the resulting events they ostensibly predicted, are preserved in numerous copies from all Mesopotamian libraries. The belief in the ominous value of such phenomena must have been widespread among Mesopotamians, both those living in the cities and those in the countryside. The signs of the gods were everywhere. The birth of a two-headed lamb in a village was highly significant and needed to be reported to the proper authorities. Extrapolations were made from observable phenomena to create fantastic situations and suggest their consequences. Thus one hypothesized about three, four, five, or six-headed lambs, and the interpretation of such impossible events was systematized. Sometimes detailed knowledge of the writing system and the various readings of cuneiform signs was indispensable for the understanding of an omen, a knowledge lacking outside cities. The omens are presented to us in a rigid format: the lists of observations and predictions were produced in a 'canonical' form from the late second millennium on. The order of the omens and their division by tablet, sometimes more than 100 in number, were standardized, a work that was undertaken in 'academies', which again existed only in urban settings.

Monumental royal inscriptions had their origins in commemorative building accounts that glorified the king's activities as the founder or restorer of temples, palaces, or city walls, all urban features. The so-called historiographic texts, relating primarily the king's military feats, were engraved on monuments within the cities: individual stelae, reliefs that decorated the palaces, colossal representations of winged bulls that guarded the monumental buildings, doorways, and so on, were inscribed with accounts of the king's actions. The only exception for the urban context of royal inscriptions is found with the rock reliefs, carved onto mountainsides in areas surrounding Mesopotamia. Interestingly, these were originally only sculpted for rulers not native to Mesopotamia, such as the Elamites and Gutians.[4] Among the Mesopotamians themselves, only the Assyrian kings of the late second and first millennia are known to have left such images behind. The kings commemorated military feats in remote areas by engraving images or texts, or a combination of both, on the mountains of distant regions reached in their campaigns. As these reliefs were usually located in places of strategic importance, such as

---

[4] The so-called rock relief of Naram-Sin of Akkade at Darband-i-Gaur, without an inscription, has been assigned to that ruler solely on stylistic grounds, e.g. Eva Strommenger, 'Das Felsrelief von Darband-i-Gaur', *Baghdader Mitteilungen* 2 (1963), 83–8. The image could represent any victorious king, and has been assigned to later periods as well (e.g. Winfried Orthmann (ed.), *Der Alte Orient* (Berlin, 1975), 202–3). As far as I can see, there is no evidence that it represents a ruler of the Mesopotamian lowlands.

mountain gorges, which future Mesopotamian armies would need to pass on their campaigns abroad, they were most likely intended for the Mesopotamian audiences rather than for the natives who could hardly have been able to read the texts. These reliefs accentuate the lack of any other type of rock inscription in Mesopotamia and its environs: no graffiti by soldiers, merchants, or shepherds are known, no stones are found in the desert with someone's name scratched on them. The total lack of such written remains may of course be due to the accident of recovery, or to an assumption by modern travellers and scholars that they are not to be found and therefore unrecognized. Yet, that seems unlikely. The rock inscriptions left by Sennacherib to describe his building of the aqueduct for Nineveh, for instance, would seem a tempting place to scratch a graffito, and such secondary carving would have been noticed by scholars.

This lack of writing in a non-urban setting probably indicates that literacy was limited to urbanites. Although I believe that more Mesopotamians knew how to read and write than seems commonly accepted by scholars, the means to acquire these skills were to be found in cities only. It has been standard opinion that scribal instruction was given in schools from the invention of writing to the early second millennium, replaced by a system of personal instruction, by fathers to their sons.[5] This idea is questionable today, and education may have remained of the same nature throughout Mesopotamian history, although we have found no physical evidence of schools so far. The school libraries of the early second millennium supposedly found by archaeologists in Ur and Nippur have turned out to be accidental accumulations of tablets from unknown origins.[6] The evidence for drastic changes in education after the mid-second millennium is not decisive. The latter idea was seemingly inspired by Diodorus who states: 'For among the Chaldaeans the scientific study of these subjects is passed down in the family, and the son takes it over from the father, being relieved of all other services in the state.'[7] Yet, Diodorus talked about

---

[5] B. Landsberger in Carl H. Kraeling and Robert McC. Adams (eds.), *City Invincible* (Chicago, 1960), 94–101.

[6] See Dominique Charpin, *Le Clergé d'Ur au siècle d'Hammurabi* (Paris, 1986), 482–5, and 'Un quartier de Nippur et le problème des écoles à l'époque paléobabylonienne', *Revue d'assyriologie et d'archéologie orientale* 84 (1990), 1–8.

[7] *Library of History*, Book II 29, trans. C. H. Oldfather, *The Loeb Classical Library. Diodorus of Sicily* I, (Cambridge, Mass., and London, 1933), 447.

divination rather than scribal activity in general. The so-called scribal families of the first millennium are not necessarily indications of real blood relations, as I pointed out before. Moreover, texts describing life in a Sumerian school were maintained in the literary canon, and traditional school texts remained commonly in use in Mesopotamia throughout its history. The recent find of hundreds of them in the temple of Nabû ša harê in Babylon shows that clearly.[8] So, a type of education in schools may have been a permanent feature in Mesopotamia. Scribal training was a long process, supervised by skilled professionals, such as priests,[9] with long practice in the uses of writing. It involved many aspects in addition to reading and writing, such as literature, grammar, calculus, geometry, and music.[10] As time went on, this training became more esoteric, as the written and spoken languages diverged, and the means of writing became more arcane. Specialists who knew the scribal techniques were only to be found in cities.

In his investigation of the position of the intellectual in Mesopotamian society, A. Leo Oppenheim distinguished between three types of scribes: the bureaucrat, the poet, and the scholar. The Mesopotamians themselves did not see them as separate specialists until the first millennium, when the scholar was regarded as distinct. The bureaucrats produced the majority of the written documentation: the palace and temple economies as well as the affairs of prominent businessmen, depended on their work. Their functions were probably not limited to bookkeeping, but also included deciding actions, such as the disbursement of goods, to keep the system going smoothly. Their employment outside the public institutions should not be underestimated. A study of Babylonian texts of the first millennium found 3,060 names of scribes who wrote Akkadian on clay tablets. Of those 2,681 worked for private individuals, 11 for the palace, and 368 for the temples. Many of the private scribes probably made a living by helping citizens with paperwork, as professional scribes still do today in the Middle East.

---

[8] See Antoine Cavigneaux, *Textes scolaires du temple de Nabû ša harê* (Baghdad, 1981). Note that A. Leo Oppenheim categorically rejected the idea that the scribal craft was passed on from father to son, *Daedalus* 104: 2 (1975), 43.

[9] For instance, the chief lamentation priest of Annunitum, Ur-Utu, at Tell ed-Der, see M. Tanret, 'Les Tablettes scolaires découvertes à Tell ed-Der', *Akkadica* 27 (1982), 46–9.

[10] See Å. W. Sjöberg, 'The Old Babylonian Eduba', in S. Lieberman (ed.), *Sumerian Studies in Honor of Thorkild Jacobsen* (Chicago, 1972), 159–79.

The poet-scribes were crucial in the creation and preservation of the royal ideology: epics, hymns, and royal inscriptions were composed and copied by them. They kept alive a cultural tradition in Mesopotamia that persevered despite numerous political changes and the arrivals of foreign rulers. Hence, the Kassites, for instance, could portray themselves as traditional Babylonian monarchs without difficulty.

Scholar-scribes were experts in scientific knowledge, especially in divination. Private citizens and the court could turn to them for predictions of future events, cures for illnesses, or rituals to avert evil. Their knowledge was entirely based on standardized lists of interpretations of omens or medical symptoms, annotated and explained with glosses and quotes from other literary material. Oppenheim stressed that all these intellectuals prospered in Mesopotamia because of their relationship to the court or their employment by private citizens in an urban environment. In the latter case, unattached professionals sold their services to private customers, who in the first millennium enjoyed increased wealth thanks to the general economic flourishing of Mesopotamia.

The role of cities as centres of religion and learning in Mesopotamia can be exemplified by two cases that excelled in these respects, Nippur and Babylon: these cities were unusual in the extent to which they administered these functions. Nippur, in the centre of Babylonia, had the unique position of never having had its own dynasty; but the city was of crucial importance for the political ideology of the rulers of other city-states. From the twenty-fifth until the eighteenth century BC, dynasts of Akkade, Ur, Isin, Larsa, and others strived for control over Nippur in order to justify their claim to kingship over Sumer and Akkad. The priesthood at Nippur seems to have had the authority to grant that title, which could only be held by one ruler at a time. The power derived from its association with the god Enlil, head of the Sumerian pantheon. Some time in the third millennium, a regional pantheon had developed in Babylonia under the leadership of the air god Enlil. In the mythology the city of Nippur became the locus where the gods gathered for the discussion of important problems, and several myths describe the visits of deities to Enlil's temple in Nippur, the Ekur. When the ideology of regional kingship was introduced with the Akkade dynasty, the support of Enlil's priesthood seems to have become crucial to further that ideology. Special attention was thus paid to the city and its shrines, booty and prisoners of war were offered to it, while statues and inscriptions glorifying the king's military feats were erected in the Ekur's courtyard. The rulers of the so-called Third Dynasty of Ur made Nippur their religious capital, perhaps even their dynastic seat, and promoted its cults by forcing other regions of Babylonia to contribute food products and livestock on a rotating basis. When Ur's hegemony over Babylonia devolved to a number of competing city-states, the struggle over Nippur became constant, although not necessarily violent. Acceptance by the Nippur priesthood provided a number of important ideological benefits. The dynasty was integrated into the Sumerian King List; the king was honoured in royal hymns; and he was crowned as king of Sumer and Akkad, not merely as king of his city. How the support from Nippur was obtained is not entirely clear. Certainly at times the priesthood had no choice but to acknowledge the supremacy of a particular ruler, when his military dominance was obvious. At other times, kings may have bought the goodwill of the priests by showering gifts upon their temple.

Nippur was important in other aspects of Babylonian culture as well. In the early centuries of the second millennium the religious ideology of southern Babylonia became codified. Possibly because of the death of Sumerian as a spoken language, its literature was written down. Much of this activity seems to have taken place in Nippur. A scribal school, which may have been established there by King Shulgi (ruled 2094–2047), was pre-eminent in the formation of the corpus of Sumerian literature. In the 'scribal quarter' of the city, thus outside the temple complex, thousands of manuscripts of literary texts were found. Unfortunately, these texts were discovered in the early stages of archaeological exploration in Mesopotamia in the late nineteenth century, and spurred an acrimonious debate between the principal scholars involved, Peters and Hilprecht, which resulted in a total lack of information about their exact provenience. Renewed excavations in the 1950s discovered school texts as well, in much smaller numbers, however, and still with a confused archaeological context. But they were certainly found in domestic dwellings, where students were taught Sumerian by memorizing literary passages of increasing difficulty, and where a preservation of Sumerian literature seems to have been consciously pursued. The output was enormous. The texts include all the tools needed to train a skilled scribe: sign lists, lexical lists, model contracts, letters and legal decisions, mathematical problems, and all types of literature: hymns, prayers, wisdom texts, myths, and epics. The large majority of the preserved tablets was probably written in the decades just before the abandonment of Nippur due to political circumstances *c*.1720. It is clear that the scribal activity was not limited to that period but that tablets were recycled and that we only see their last use.[11] Long after 1720 the memory of a special connection between Nippur and the Sumerian language was maintained. The humorous story 'Why do you curse me?',[12] preserved in a manuscript from the sixth century, describes how a physician from Isin goes to Nippur, and fails to communicate even with the local gardening woman selling vegetables, who speaks Sumerian. We have no idea whether or not this predicament occurred in reality, but the fact that it was perceived to be possible and was understood as an amusing situation, is what shows that Nippur was considered to be a city of special knowledge in Babylonia.

The religious primacies of Enlil and Nippur were taken over in the mid-second millennium by Marduk and Babylon. Babylon had risen to become the foremost city of southern Mesopotamia by military and political means. Its first dynasty had conquered the rest of Babylonia in the eighteenth century, and since that time Babylon was considered to be the main political capital of the region until the Greek founding of nearby Seleucia around 300 BC. Because of Babylon's prominence, its city-god Marduk became the head of the Mesopotamian pantheon, a rise described in the so-called Epic of Creation, in which the former leader Enlil is among those gods honouring the new king. Again cult and political ideology were closely interwoven. The king was the only person allowed to lead the ceremonies in the annual New Year's festival, when the rise of Marduk was celebrated. Every king, whether Kassite, Babylonian, Assyrian, Persian or Greek, participated in this event when possible, from at least 1300 to 224 BC.[13] For several years the

---

[11]   See Miguel Civil, *Materials for the Sumerian Lexicon* 14 (Rome, 1979), 7–8, and Charpin, *Revue d'assyriologie* 84 (1990), 1–8.

[12]   Benjamin R. Foster, *From Distant Days*, (Bethesda, 1995), 363–4. I am not convinced by A. R. George's interpretation of the humour in this text as deriving from a confusion between two dialects of Akkadian (*Iraq* 55 (1993), 63–72).

[13]   Amélie Kuhrt, 'Usurpation, Conquest, and Ceremonial: From Babylon to Persia', in David Cannadine and Simon Price (eds.), *Rituals of Royalty* (Cambridge, 1987), 52.

maverick King Nabonidus abandoned Babylon for the Teima oasis in the Arabian desert, thereby ignoring the festival and bringing upon himself the wrath of the Marduk priesthood. The priesthood had less power than the old Nippur one, in that it did not have a choice between several candidates for the office of king and was confronted with a military *fait accompli*. Yet, it may have been able to arouse popular resentment against a king, which probably explains why the Persian ruler Cyrus was greeted as a liberator when he took Babylon from Nabonidus.

In addition to its cultic role, the priesthood of Babylon also acquired a leading position in the 'science' that was of utmost importance to the Mesopotamians: divination. The abilities to read the signs sent by the gods revealing future events, and to perform correct rituals or recite the proper prayers to make them change their minds in case the omen was bad, were greatly prized by the citizenry. Under the Assyrian kings of the seventh century a network of posts was set up across the Mesopotamian countryside for the observation of all relevant celestial signs. A constant flow of reports arrived at the court, describing the signs, interpreting them, and suggesting a means for warding off evil. A large portion of these reports came from Babylonia, and Babylon was one of the prominent centres of observation. The city's importance and fame in the divinatory sciences survived for a very long time. In the seventh century, celestial omens became of paramount importance in divination: in Babylon astronomical diaries were produced, in preparation for the composition of new lists of ominous interpretations. The diaries record on a daily basis the positions of the moon, the planets, and the fixed stars, as well as information about the weather, the level of the Euphrates river, and some historical events. They date from the mid-seventh to the mid-first century BC, and almost all those known to us were written in Babylon. These observations also provided the necessary data for mathematical astronomy, which flourished at that time. Hence, the Babylonians, under the Greek designation Chaldaeans, became the most famous astronomers of antiquity, a fame that lasted at least until the first century AD. In his *Natural History*, Pliny describes the city of Babylon as a wasteland, but for the temple of Jupiter Belus (i.e. Marduk) which survived as a school of astronomy.[14] The popular longevity of astronomy in Babylon can be explained by the fact that

[14]  6. 30. 121–3.

it was fundamentally connected with divination and religion in the Mesopotamian mind. The temple was the locus of celestial divination; this should not be disassociated from the other intellectual endeavours of the Mesopotamians, simply because in our opinion divination has nothing to do with science.

Nippur and Babylon were two prime examples of Mesopotamian centres of learning. The strength of their cultural contributions can only be explained because of the inherent connection with the temple; similarly temples flourished because of their integral role in the royal ideology. The culture of Mesopotamia relied thus on the presence of temple and palace, elements that were only to be found in the city. The absolute character of the urban bias of Mesopotamian culture can be understood for practical reasons. The urban background had a strong impact on the culture in general. The outlook on the world centred on the city, which was regarded as the only habitat suitable for a cultured person. Anything outside the city walls was regarded with suspicion, or even fear. There was no appreciation of wild nature and its beauty, only for nicely laid-out gardens. A few texts devote special attention to the natural environment, sometimes showing great powers of observation,[15] but their rarity stresses the usual formalism and lack of interest in such matters. Cosmogonic myths do not focus on the creation of natural phenomena and man's environment, but on the organization of that environment, especially the establishment of cities for man to live in. To a modern mind, such an outlook may have a claustrophobic feeling to it, a lack of openness and a short-sightedness. To the Mesopotamian as known to us, this closed environment seems to have been the only acceptable one, with the chaos outside as something to be avoided.

BIBLIOGRAPHY

All known rock reliefs were listed by Jutta Börker-Klähn, *Altvorderasiatische Bildstelen und vergleichbare Felsreliefs* (Mainz am Rhein, 1982). Those of Assyrian kings are conveniently indicated

---

[15] See A. Leo Oppenheim, 'Man and Nature in Mesopotamian Civilization', *Dictionary of Scientific Biography* 15, suppl. 1 (New York, 1981), 636.

on the maps in Michael Roaf, *Cultural Atlas of Mesopotamia and the Ancient Near East* (Oxford, 1990), 164 and 179.

The position of scribes in Mesopotamian society was studied by A. Leo Oppenheim, 'The Position of the Intellectual in Mesopotamian Society', *Daedalus* 104: 2 (1975), 37–46. For bureaucrat-scribes in first millennium Babylonia, see Muhammed A. Dandamaev, *Babylonian Scribes in the First Millennium B.C.* (Moscow, 1983), in Russian with an English summary on pp. 235–42.

For Nippur as a literary centre, see William W. Hallo, 'Nippur Originals', in H. Behrens, D. Loding, and M. Roth (eds.), *DUMU-E₂-DUB-BA: Studies in Honor of Åke W. Sjöberg* (Philadelphia, 1989), 237–47. The most up-to-date survey of education, based primarily on Old Babylonian sources, is provided by Miguel Civil in D. N. Freedman (ed.), *The Anchor Bible Dictionary* 2 (New York, 1992), 301–5. More detail can be found in Hartmut Waetzoldt, 'Der Schreiber as Lehrer in Mesopotamien', in Johann Georg Prinz von Hohenzollern and Max Liedtke (eds.), *Schreiber, Magister, Lehrer* (Bad Heilbrunn, 1989), 33–50. Also interesting are the observations by H. L. J. Vanstiphout, 'How did they learn Sumerian?', *Journal of Cuneiform Studies* 31 (1979), 118–26.

A clear description of the discovery of approximately 23,000 literary texts in Nippur during the excavations in the late nineteenth century is not available. H. V. Hilprecht, *Exploration in Bible Lands* (Edinburgh, 1903), 512–32, gives an account of what he calls the Temple Library. The disaster-prone early seasons of excavations at the site are described by André Parrot, *Archéologie mésopotamienne* 1 (Paris, 1946), 143–58; and in C. Wade Meade, *Road to Babylon* (Leiden, 1974), 47–63. The latter book also gives a summary account of the Peters–Hilprecht controversy on pp. 72–6. The excavation of the scribal quarter in the 1950s is published in Donald E. McCown and Richard C. Haines, *Nippur* I (Oriental Institute Publications 78; Chicago, 1967); and restudied by Elizabeth C. Stone, *Nippur Neighborhoods* (Chicago, 1987). For the latter see the important review by Dominique Charpin, 'Un quartier de Nippur et le problème des écoles à l'époque paléo-babylonienne', *Revue d'assyriologie* 83 (1989), 97–112 and 84 (1990), 1–16. For examples of school texts, see Edward Chiera, *Lists of Personal Names from the Temple School of Nippur*, (Philadelphia, 1916). On pp. 41–8 a typology of school tablets is provided, which has been refined by Edmund I. Gordon in *Sumerian Proverbs* (Philadelphia, 1959), 7–10.

The New Year's festival at Babylon and its importance in royal ideology was discussed by Amélie Kuhrt, 'Usurpation, Conquest, and Ceremonial: From Babylon to Persia', in David Cannadine and Simon Price (eds.), *Rituals of Royalty* (Cambridge, 1987), 20–55.

Divination and astronomy are discussed in many books and articles. A very useful introduction to the fundamentals of divination can be found in Jean Bottéro, *Mesopotamia: Writing, Reasoning, and the Gods* (Chicago and London, 1992). The nature of the 'canon' of divinatory texts has been discussed by Francesca Rochberg-Halton, 'Canonicity in Cuneiform Texts', *Journal of Cuneiform Studies* 36 (1984), 127–44. For the practitioners of astronomical divination see, for example, A. Leo Oppenheim, 'Divination and Celestial Observation in the Last Assyrian Empire', *Centaurus* 14 (1969), 97–135; and the papers by Francesca Rochberg and Simo Parpola in H. D. Galter (ed.), *Die Rolle der Astronomie in den Kulturen Mesopotamiens* (Graz, 1993). The contents of the astronomical diaries are discussed in the same volume by Hermann Hunger, who together with Abraham Sachs was responsible for their publication in *Astronomical Diaries and Related Texts from Babylon* 1 and 2 (Vienna, 1988–9). Hunger also recently re-edited the *Astrological reports to Assyrian kings* (Helsinki, 1992).

# 11

## The Eclipse of the Ancient Mesopotamian City

What happened to the ancient Mesopotamian city? Did it die out suddenly or gradually or did it form the basis for a long evolution leading to the medieval cities of Iraq? In this book the bulk of documentation was derived from archaeological and textual sources dating to the early third millennium through the fourth century BC, the period traditionally identified as that of ancient Mesopotamian history. Scholars have rarely addressed the issue of when this period ends, and various dates seem to be tacitly accepted for different purposes. Some define the end of Mesopotamia as when it ceased to exist as an independent political entity by its integration in the Persian empire in 539;[1] while this is seen as a convenient date, most scholars see the conquest by Alexander of Macedon and the coming of Hellenism as the decisive moment. But scholars working with sources written in cuneiform from the Persian and Seleucid periods are readily considered ancient Mesopotamian specialists and themselves often emphasize the continuity with earlier periods. Alexander has been called the last of the Achaemenids, ending a period of Persian reforms based on Assyrian antecedents,[2] while the end of Babylonian culture has been seen as caused by Iranization under the Parthians starting in the second century BC, rather than by Hellenization under the Seleucids two centuries earlier.[3] It is often forgotten that only four successive foreign imperial regimes controlled all or part of the region of ancient Mesopotamia from the defeat of the last

[1] William W. Hallo and William K. Simpson, *The Ancient Near East: a History* (New York, 1971).

[2] P. Briant, 'Des Achéménides aux rois hellénistiques: continuités et ruptures (Bilan et perspectives)', *Rois, tribus et paysans* (Besançon, 1982), 291–330.

[3] Joachim Oelsner, 'Kontinuität und Wandel in Gesellschaft und Kultur Babyloniens in hellenistischer Zeit', *Klio* 60 (1978), 101–16.

independent Babylonian dynasty to the Muslim conquest of Iraq: Achaemenid Persians from 539 to 331 BC, Seleucid Greeks from 331 to 141 BC, Arsacid Parthians from 141 BC to AD 226, and Sasanian Persians from AD 226 to 637. Even the Muslim conquest can be seen as the imposition of a new foreign government upon the area. The dynastic struggles of the successive regimes were highly intricate, and the area of Mesopotamia was often divided among various powers: Iranian, Roman, or Byzantine, alongside more or less independent kingdoms, such as Characene, Adiabene, and the Lakhmid kingdom, to name just a few. All of these left historical records, minted coins, and are discussed in a wide variety of sources, so that the political history of the region becomes a labyrinth of names, dates, and events. But are we justified is speaking of the end of a historical era, simply because of the conquest of Mesopotamia by a foreign dynasty? Was there really a difference between the Kassite invasion of Mesopotamia in the sixteenth century BC and the Achaemenid Persian annexation of the region a millennium later? Was the history of the region more homogeneous previously, or do we just lack insight because we lack documentation?

The limits traditionally imposed upon Mesopotamian history have less to do with historical reasoning than with the fact that the nature of the textual sources changed entirely. The use of cuneiform slowly died out in Babylonia at the same time as the coming of a Greek administration, and neither the reasons for that disappearance nor the exact moment of its occurrence are entirely clear to us. We see a gradual decline in the number of textual types written in cuneiform during the Seleucid period, with the variety of legal documents decreasing, and fewer genres of literature at first being composed, later only copied. Only astronomical material, the evidence of 'Chaldaean' science famous throughout the classical world, was still being created well into the first century AD, the latest text known so far dating to the year 75. But cuneiform writing and Akkadian as a literary and an administrative language remained in use at least until the early first century BC, thus well into the Parthian period. Literary material is copied into the mid-first century BC. The most recent administrative text known so far was found in Babylon and dates to the year 92 BC,[4] and texts from

---

[4] See R. J. van der Spek, *Grondbezit in het Seleucidische Rijk* (Amsterdam, 1986), 71.

Kutha and Borsippa are known from only a few years earlier. Cuneiform was thus still in daily use in several places in the late second century BC, and possibly more archives from this poorly researched period are still to be found. The 'death' of cuneiform was surely not due to the fact that alphabetic writing systems appearing in the first millennium would have been somehow superior in communicating messages: cuneiform had been found perfectly acceptable for expressing whatever was needed for millennia.[5] The loss of cuneiform's cultural foundations, which has been blamed as the cause of its demise,[6] seems to me something we should set out to demonstrate, rather than to presume. Another theory asserts that the Seleucid administrators demanded records of taxable transactions to be written in a language understandable to them—Greek or Aramaic—and that these records consequently were penned down on parchment or papyrus, materials that did not survive in the Mesopotamian soil.[7] This idea is certainly appealing, but evidence that some transactions, such as slave sales, were taxed by the central administration when cuneiform records of them were still in use, shows that it does not explain the entire process; moreover, it fails to demonstrate why the interactions between the native Babylonian communities did not remain recorded in Akkadian written in cuneiform on clay tablets.

In order properly to understand the periods after 331 BC, the ancient Near Eastern historian, trained to work with cuneiform tablets, is thus forced to consider very different materials, either written in difficult languages, such as various dialects of Aramaic, and Old and Middle Persian, or classical sources which are thought to require an entirely different approach. Hence, it is a convenience to consider these periods as irrelevant to the field of study. Archaeologists too, are usually not interested in Parthian and Sasanian remains, as they merely prevent access to older deposits, which are considered 'genuine' ancient Mesopotamian.

This issue involves many aspects of society other than urbanism, and it merits a separate discussion. Here, I want only to review

---

[5] Mogens Trolle Larsen, 'What They Wrote on Clay', in K. Schousboe and Mogens Trolle Larsen (eds.), *Literacy and Society* (Copenhagen, 1989), 121–48.

[6] Marvin A. Powell, 'Three Problems in the History of Cuneiform Writing: Origins, Direction of Script, Literacy', *Visible Language* 15: 4 (1981), 435.

[7] See L. T. Doty *apud* William W. Hallo, 'God, King, and Man at Yale', in E. Lipinski (ed.), *State and Temple Economy in the Ancient Near East* I (Orientalia Lovaniensia Analecta 5; Louvain, 1979), 110–11.

briefly what we can discern in the meagre and undigested material from the sixth century BC to the seventh century AD about the survival or death of the ancient Mesopotamian city. This question cannot be answered by considering all aspects of urban life simultaneously. It seems more useful to isolate the problems discussed in the earlier chapters, and to see whether substantial changes took place starting with the Persian conquest of Mesopotamia.

First, there is the question of what cities continued to exist, and whether and where new cities were built. We see both a continued use of older settlements and the foundation of new ones by the ruling dynasties. Many of the old cities of Babylonia remained inhabited and important for several centuries. For instance, Babylon itself was the political capital of Asia until Alexander's successor, Seleucus I, founded Seleucia-on-the-Tigris nearby around 300 BC. The city suffered from the new foundation, mainly because Seleucia was settled by displaced Babylonians. But Babylon remained an important cult centre, and a centre of astronomy into the Parthian period, at least until the end of the first century AD. Other cities of Babylonia that show Parthian remains are Larsa, Uruk, and Nippur, while Kish contains the ruins of a considerable Sasanian town. The new royal foundations in Babylonia often caused a shift away from the older urban centres. Thus was Seleucia-on-the-Tigris built at the expense of Babylon, and Ctesiphon surpassed its neighbour Seleucia in the Parthian period. Finally, the Sasanians built Veh-Ardashir (Coche) in the same neighbourhood, which became so densely urbanized that the Arabs referred to it as al-Madā'in, 'the cities'. The intense concentration of urbanism at that point can be explained by its location in the centre of many trade routes. Other trading centres, such as Charax Spasinu on the Shatt al-Arab, were probably also established at the expense of older cities.

According to Adams's analysis of central Babylonian settlement patterns, the region flourished from the neo-Babylonian period well into the early Islamic period because of its agricultural resources. In the Seleucid, Parthian, and Sasanian periods total settlement reached an extent unparalleled in earlier history with a high percentage of people living in urban centres.[8] The same cities did not necessarily remain inhabited, however. With the Islamic

---

[8] Defined as more than 10 hectares in size.

conquest, the Sasanian cities suffered a loss of inhabitants who moved to the new military settlements such as Basra, Kufa, and Wasit. Also, there had previously been a general shift of settlement eastwards, as the water of the Tigris river was now integrated into the irrigation system of Babylonia. A canal joining Tigris and Euphrates in the north of Babylonia drained much of the water of the Euphrates and caused a gradual reduction of settlement further south.

The period after 500 BC was not one of decline in Babylonia. Quite the opposite was true. The region flourished, supported by a strong agricultural base. It was only after the eighth century AD that the agricultural economy collapsed, and that permanent settlement virtually ceased to exist in Babylonia. This collapse seems to have been the result of a cumulative process involving wars, administrative mismanagement, and excessive taxation, causing a spiral of rural resistance and subsequent repression, and perhaps also a string of plagues.[9] Many of these problems may have developed in pre-Islamic times, yet they did not cause havoc until much later.

In the North of Mesopotamia, the situation is more difficult to assess, primarily because of the lack of a systematic archaeological survey. We see the survival and creation of several important urban centres. Assur has substantial Parthian remains, while Nineveh, Shemshara, and Erbil were settled at that time as well. Nimrud contained a Hellenistic village, abandoned in the second century BC. The most important city of northern Iraq became Hatra on the Wadi Tharthar, originally built by the Parthians as a fortress against Rome. The city came to have a crucial strategic importance in the struggles between Rome and the Parthians and Sasanians, ruled by a native dynasty that shifted its allegiance back and forth between East and West. It withstood several Roman attacks, and was finally destroyed by the Sasanians, probably around AD 240. The city may be indicative of the pattern of urbanization in the North after the eighth century BC. It was located in a barren countryside without a hinterland able to feed its inhabitants. Its fortunes depended on caravan trade, not on agriculture.

Northern Mesopotamia in the period from 612 BC to the AD 630s

---

[9] See Peter Christensen, *The Decline of Iranshahr: Irrigation and Environments in the History of the Middle East 500 B.C. to A.D. 1500* (Copenhagen, 1993).

seems not to have known much rural settlement, but was gradually taken over by semi-nomadic tribesmen. It was exposed to numerous military incursions, as it was located between Rome and its successor state Byzantium trying to extend their influence eastward to the Tigris, and the Iranian dynasties attempting to maintain the Euphrates, with the Balikh or the Habur, as their western border. The political uncertainties of the region may have caused its sparse population, as there is no evidence for droughts or environmental decline. The potential for the economic development of the region was always great, if the right political conditions existed. In the eleventh to thirteenth centuries AD, an independent and stable dynasty in Mosul brought great prosperity to the region which became densely inhabited at that time.

The middle Euphrates valley shows a different pattern of occupation from northern Mesopotamia. The river was extremely important for strategic purposes and often formed the border between the eastern and western empires. Politically, it changed hands many times, its northern section often controlled by Rome or Byzantium, its southern section usually in Parthian or Sasanian hands. Despite the ravages that must have been imposed upon it by military activity, the valley seems to have thrived economically. The names of many cities in the Euphrates valley are preserved in the accounts of classical geographers. The most important city by far was Dura Europos, founded in 303 BC midway between the Seleucid capitals of Seleucia and Antioch. From 113 BC on it was a Parthian city, and in the second century AD it became Roman, until it was sacked by the Sasanian ruler Shapur in 256. Subsequently, it seems that the Euphrates valley lost its prosperity, due to a Byzantine emphasis on the cities of northern Syria.

These remarks on the location of sites are extremely superficial, due to the lack of solid data, caused partly by archaeologists' lack of interest, and partly by the fact that remains of these periods are often concealed underneath subsequent Islamic settlements. It is important to remember that many variations according to period and region existed, and that the political situation often differed in neighbouring regions that had earlier been ruled by the same regime. It seems, however, that we can state that settlement trends in Babylonia, started in the sixth century BC with the neo-Babylonian dynasty, continued with a great agricultural flourishing of the region and an increasingly dense population, a trend that culminated in late Sasanian times. Older cities were gradually surpassed in importance by the new foundations of successive regimes. In Assyria settlement seems to have become sparse after the fall of the neo-Assyrian empire in 612 BC, and a process of 'Bedouinization' is at the latest obvious in the first centuries AD. Some urban centres in this area were very prosperous, however. These seem to have been isolated cities in a deserted hinterland, whose survival depended on trade, not on the exploitation of local resources, a subject I will discuss in more detail presently. The Euphrates valley seems also to have benefited from international trade; its prosperity lasted until the third century AD.

The layout of the cities in these periods depended greatly upon the time of their foundation. The old centres seemingly continued with the same basic patterns as before. In Babylon, for instance, a theatre and perhaps also a gymnasium and an agora were built in the Seleucid period, but the city did not lose its Babylonian character. The new royal foundations were planned in advance, however, and Seleucia and Dura Europos have a strict Greek Hippodamian layout. The Parthian city of Hatra (Fig. 11.1) reflects an entirely different plan. It was a round city, 320 hectares in size, surrounded by two concentric walls. In its centre was located a large rectangular official complex, 437 by 322 metres, separated from the rest of town by a massive wall. Four gates gave access to the city. Almost its entire surface was covered with houses, grouped in insulae, formed by streets that were not laid out in a regular pattern. The circular plan of the city was new in Mesopotamia, but in Iran several older examples of it are known; thus we see here Parthian influence in city planning. This plan was adopted by the Sasanians who used it for the layout of their new foundation Veh-Ardashir, near Seleucia.

In western Syria, a gradual reformation of the Hellenized cities to the early Islamic *madina* has been observed in late antiquity, their 'decline' due to overpopulation, imperial neglect, and changing ideas about property,[10] but such an evolution cannot be discerned in Mesopotamia. The only planned Hellenized cities, Seleucia and Dura, did not survive the Sasanian period, and the other cities already had many of the aspects of the early Islamic

[10] Hugh Kennedy, 'From *Polis* to *Madina*: Urban Changes in Late Antique and Early Islamic Syria', *Past and Present* 106 (Feb. 1985), 3–27.

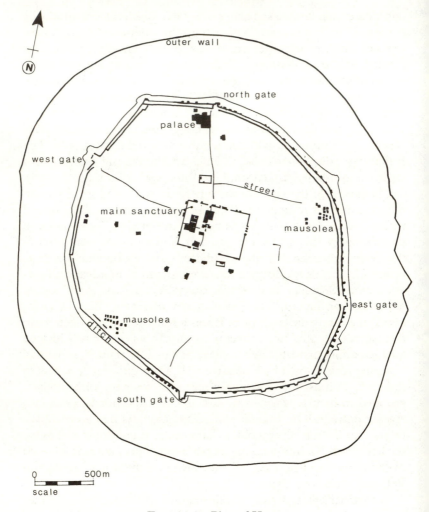

F<sub>IG</sub>. 11.1   Plan of Hatra

town layout. The only difference was in the layout of the cult complexes—mosques, Christian churches, or synagogues—and perhaps in the introduction of the Muslim school, the *madrasa*. Throughout the periods after 500 BC the majority of urban citizens must have lived in conditions similar to those of their ancestors. Streets remained primarily narrow and winding. Houses maintained the same courtyard plans as before. Only rarely were Greek architectural forms adopted. Even traditional public buildings at first remained Mesopotamian in outlook. Parthian architecture became a mixture of many different styles, including ancient Mesopotamian forms: the ground plan of the Gareus temple at Uruk, for instance, is traditional Babylonian.[11] Architectural historians of the Islamic city have emphasized the continuation of traditions going back to the second millennium BC,[12] but one should be careful not to see this too much as the result of a conscious policy. The winding streets and courtyard houses provide the best protection against the heat and dust of the region, and it is likely for this reason that they remain popular to this day.

When we look at the economy of cities after 539 BC, we see many elements of continuity, but also fundamental changes. Continuity can be seen in agricultural practices. Even if such new crops as rice were introduced, they did not change the basic provisions of food available. Starting in the neo-Babylonian period, Babylonia's agriculture revivified, continuing into the early Islamic period, based on the traditional irrigation techniques and crops of wheat, barley, and dates. The decline of agriculture in the North of Mesopotamia, due to extensive military activity in the region, explains the rarity of urban centres there. Cities such as Hatra, located in a barren hinterland, must have imported their food.

Industrial activity also remained the same as in earlier centuries. The same products were made with the same resources as before, and political changes did not alter these activities. Borsippa, for instance, was famous as a centre of linen production from the Seleucid to the early Islamic periods.[13] However, it is likely that the manufacture of certain products was intensified due to increased demand for export. The centralization imposed by Sasanian administrators affected both agriculture and industry, especially in the late fifth century AD. The Sasanians may have organized shipments of food and basic craft products over long distances, and caused an unprecedented regional specialization of agriculture and industry. Indicative of such specialization are the enormous

---

[11] Ernst Heinrich, *Sechster vorläufiger Bericht . . . Uruk-Warka* (Berlin, 1935), 33.
[12] e.g. Besim S. Hakim, *Arabic-Islamic Cities: Building and Planning Principles* (London and New York, 1986).
[13] *Pauly's Real-Encyclopädie der klassischen Altertumswissenschaft* 3, Georg Wissowa (ed.), (Stuttgart, 1899), 735.

mounds of glass slag found north of Uruk, which suggest that production for the entire Sasanians empire took place there.

A radical change in the economy did take place, however, in the area of international trade which underwent an enormous expansion starting in the sixth century BC. Two factors contributed to this growth: the use of camel caravans, and the integration of Mesopotamia into empires with enormous geographical extent. The domestication of the camel and its use as a pack animal in the early first millennium BC, opened up an entire network of trade routes crossing the interior of Iran and the Syrian and Arabian deserts. The dependence upon river valleys for the water supply of travelling caravans disappeared, and oasis cities could become transit stations for long-distance trade. Palmyra in Syria, for instance, enjoyed an ideal location halfway between the Euphrates valley and the Mediterranean coast. Travel time between Mesopotamia and the Mediterranean Sea was substantially reduced by using a direct road through the desert, while camels also had greater speed and endurance than other pack animals previously used, covering a much greater distance in one day. A wide array of new trade routes from east to west and north to south became thus accessible, and areas previously out of the reach of Mesopotamian traders, such as south and central Arabia, now became frequent destinations.

But the new means of transportation by itself would not have been sufficient to have caused the enormous expansion of international trade. The fact that Mesopotamia became part of a succession of enormous empires gave its traders freedom of movement in a wide geographical area and imperial diplomatic protection in foreign lands. Already the neo-Babylonian empire stretched from western Iran to Egypt, providing traders safe passage from the Persian Gulf to the Mediterranean Sea. Under the Achaemenids, this area was extended permanently to include Egypt and Anatolia in the west, and Iran, Afghanistan and India in the east. Under the Seleucids, Arsacids, and Sasanians this area had shrunk somewhat, but still enormous regions were ruled by the same regime that controlled Mesopotamia. Emperors provided diplomatic assistance to traders in their interactions with foreign powers. Direct contacts between Parthian and Chinese rulers are attested in the first centuries AD, including trade along the famous 'Silk Route'.

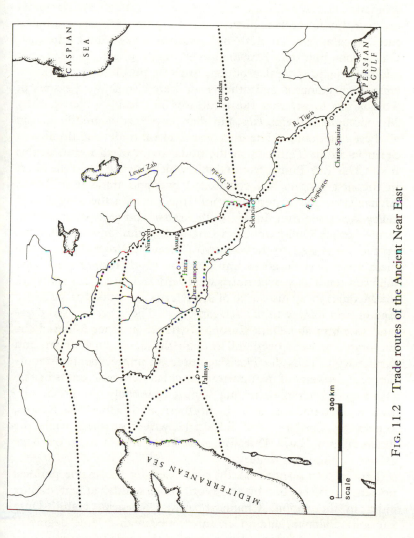

FIG. 11.2   Trade routes of the Ancient Near East

Moreover, the existence of the Roman and Byzantine empires, with a clientele that desired supplies of exotic products from the East was all to the benefit of Mesopotamian traders. Silk, spices, aromatics, slaves, gold, and silver all passed through Mesopotamia on their way to markets in the west. In return, primary manufactures, such as woollen cloth and glass, were exported to the east. Glass from Iran and Babylonia was highly prized in China. In addition, some natural products, such as purple dyes, olive oil, wine, pomegranates, and other fruits were also shipped eastward. This is not to say that the trade was physically undertaken by Mesopotamians themselves, but that they acted as middlemen in all these transactions. The trade was a transit trade, and the area of Seleucia-on-the-Tigris lay at the nodal point of all routes of this trade. The 'Silk Route' from China, which opened up at the latest in the first century AD, channelled overland trade from India, Afghanistan, and eastern Iran into the west via the Diyala river valley. Sea trade from India, south Arabia, and east Africa arrived at the Persian Gulf harbour of Charax Spasinu, and was directed up the Tigris river to the vicinity of Seleucia. From Seleucia two main routes were used to transport the goods further west. One followed the Tigris river north-westward and either cut across to the Mediterranean just south of the Taurus mountains or went into Anatolia on its way to the Aegean coast. The other crossed overland to Hatra and Dura Europos, whence it either followed the Euphrates or went overland through the desert to Palmyra and further west. Thus the Tigris acquired an unprecedented importance, and several of the new trading cities were built on its banks. Older cities such as Assur and Nineveh probably owed their survival to that trade as well. In northern Syria cities like Nisibis, Harran (= Carrhae), and Edessa likewise flourished, while the desert cities of Hatra, Dura Europos, and Palmyra could not have existed without this trade.

This trade was not directly controlled by the major political powers, however, but by the more or less independent trading cities in the region. Charax Spasinu, Seleucia, Hatra, Dura Europos, Palmyra, and so on functioned with a large degree of autonomy. Their independence enabled the trade to continue during the long and devastating territorial wars between eastern and western powers, often fought out on Mesopotamian soil. The imperial authorities encouraged this situation: they benefited from the transit taxes and the selection of goods made available to them. Consequently, the fate of these trading cities did not depend directly upon their geographical surroundings. Politically and economically, they were like oases, rather than cities integrated within their hinterlands. Although similar situations had existed previously in the Near East—for instance with the Phoenician trading centres of the early first millennium—the heartland of Mesopotamia had never known such conditions. There, international trade had always been an aspect of the urban economy, integrated with agriculture and industrial production. The caravan cities were thus innovations in the Mesopotamian environment.

A tremendous amount of financial activity probably took place in these trading cities, and in other cities as well. During the Achaemenid period, private 'banking' houses such as the Egibi in Babylon and the Murashû in Nippur were extensively involved in the financing of agriculture and trade. Credit operations were widespread at that time, both for consumer and investment purposes. No basic differences with the earlier periods are noticeable. But with the Seleucid period, evidence for such activity becomes rarer. The records start focusing upon the transactions of the temples, which continued to function as in the past. The economy was entirely run upon a monetary basis with silver used for every transaction.[14] Financial activity by private individuals is clear from parchment and papyrus records found at Dura,[15] but the number of these records remains limited. Coinage, introduced into the area by the Achaemenids, does not fill the documentary gap. We know that Seleucia was a royal mint into the Parthian period, but we do not know what was done with the coins, or how extensive their use was among private citizens. The lack of documentation should not be taken as indicative of a change in the financial role of urban residents in the economy, only as the unfortunate loss of evidence for such activity.

Changes in the political structure of Mesopotamian cities have been hotly debated by scholars attempting to determine the impact

---

[14] See e.g. the records published by Gilbert McEwan, 'Arsacid Temple Records', *Iraq* 43 (1981), 131–43.

[15] e.g. C. Bradford Welles, *The Parchments and Papyri* (Excavations at Dura Europos. Final Reports V/1; New Haven, 1959), 109–22 where several loan records are published, stating circumstances and conditions similar to those found earlier in Mesopotamian material.

of Hellenism on the ancient Near East. In a sense, the discussion is futile, as it often ignores the earlier civic institutions of Mesopotamian cities, while portraying the Greek *polis* as an idealized democratic urban society that certainly did not exist in the late fourth century, if it had ever existed at all. As I pointed out in an earlier chapter, many aspects of urban government continued from the neo-Babylonian/Achaemenid into the Seleucid periods. Cities had a great deal of autonomy and maintained political institutions, such as the assembly. That assembly may resemble the Greek *boule*, but that does not mean that its activities changed from pre-Greek times. The temple organization and its importance in Babylonian society remained. Officials with Greek titles, such as *epistates*, were introduced within this existing structure, and their responsibility remained the representation of the community in its interactions with the royal administration, as had been the case before with officials with traditional Babylonian titles. The latter continued to use their old titles when dealing with the native community. There is no indication that the new Seleucid cities were treated differently from the older ones. Their governmental structure, including Seleucia's, is not really known to us in this period. But in the Parthian period assemblies still existed there. According to a Syriac text of the seventh century, Seleucia had three assemblies in the first and second centuries AD: for the elders, for the young men, and for the boys. The Aramaic term used for assembly was *puhra*, obviously a survival of the identical ancient Akkadian term.[16] The Parthian kings allowed cities a great deal of autonomy: their trading activities brought substantial income to the crown, and the new rulers may not have had the experience needed to administer the vast geographical area they controlled. There was no need to change existing mechanisms that had proved their worth. The Sasanians may at first have continued this practice, but they finally limited urban autonomy. Both new foundations and older cities were instituted under a policy of political and economic centralization, and cities turned into military garrisons and centres of royal administration. Early Muslim rulers continued this trend, clamping down on urban autonomy. We can, however, say that the concept of the Mesopotamian urban community as an autonomous

---

[16] N. Pigulevskaja, *Les Villes de l'état iranien aux époques parthe et sassanide. Contribution à l'histoire sociale de la Basse Antiquité* (Paris and The Hague, 1963), 84–5.

body, represented to the crown by selected individuals, survived for many centuries of foreign rule over the region. Thus a situation that had originated under local dynasties was perpetuated once independence was lost.

Socially, the ethnic diversity of the urban populations increased with the ability of various peoples of the empire to settle in Mesopotamia, which was always one of the most prosperous regions. Again, this was a continuation of trends that had started earlier, especially by the deportation policies of the Assyrian and neo-Babylonian kings. Already under the Achaemenids, Babylonia housed a great variety of foreign people, including Phoenicians, Judaeans, Egyptians, Arabs, Phrygians, Lydians, Carians, Armenians, Indians, and Persians, mixing with indigenous Babylonians—whatever that meant in this period—and Chaldaeans. Certain of these communities may have resisted assimilation, but a great deal of cultural and ethnic mixing took place. All spoke Aramaic and adopted Babylonian names. The Macedonian conquest introduced a European element in this mixture. Despite Alexander's alleged desire to merge Asiatic and European cultures and peoples, the Greek and Macedonian populations seem to have maintained a distance from the Mesopotamians. In Babylon, evidence of Greek occupation is limited to a small area in the north-east sector of the city, and Seleucia-on-the-Tigris was seemingly built as a Greek counterpart of the Mesopotamian metropolis. A number of Babylonians were allowed to adopt Greek names and to work in the Greek administration, but apparently no Greek wanted to do the reverse. It is quite likely that new immigrants from Europe continued to arrive throughout the Seleucid period,[17] so a policy of segregation could be maintained. Yet, we should not exaggerate the Greek lack of interest in the natives and their culture. Some adoption of Babylonian practices, among them the use of clay tablets, is attested. Why should we assume that Greeks did not marry native Babylonians? They could not have avoided seeing them, even in cities such as Seleucia, and we know that they were not averse to mixed marriages in places like Egypt.

The situation changed when the Parthians took over control of the area. We have no idea what happened in most cities due to a

---

[17] See Pierre Briant, 'Renforts grecs dans les cités hellénistiques d'Orient', in *Rois, tributs et paysans* (Besançon, 1982), 263–79.

lack of documentation. In the trading cities founded by the Greeks, such as Seleucia, Greeks seem to have continued their control. But other ethnic groups gradually gained a foothold in them as well. In Dura Europos we find traces of the cultural traditions of many ethnic groups: Greeks, Romans, Jews, Arabs, and Parthians. A crucial change took place in the social organization of urban communities in the Sasanian period, however. Religion became the dominant element in determining one's affiliation with others, replacing language, occupation, or ethnicity. Religious communities with separate organizations and legal institutions became the main social unit for an individual: Zoroastrian, Christian, Jewish, pagan, and later Muslim. Although ethnicity often coincided with religion, ethnic borders could be crossed: the Arameans, for instance, formed the majority of both the Jews and the Christians. The preponderance of such religious communities became a determining element of early Islamic society, and indicates a major difference with earlier history.

Urban culture clearly changed, mainly because of the increased religious diversity. While Mesopotamian culture and religion had been able to absorb and inspire new arrivals during its long history, it failed to do so with the Greeks, and later with the Parthians. Yet elements of Babylonian culture, such as astronomical sciences, survived into the first century AD, and the age-old literature disappeared only in the first century BC. The literature failed to be preserved in non-cuneiform writing except in vague references. Hence, the literary tradition seems to have been perpetuated only by native Babylonians. Official cults seem to have been either assimilated with new foreign deities, or to have disappeared altogether. When the Babylonian temple complex at Uruk was destroyed around 100 BC, it was replaced by a Graeco-Iranian temple for Gareus. In popular cults, Babylonian influence continued much longer, even among members of the monotheistic religions. In late Sasanian Iraq, gods such as Shamash, Sin, Bel, Nanai, and Nergal were still invoked. A form of Ishtar was still the patron-goddess of Erbil, as she had been 1,500 years earlier. The disappearance of official Mesopotamian cults was not, therefore, the result of government policy. Neither the Seleucids nor the Parthians seem to have forced their gods upon local populations. So the disappearance of ancient Mesopotamian cults is shrouded in mystery. The loss of the economic role of the temples, the lack of royal patronage, and the drowning of the 'Mesopotamian' in a sea of new immigrants all may have played a role, but we do not have the evidence to study these issues.

Even though the culture in the cities changed, the idea of the city as the centre of culture did not disappear. Zoroastrian fire altars or Christian monasteries may have appeared as non-urban centres of religion, but the cities remained the focal points of cultural and religious developments. Religious ideologies of these periods are entire fields of research by themselves, and their liveliness shows that intellectually and culturally, Mesopotamia was flourishing. The splendours of Abbasid Iraq were certainly not created *ex novo* by the Muslim rulers, but must have had some of their roots in the ancient traditions of the region.

Thus, on balance, I think that we can say that the ancient Mesopotamian city did not die out with the end of Mesopotamia's political independence—certainly not suddenly, at any rate. Many traditional aspects of urban life continued to exist from the fifth century BC long into the first centuries AD. New influences altered aspects of religion and culture, and the economy of certain cities was changed due to the enormous expansion of international trade. Social changes were fundamental in late Sasanian times. But the urban civilization of Mesopotamia did not really disappear, in my opinion, until the agricultural decline of the region in the early Islamic period. Even then, centres like Baghdad perpetuated earlier traditions, and perhaps only the Mongol sack of that city in AD 1258 marks the end of an era.

BIBLIOGRAPHY

The end of 'Mesopotamian civilization' is usually left unexplained by scholars; it is apparently regarded as having resulted from the loss of political independence at the hands of the Persians. Recently Norman Yoffee explained the culturally devastating impact of that conquest by the fact that it ended the peculiar ideal of a Mesopotamian state which had for millennia enabled various foreign groups to legitimize their rule, in Norman Yoffee and George L. Cowgill (eds.), *The Collapse of Ancient States and Civilizations* (Tucson, 1988). Mogens Trolle Larsen sees an intellectual malaise reflected in Mesopotamian literary texts, some of which date to the end of the second millennium, which would have made the 'stream of tradition' meaningless, 'The Collapse of Civilizations: The Case of Mesopotamia', in Jens Christian, V. Johansen, *et al.* (eds.), *Clashes of Cultures: Essays in Honour of Niels Steensgaard* (Odense, 1992), 107–29. Both of these explanations take the disappearance of cuneiform texts as an indication of the end of Mesopotamian civilization.

Much of the information on Mesopotamia in the periods after the Persian conquest in 539 BC has to be culled from books that deal primarily with other areas, especially the Hellenistic world and Iran. However, the Achaemenid and Seleucid periods in Mesopotamia are currently very popular subjects among cuneiform scholars. The works by Mohammed Dandamaev for Achaemenid Babylonia are crucial, see e.g. his (with V. G. Lukonin), *The Culture and Social Institutions of Ancient Iran* (Cambridge, 1989). For the Seleucid material, the work by Joachim Oelsner, *Materialien zum babylonischen Gesellschaft und Kultur in Hellenistischer Zeit* (Budapest, 1986), is very convenient and complete. Of interest are the articles by Pierre Briant collected in *Rois, tributs et paysans* (Besançon, 1982). A recent re-evaluation of the Seleucid state as an eastern empire by Susan Sherwin-White and Amélie Kuhrt, *From Samarkand to Sardis: A New Approach to the Seleucid Empire* (London, 1993), contains much of interest on Babylonia. M. Rostovtzeff's majestic work, *The Social and Economic History of the Hellenistic World* (Oxford, 1941), is still of great importance.

For the Parthian and Sasanian periods the *Cambridge History of Iran* 3, E. Yarshater (ed.) (Cambridge, 1983), contains good information. The book by N. Pigulevskaja, *Les Villes de l'état iranien aux époques parthe et sassanide: Contribution à l'histoire sociale de la Basse Antiquité* (Paris and The Hague, 1963), provides a good introduction to the sources available for the study of cities; but the work focuses primarily upon the evolution from a community-based, slave-owning society to a feudal society in Sasanian Iran, and this emphasis prejudices the discussion. The social and administrative conditions in the late Sasanian and early Islamic periods are thoroughly discussed by Michael G. Morony, *Iraq after the Muslim Conquest* (Princeton, 1984).

A nice historical survey of the city of Babylon in the late periods is provided by Horst Klengel, 'Babylon zur Zeit der Perser,

Griechen und Parther', *Forschungen und Berichte. Staatliche Museen zu Berlin* 5 (1962), 40–53.

For archaeological information on the periods discussed in this chapter one has to go through the excavation reports of various sites. Assur, Coche, Dura Europos, Hatra, Nippur, Seleucia, and Uruk have been well excavated. Robert McC. Adams's *Heartland of Cities* (Chicago and London, 1981) is a mine of information on Babylonia. Aharon Oppenheimer, *Babylonia Judaica in the Talmudic Period* (Wiesbaden, 1983), provides a long list of place names found in Talmudic literature, with classical references, and much archaeological and historical information on the cities of Babylonia in the Hellenistic through Sasanian periods. For settlement in northern Mesopotamia see David Oates, *Studies in the Ancient History of Northern Iraq* (London, 1968): chapters 4 and 5, and for the Euphrates valley see the contributions by Pierre Leriche and Georges Tate in Olivier Rouault and Maria Grazia Rouault (eds.), *L'Eufrate e il tempo* (Milan, 1993), 98–104.

# CONCLUSIONS

## The Ancient Mesopotamian City

The ancient Mesopotamian city has a particular position in history, which can be fully appreciated only when placed within the context of urbanism in the ancient Near East, and in the ancient world in general. After establishing the unique position of Mesopotamian urbanism within its ancient Near Eastern setting, I will argue that it can be integrated within Max Weber's ideal type of the ancient city, a concept frequently employed by Graeco-Roman historians, despite the orientalist foundations of that model. Finally, I will discuss how Mesopotamia can be seen as a single entity with respect to urban history, with Babylonia and Assyria as mere variants of a common tradition.

The ancient Near East outside Mesopotamia includes a large area with many regions that have distinct geographies: the Iranian plateau, the Arabian desert peninsula, the Anatolian mountains, the Levantine Mediterranean coast, and the Egyptian Nile valley, all with abundant natural diversity within them. Cities appear in all these regions at various moments in the period paralleling Mesopotamian history, but nowhere are they such a crucial and dominant element as in Mesopotamia. In many cases urbanism in these regions seems to have been inspired by Mesopotamia, but urban life was less an integral part of their civilizations. A comparison of the Mesopotamian city with those of the other regions is made difficult by the lack of comprehensive studies on any of them, but a broad survey of the characteristics of urbanism in a selection of those areas will elucidate some of the fundamental differences.

The best studied region with respect to urbanism is Syria–Palestine, an area that can be regarded in many respects as an extension of Mesopotamia proper. Geographically it forms the western and southern segment of the so-called 'Fertile Crescent'. The border between northern Mesopotamia and northern Syria is especially indeterminate. In every respect, the Syro-Palestinian area was in closest contact with Mesopotamia proper, either through trade relations or as the primary victim of military expansion. Its political life was greatly influenced by Mesopotamian powers and many aspects of its culture derived thence. The late fourth-millennium Uruk expansion caused the rise of settlements with urban characteristics in the Upper Euphrates valley, including ephemeral ones such as Habuba Kabira. Urban centres survived throughout the Syro-Palestinian area for most of the period between 3000 and 2400, seemingly influenced by trade contacts both with southern Mesopotamia and with Egypt.

The Bronze Age cities of the Syro-Palestinian area experienced several changes in their fortunes until the final collapse of the culture around 1200 BC, but one characteristic seems to have remained a constant throughout the period: the cities were dominated by a small élite associated with their palaces, which exploited the agricultural village populations to maintain their consumption of refined craft products. These cities were the centres of small regional states whose territories probably did not extend beyond a 50 kilometre radius. The political and military powers were held by a secular hierarchy which kept political and commercial contacts with equals nearby, and with the major political powers in Mesopotamia, northern Syria, Anatolia, and Egypt. Archaeologically, their distinct status is indicated by palaces with their own defensive structures, separated from the rest of the city.

Some of these cities owed their livelihood almost entirely to long-distance trade. Byblos on the Lebanese coast, for instance, acted as the main port for Egyptian commercial contacts with Syria. In general, one has the impression that the Syro-Palestinian cities of the Bronze Age were somewhat artificial foundations, maintained through trade or through the exploitation of the surrounding countryside by political and military means. Hence, their collapse around 1200 is seen by some scholars to have been the result of social upheaval, although invasions and population movements have also been blamed.[1]

Not all of these cities disappeared around 1200, but the succeeding centuries are very poorly known in historical terms. When we

[1] See W. A. Ward and M. S. Joukowsky (eds.), *The Crisis Years: The 12th Century B.C.* (Dubuque, 1992) for a survey of current opinions.

obtain more information, in the tenth century, many cities were situated in new locations and they were almost always part of new political entities, nation-states of a greater extent than the Bronze Age states. Some scholars have seen this as an indication that the role of the city was greatly reduced in this period,[2] which may have been true in political terms, but does not necessarily apply to the economy, culture, and society. We do observe a hierarchy of variously sized cities throughout the area, and cities remained a crucial part of the settlement pattern. On the Levantine coasts the trading cities, now especially Tyre, flourished despite the lack of good agricultural hinterland. When the Assyrians and Babylonians conquered and ruled the area of Syria–Palestine, they destroyed many of the existing cities and deported large segments of the population. Yet, the Assyrians at least, also established some administrative centres of their own throughout the region. About the Persian rule over the area, little is known beyond the fact that they had problems with the Phoenician cities. It is unclear what the level of urbanization in the area was when the Macedonians conquered it, and started their policy of city foundations. Recently it has been suggested that Syrian society at that time was primarily rural,[3] a view that needs further argumentation.

Cities in the Syro-Palestinian area were thus a common feature of settlement throughout ancient history, yet seemingly less integrated in their immediate environments than those in Mesopotamia. They were reliant on long-distance trade or political domination for their survival, and were not integrated within the rural economy. They were smaller than the Mesopotamian cities, and probably only a restricted segment of the population lived in an urban environment.

In Anatolia, the evolution of urbanism seems to have been similar to that in Syria–Palestine, although the political geographies of the two regions differed. Cities appeared in the third millennium. They flourished in the second millennium within a large Hittite state, a conglomerate of various regions in Anatolia and northern Syria, ruled from the capital Hattusas in central Anatolia. Most cities were located in the valleys, except for Hattusas itself. Hittite cities are characterized by their citadels, containing the major

---

[2] Giorgio Buccellati, *Cities and Nations of Ancient Syria* (Rome, 1967), 109.

[3] John D. Grainger, *The Cities of Seleukid Syria* (Oxford, 1990), 23–30.

secular and religious monumental buildings, and separated by a wall from the rest of the town. The Hittite state was destroyed around 1200, and several cities disappeared at that time. In the first millennium, new political entities emerged with cities as important political centres: in the west, the Phrygians, about whom relatively little is known; in the east Urartu. In the latter area several fortress cities, built on mountain peaks, were created, some very carefully planned. The role of these cities within their environments is hard to reconstruct, due to the lack of relevant textual information.

The city in ancient Egypt is a subject that has only recently received proper scholarly attention. Archaeologically, non-monumental urban remains can rarely be uncovered, due to later settlements or monumental buildings that have destroyed what lies underneath them. The textual evidence concerning cities is also extremely scarce. Some exceptions exist, however, only from places that were occupied for a short periods: their representative nature for Egyptian cities can be doubted. The town of Kahun from the early centuries of the second millennium, with its houses and streets laid out in rectangles along straight lines, was probably a pyramid city to house the personnel attending the cult of the dead king Sesostris II, and may exemplify a common settlement near pyramids. The totally planned capital city of Akhetaten, modern el-Amarna, built in a few years by Akhenaten in the fourteenth century, and abandoned upon his death, may be a good example of a major Egyptian city, but it also may have been highly atypical. The important political and economic centres of Egypt—Thebes, Memphis, and later Pi-Ramesse—are virtually unknown archaeologically, and cannot be compared to Akhetaten.

Politically, the cities of Egypt played a very different role from those in Mesopotamia, since the Egyptian nation-state developed at the same time as its cities. Moreover, the Nile River's ability to act as a major transport route allowed for the provisioning of urban populations with the agricultural produce from remote regions. Yet the existence of a hierarchy of settlements with a very few major cities, some forty nome-capitals the size of small towns, and numerous surrounding villages can be hypothesized. If this is correct, it would show that the settlement patterns in Egypt were not entirely determined by political considerations, but that the processes of local economic exchange also played a role.

Although cities were thus common in these three Near Eastern regions, they seem to have played a less crucial role in their civilizations than did the city in Mesopotamia. The cities were modest in size, a smaller percentage of the populations was urban, and the cities were less an integral part of the economy and the culture. We have to be cautious, however, not to reduce the role of the cities within these civilizations too much. When studying them, the focus of scholarly attention has often been on other aspects of their cultures. The study of cities has usually been the study of city-states, which were less important in Anatolian and Egyptian history, and which are thought to have been only dominant in Syria–Palestine during the Bronze Age. Little attention has been paid to cities within nation-states, but this scholarly selection should not lead us to believe that cities were less important then. In any case, Mesopotamia stands out as the region where cities did play a crucial role in every aspect of the culture, and this, combined with the fact that cities originated there, shows the special nature of Mesopotamian urbanism within its Near Eastern context.

The position of the ancient Mesopotamian city within ancient urbanism in general needs to be seen in the context of the idea of the 'ancient city'. This concept is rooted in the work of the German sociologist Max Weber (1864–1920), who did not develop a typology of urbanism in world history, but who wanted to explain the rise of capitalism in Western Europe and the role of the 'occidental city' in that process.[4] As was normal in his days, Weber was convinced of the uniqueness of historical evolution in the West, and he wanted to emphasize this by contrasting it to the situation in the East. The opposition between Occident and Orient was fundamental in his mind, and he saw its roots in antiquity. Although Weber did inform himself of the little Mesopotamian evidence that was accessible to him in the early twentieth century,[5] he was unable to see Mesopotamia in any other light than in contrast to the West, represented by its most illustrious civilization, Greece.

[4] The manuscript was only published after Weber's death, and has been later integrated in his posthumous work *Wirtschaft und Gesellschaft*. The original text was translated into English and edited by Don Martindale and Gertrud Neuwirth, *The City* (New York, 1958).

[5] See Weber's entirely ignored chapter on Mesopotamia in *The Agrarian Sociology of Ancient Civilizations*, translated by R. I. Frank (London and New York, 1988), 83–104.

The basic opposition between East and West according to Weber related to the issue of power: the East was identified by despotism, the West by freedom of the individual. This distinction affected city life in that only the occidental city could obtain the status of an autonomous political centre, while in the East the city was always subject to larger political entities. Weber characterized the oriental city by its lack of autonomy and autocephaly, without its own constitution, administration, tribunal, or military force. In contrast, both in antiquity and in the Middle Ages, the western city was able to develop a type of democracy. He based these statements upon his ideas on India, China, and Japan, and it has to be said, by way of explanation, that he never really studied the oriental city on its own merits, but only as a foil for the occidental city. Obviously, by opposing the Orient to the Occident, he placed himself firmly within the Orientalist tradition, so prevalent in his days that its absence in Weber's work would have been more of a surprise than its presence. I am far from condoning this attitude. We must realize that Weber did not claim to have provided an in-depth study of non-western cities or that his thoughts on them were to be uncritically adopted. Other scholars have used his statements about the uniqueness of the occidental city without much thought, however. The idea that the ancient Near Eastern city was dominated by the temple or the palace is still popular among ancient historians.[6] I hope to have shown that it is false to state that in Mesopotamia royal power was absolute, and that all citizens had to obey the king's orders. At times indeed 'city air made man free' in Mesopotamia, and urban autonomy was not to be ignored. How this compares to the situation in classical Greece seems to be a matter of personal sympathy. In many discussions complex and intricate political relationships seem often to be reduced to empty slogans. It is still common to identify 'the dawn of democracy' in classical Greece, and to oppose the political situation there to the 'oriental despotism' of Asia. Yet such catchy phrases have little meaning, and obscure the nuances of the political realities in both regions. When the Greeks colonized Mesopotamia, the political organization of cities there did not change much. I would not explain this as a result of the survival of an oriental tradition in the

---

[6] See, for instance, M. I. Finley, *The Ancient Economy*, 2nd edn. (Berkeley, 1985), 28.

eastern Greek world, distinct from the ancient tradition in Europe,[7] but as an indication that the differences between East and West were not so fundamental. Mesopotamian cities were often autocephalous units in political terms, with long traditions as political entities, and with conflicts between these cities and the governments of territorial states and empires.

If we abandon the unconditional opposition between East and West in Weber's writings, however, we can make use of his other theories regarding urbanism in the study of the Mesopotamian city. In addition to the East–West opposition, Weber saw a second crucial distinction between ancient and medieval, placing him firmly in the primitivist camp in the primitivism–modernism debate. This view held that the ancient city differed fundamentally from the medieval European one, primarily because the ancient city was a consumer, while the medieval one was a producer. This interpretation seems now universally accepted by scholars, whether accepting or challenging Weber's views, and is a common starting point for discussions of aspects of ancient urbanism.[8] The influential ancient historian Moses Finley identified the role of consumer as the primary characteristic of the ancient city, which, in his opinion, was only to be found in the Graeco-Roman world.[9] The townspeople lived from rents and taxes derived from the agricultural hinterland, and the majority of manufactured goods and services generated within the city was for local consumption. This is in contrast to the medieval European city, which was a net producer of goods and services, and thus generated the economic conditions for the rise of capitalism. Finley acknowledged that the ideal type of the ancient city as a consumer had many variations that merit investigation. It is thus worthwhile to see whether the ideal type applies to ancient Mesopotamia.

I have tried to show that all three sectors of the economy— agriculture, manufacture, and services—were of importance to Mesopotamian cities. There is a major problem in establishing

---

[7] See Finley, ibid. 183. Admittedly, he refers there to social and economic systems, not to politics, but it seems that his belief in the absolute distinction between East and West is all-encompassing.

[8] See e.g. John Rich and Andrew Wallace-Hadrill (eds.), *City and Country in the Ancient World* (London and New York, 1991).

[9] M. I. Finley, *Economy and Society in Ancient Greece* (London, 1981), 3–23.

their relative worth, but this is far from clear in the Graeco-Roman world as well. There is no means of quantifying the evidence, despite the countless Mesopotamian records available to us, and we are left with informed guesses. It seems reasonable to state that agriculture was the basis of the economy of most Mesopotamian cities. In Babylonia we see that agricultural development and urbanism coincided, while food from the hinterland seems to have been sufficient to feed the cities, rendering long-distance imports unnecessary. Although manufacture was not just 'petty commodity production' intended for local consumption,[10] and exports of basic goods such as textiles are well attested, we cannot say that any city made its fortune as a manufacturing centre. Similarly, services, such as trade, never seem to have made the principal contribution to a Babylonian city's wealth. In Assyria, the situation is more difficult to assess. The metropolises of the first millennium were clearly enormous consumers of goods, both agricultural and manufactured, but can hardly be regarded as producers in economic terms. The primary difference with Babylonia is that in order to find the necessary supplies they needed to rely on a larger hinterland, either in the territorial states controlled by them, or in the surrounding areas within the reach of their armies. Yet, some Assyrian cities, like Assur, may have acquired a substantial amount of wealth through trade, which would make it somewhat like the medieval towns of Europe. Moreover, by the mere fact that cities like Nineveh were great consumers, they did stimulate the economy, something that was true as well for the consumer city *par excellence* in antiquity, Rome.[11] The label of consumer city seemingly can be applied to the ancient Mesopotamian city, in that it drew more resources from the surrounding countryside than it delivered. The urban population lived off the income from land it either owned itself or which was owned by the public institutions which were located within the cities, the temples and the palaces.

But was this consumption entirely of a parasitical nature? Did these cities give nothing in return to the exploited rural

---

[10] As M. I. Finley would say. See e.g. ibid. 22.

[11] See H. W. Pleket, 'Rome: A Pre-industrial Megalopolis', in Theo Barker and Anthony Sutcliffe (eds.), *Megalopolis: the Giant City in History* (New York, 1993), 14–35.

populations? This issue seems to be the crucial point of dissent with the Weber–Finley model among ancient historians.[12] In the case of Babylonia it seems unreasonable to see the city entirely as a negative element in the agricultural development of the region, as a parasite living off the fat of the land. Agriculture could not have flourished to the extent it did without cities. By the fact that cities and urban institutions acted as loci and organizers of distribution and exchange, they enabled the specialization of different food producers: farmers, gardeners, herders, fishermen, and hunters. Financial transactions, such as the provision of credit, facilitated the contacts between landlords and tenants and the collection and distribution of produce in an economy without well-developed market mechanisms. Moreover, cereal agriculture came to rely on increasingly extensive irrigation works, which were maintained by urban institutions. Thus, despite the total fallacy of her statement 'Cities First—Rural Development Later', Jane Jacobs did have a valid point when she stated that agricultural development cannot be seen as a gift from nature requiring no organization.[13] Rural productivity did benefit from urban stimuli, and the Babylonians did not live in a God-given garden of Eden. In Assyria the cities played less of a role in agricultural development, which could flourish in an environment of self-sufficient villages, although on a smaller scale. Certain aspects of increased production relied on urban institutions, especially the palace. Kings could order irrigation systems to be laid out or marginal zones to be developed, but it is remarkable that the texts describing such works do not emphasize their benefit to the basic food supply of a city. Aqueducts were built to water exotic gardens. It seems that the region was able to support settlements of up to 100 hectares in size without great difficulties or organization, that such cities were properly integrated within their rural surroundings, and as such may have stimulated agricultural development. But once they surpassed this size they became difficult to feed, a burden upon the rural economy.

Whether the manufacturing and service aspects of the urban economy benefited the rural residents is difficult to say. Obviously, certain goods and materials became available to them, but it is

---

[12] See e.g. Philippe Leveau, 'La Ville antique et l'organisation de l'espace rural: *villa*, ville, village', *Annales* 38 (1983), 920–42.

[13] Jane Jacobs, *The Economy of Cities* (New York, 1969).

likely that they would have remained unaffordable. I do not see how organized religion or the state apparatus could have been a great asset to them, and the products of high culture generated in cities were probably entirely beyond their reach. Thus the position of the Mesopotamian cities in their regional economies, and their relationships with the agricultural hinterland seem similar to what we find in the rest of the ancient world. They were great consumers of resources, yet their presence did not have purely negative effects. In Babylonia cities provided an important benefit to agricultural development with their managerial services. In Assyria cities were not crucial to agriculture and their relationships with their hinterlands may have been of a more parasitical nature. Hence, in this respect these cities present variants to the 'ancient city' as visualized by Weber, yet they are sufficiently close to his ideal type to deserve the same designation.

As a sociologist, Weber was obviously interested in the social structure of cities. In his opinion, the medieval European city was unique because of its ability to integrate individuals within the citizenry, while in the ancient city an individual could only be a citizen as a member of a clan.[14] Weber was also the most outspoken opponent of his time to the prevalent evolutionary model that saw a progression from a tribal society to one based on nuclear families in a territorial state.[15] His statement has thus to be seen distinct from that model, and if we allow the term 'clan' to refer to a kinship group with common interests, rather than to a group of blood relatives, his characterization of ancient citizenship as based on clans fits the Mesopotamian model as well. In that sense the ancient Mesopotamian city is also an example of the ancient city. In the ancient Mesopotamian city individuals did not count as citizens. As I pointed out before, cities were made up of various groups, which could be familial, ethnic, residential, or professional in nature. An individual outside any of these groups did not have a means to participate in the social and political life of the town.

I would disagree with some classical historians' statements about differences in the social structure of the Graeco-Roman and Meso-potamian cities. Frank Kolb, for instance, who seems to find little of value in Weber's ideal types of cities, sees a major distinction

---

[14] Weber, *The City*, 101.
[15] See M. I. Finley, *Ancient History: Evidence and Models* (Harmondsworth, 1987), 90–3.

between the ancient Near Eastern and Graeco-Roman cities in their social organization. In his opinion, the ancient Near Eastern city, and for that matter the medieval European city as well, shows a division in quarters for specific ethnic and professional groups, inaccessible to outsiders. On the other hand, the Graeco-Roman city, especially in its Hippodamian layout, was entirely open to all citizens who were drawn together by public places (like the agora, forum, or baths) and institutions (like the assembly).[16] He sees thus a strong community encompassing the entire Graeco-Roman city, which he finds lacking in the ancient Near Eastern city. Although the social coherence of the Mesopotamian city is hard to appraise, it seems mistaken to see it as a loose conglomerate of disjointed groups. The entire city could act as a community. As in classical Greece, there was a general city assembly in Mesopotamia. And there must have been some type of civic pride which led people to name their children after their home town, 'Dilbat is my father' and so on. This sense of community was not enforced upon the citizens, who cannot be regarded as mere servants to the city gods or their representatives, be they kings or priests, as Kolb states. If this were true we would have to envisage all the Mesopotamian urban residents as dependants of the public institutions of temples and palaces. Although these institutions may have provided social networks for a substantial segment of the urban population, it seems clear to me that they were not all-encompassing and that independent individuals and families resided in cities as well, with other social structures available to them. These also had civic pride and belonged to the urban community very much like their Greek counterparts, I would think.

In conclusion, I think that we can say that the ancient Mesopotamian city fits the type of the ancient city as described by Weber and Finley, if we allow for a certain number of peculiarities. Economically and socially, the similarities with ancient Greece and Rome were greater than the differences. Subsequently, Fernand Braudel's insistence on looking at the Mediterranean world as an entity, not as an area divided between Europe and Asia,[17] might be fruitfully applied to the study of antiquity as well. Certainly, the unity of the Mediterranean world in antiquity is a historical ques-

---

[16] Frank Kolb, *Die Stadt im Altertum* (Munich, 1984), 261–70.
[17] See Fernand Braudel, *The Mediterranean and the Mediterranean World in the Age of Philip II* (New York, 1973).

tion that extends far beyond the issue of urbanism and that needs much more exploration. It is hoped that it will be given serious consideration by scholars both of the ancient Near East and the Graeco-Roman world.

Can we say that there was a Mesopotamian city, i.e. a type that can be found both in Babylonia and Assyria? Here again the answer depends on how far one is willing to make abstractions. It seems that there were differences between Babylonia and Assyria in the role and importance of the city, differences that at some times of their histories may have been more acute than at others. In origin, the divergences were due to the ecological conditions of the two regions. In Babylonia, the arid countryside and the dependence upon irrigation for agriculture limited the possibilities of settlement and caused the need for redistributive centres. In the rain-fed areas of Assyria, settlement in self-sufficient villages throughout the countryside was possible. The first cities in Assyria were artificial foundations for political or trading purposes, often inspired by southern stimuli.

Urban life in the two regions has to be considered separately, although mutual influences have led to many similarities between them as well. In Babylonia, the city was the most important social and economic institution for the entire society. Babylonia is one of the few areas in the world where an urban society developed without outside influence, entirely due to local circumstances. In most periods of its history, from roughly 3000 to 1600 BC and from 700 BC to AD 700 the level of urbanization was extremely high, with major urban centres within sight of one another. Cities were the centres of the economy, the political institutions, and the culture. Whenever Babylonia flourished economically, cities were needed to enable the exchange of locally produced agricultural and manufactured products. Either the public institutions situated in the cities distributed these goods to their dependants, or an urban market financed and organized by private entrepreneurs enabled their acquisition. International trade was of secondary importance in that it procured prestige goods for a small élite, not for the majority of the Babylonians, and, until the Seleucid period, no city seems to have been founded there for trading purposes only.

The city was of paramount importance in the political life of Babylonia: no ruler could claim real power without an urban base. Such an attitude can be well understood, since no positive economic role could be played without access to a city. In ideology and in practice, the city dominated political life. Non-urban segments of the society, such as villagers and pastoral nomads, were considered to be dependent upon a particular town. People who did not have such an affiliation were outcasts, brigands. The king resided in the city to be with his gods and his bureaucracy. He could not be a tribal leader, using existing cities for trading purposes or the like. The entire high culture of Babylonia was also focused upon the city in that it housed its primary patrons, the temples and the court. Babylonian civilization cannot be imagined without cities.

The situation was different in Assyria, although Babylonian influence also generated many similarities between the two regions. Since cities were not needed for the exchange of locally produced goods, they did not develop independently. They were created for long-distance trading or for political purposes. The ephemeral urban foundations of the North in the third millennium were organized under Babylonian influence, for trade and perhaps for political control of the region. Most of these cities disappeared when southern influence waned. Those that survived, like Assur, were perhaps primarily trading centres, specializing in transit trade between various regions. When a second wave of urbanization took place in the early second millennium, the cities were primarily bases of political control of the region. Assyrian rulers founded them for administrative purposes throughout the territorial states they tried to create. In Assyria the political powers created the cities; in Babylonia the cities created political power. The dominant element in Assyrian society was the court, which used the cities for its own purposes. In economic terms, many Assyrian cities, such as the imperial capitals, were a drain upon the region rather than an asset. They disrupted the rural economy by their excessive demands—consumer cities *par excellence*.

But the regions had such close and permanent contacts that the mutual influences were great, and over time these differences were smoothed out. The similarities in their attitude towards urban life are most obvious in the ideology towards cities and in the cultural role of the cities. Both Babylonians and Assyrians saw the city as the centre of the universe, the heart of their culture and religion, the proper habitat of a civilized person. The social role of the city, with its ability to gather people of different backgrounds and separate affinities, was also the same. And, over time, the relationship between cities and the state became also more alike: Assur, the cultural centre of Assyria, claimed the same urban privileges as did the Babylonian cities of ancient standing.

I think thus that we can speak of an ideal type of the ancient Mesopotamian city, which showed different characteristics in Babylonia and Assyria. A lot more work needs to be done to improve our knowledge of Mesopotamian urbanism. Problem-oriented research, both by archaeologists and philologists, can elucidate many of the topics discussed in this book, and several projects of this nature are in progress. Archaeologists can devote more attention to the residential areas of the walled cities, to suburbs, and even to villages. Reconstructions of entire town plans have been attempted through aerial photography and surface scraping, but still the focus of excavations is on monumental buildings. It is, obviously, impossible to excavate an entire city, thus only sample areas in residential zones can be investigated in this manner. Remains of villages are not so easy to identify in the countryside, while grant agencies and archaeological services seem to show little interest in providing funding or permits for their excavation. Yet, in order to understand aspects of urban geography, it is necessary to contrast the city to non-urban settlements.

There is also a great need to understand the natural environments of cities, and to determine their agricultural potential in antiquity. Such research would enable us to study the availability of foods, their procurement by citizens, and the ability of the hinterlands to support cities in individual cases. Projects of this nature are now regularly undertaken, around the Assyrian city Dur-Katlimmu on the Habur in Syria, for example,[18] and will yield crucial insights on the basis of the Mesopotamian economy, agriculture.

Philologists can analyse materials already available to them in order to elucidate many of the problems of urban life. Information on the governmental structure, for instance, could probably be culled from the abundant business correspondence of several periods of history. If backed by a concern to understand the role of the

---

[18] Hartmut Kühne, *Die rezente Umwelt von Tall Šēḫ Hamad und Daten zur Umweltrekonstruktion der assyrischen Stadt Dūr-Katlimmu* (Berlin, 1991).

city, the writing of social histories of particular cities would seem very useful and feasible, especially in periods other than the early second millennium, for which such studies already exist. Such histories will be filled with lacunae because of the total absence of data on many questions, but even in that form they can lead to a better understanding of temporal and regional variations in urban life.

In general, Mesopotamian historians should be aware of the urban bias of the documentation available to them, and evaluate that material in this light. Land sales, rental contracts, business agreements, and so on, are evidence of activities by urban landlords and businessmen. They do not necessarily reflect the most common situations in Mesopotamia. An understanding of life in the countryside, even if it is based on scanty evidence, is needed to provide a foil for our image of the city. Projects of this nature require the careful analysis of numerous documents, edited and unedited, and need to be undertaken by a large number of individual researchers concentrating on a particular place or time. They provide the necessary basis for more general studies of urbanism.

On the other hand, we have to resign ourselves to the fact that certain aspects of urban life in Mesopotamia will never be known to us, or that our reconstructions of them will be extremely tentative. We will never obtain a clear portrait of daily life in the Mesopotamian city, an unreasonable aim in any case as there is no paradigmatic city. Essays which hope to show 'a day in the life of' an individual of a particular city are similarly impossible. The lack of narrative sources in Mesopotamian historiography makes it impossible to do more than imagine how one of the innumerable men and women known to us by name spent the day at work, at home, with friends, or wherever. Except for a few kings, whose personality is to some extent revealed to us, the Mesopotamian person we study is a faceless one, a name with a profession, some records and earthly goods. We can develop vivid images of a citizen of Uruk or the like, but most of that would be in the realm of fantasy. What a Mesopotamian city would have looked like during the day is hard to say. But at night, peace and quiet descended when people had gone to sleep, as this testimony of a diviner, forced to stay awake, attests:

The noble ones are safely *guarded*, doorbolts drawn, rings in place.
The noisy people are fallen silent, the doors are barred that were
    open.
Gods of the land, goddesses of the land,
Shamash, Sin, Adad, and Ishtar are gone off to the lap of heaven,
They will give no judgment, they will decide no cases.
Night draws a veil, the palace is hushed, the open land is deadly still,
The wayfarer cries out to a god, even the petitioner ⟨of this omen⟩
    keeps on sleeping!
The true judge, the father to the orphaned, Shamash has gone off to
    his bedchamber.[19]


### BIBLIOGRAPHY

On Syro-Palestinian cities, see Giorgio Buccellati, *Cities and Nations of Ancient Syria* (Rome, 1967). The archaeological information, primarily from Palestinian sites, has been summarized by Ze'ev Herzog, 'Cities in the Levant', *The Anchor Bible Dictionary* 1 (New York, 1992), 1032–43. For the Bronze Age, see Jean-Louis Huot *et al.*, *Naissance des cités* (Paris, 1990).

For Anatolia the literature is very slim. Some remarks on urban settlements in the third and second millennia can be found in Rudolf Naumann, *Architektur Kleinasiens*, 2nd edn. (Tübingen, 1971), 204–35.

The literature on Egyptian cities is steadily growing. See most recently the contributions by Fakri A. Hassan and David O'Connor to Thurstan Shaw *et al.* (eds.), *The Archaeology of Africa: Food, Metals and Towns* (London, 1993), 551–86. Also important are the insights in Barry J. Kemp, *Ancient Egypt: Anatomy of a Civilization* (London, 1989).

---

[19] Trans. Benjamin R. Foster, *Before the Muses* (Bethesda, 1993) 1, 146, quoted by permission.

# INDEX